THE FUGITIVES

The FUGITIVES
A CRITICAL ACCOUNT

by

JOHN M. BRADBURY

Chapel Hill
THE UNIVERSITY OF NORTH CAROLINA PRESS

Manufactured in the United States of America

To My Father,

WILLIAM F. BRADBURY

who, early in life, made me deeply aware of the excitement, as well as of the permanent values, which literature offers.

Foreword

IN THE FUTURE history of American letters, the Fugitive group almost certainly will occupy a position analogous to that of the Transcendental group of the mid-nineteenth century. Like their New England prototypes, the Southern Fugitives have been rather consistently over- and underrated by their contemporaries on grounds essentially irrelevant to their achievements. The fact that the major Fugitives engaged in the Agrarian movement of the early thirties and the further fact that they have insisted upon defending "reactionary" political positions have led many social-minded critics to condemn them out of hand. They have been called "young Confederates" and "defenders of the faith," scored for "cozy self-satisfaction" in their reactionism and for "anti-intellectualism . . . in the interests of tradition." On the other hand, they have been extolled as preservers of American tradition by patriotic regionalists. But these are extraliterary considerations, interesting sociologically and in the "history of ideas," but largely irrelevant to the present study of the specifically literary and critical performances of the group.

The Fugitive penchant for polemics and their dogmatism in critical theory has tended to alienate not only their avowed enemies, but their potential allies as well. Fellow-traditionalist groups, such as the Neo-Humanists and the Chicago Aristotelians, have been attacked by Ransom and Tate with the same vigor they have marshaled against the "positivists." Ransom has severely criticized T. S. Eliot, apparently a natural ally, and even his fellow Fugitives. The result of this individualism has been a gradual narrowing of the circle of eager followers among American critics. Nothing like an influential "Fugitive

School" of criticism has been developed in this country, therefore. As in the case of the similarly individualistic Transcendentalists, however, the basic ideas, the approaches both to creative writing and to critical practice, have been very widely disseminated. Fugitive dicta have had already a profound effect on the practice of American letters, not alone in the South, and not alone among those who approve their political and social doctrines.

This book presumes neither to be a definitive history of the Fugitive writers themselves, nor to offer a final judgment of their literary contributions. Their history is by no means complete in 1956. This volume can be justified only as an attempt to set the Fugitive group as a whole in its proper historical place, and to indicate the nature of the contributions which each has made thus far to our literary heritage. The kind of wholesale rejection and only less critical praise which has characterized so much of the discussion of the group thus far indicates the need for such an attempt. No one interested in American literature can afford to dismiss poets like Ransom, Warren, and Tate, or a novelist like Warren. And no theoretic disapproval of "traditionism" should blind any reader interested in the broader aspects of our culture to the significant and influential body of ideas which Fugitive critics have developed and applied to literary criticism. On the other hand, failure to recognize certain limitations in the theory and practice of criticism as it appears in Fugitive writing well could lead to a narrowing conception of literature and even to cultism.

In preparing this book, I have avoided on principle all biographical data which has not appeared in print. In dealing with living writers, there is always a problem of decorum, as well as one of bias on the ground of personality. Any conclusions which I have expressed in regard to personal characteristics of the authors considered—and they are very few—have been influenced, I trust, entirely by the printed word. I have attempted no psychoanalyses and made no assumptions in regard to personal relationships without the warrant of the record. In general, I have endeavored to guide myself by Fugitive practice, which, despite many private strains and stresses within the group, has exhibited a model discretion in public.

In an era such as ours when literary, as well as general, values are in a state of flux, it becomes the duty of the critic to indicate, at least, the criteria upon which his judgments are based. Inevitably, the critic of the Fugitives is influenced to employ some of the techniques of close textual analysis which his subjects have developed and found rewarding. To the extent permitted by the scope of this work, I have used such techniques. However, one of the lessons which the Fugitive example enforces, if I am correct, is that dogmatic application of a single methodology entails a sacrifice out of proportion to its advantages. The canonization of certain practices of John Donne and his followers has led Ransom and Brooks, for example, to depreciate or distort Shakespeare; and Tate, Brooks, and Ransom to pillory Shelley and dismiss practically the whole nineteenth century in English literature. On the other hand, no critic in a rationalistic age can afford the lack of precision to which an indiscriminate eclecticism must conduce.

The basic assumption of this book is that art is an organic phenomenon, that it relates to life itself as imagination relates to action. The prime criteria for the judgment of art, therefore, are those by which we judge life, but at an imaginative remove from consequences in action. The work of art, like the person in life, must be judged in totality, as an extremely complex set of relationships functioning organically. This is not, however, to remove criticism into the realm of the subjective. As we can point to this or that objective feature or act of the person and say that just here his quality is displayed, so we can point to the passage, the controlling image, the particular aesthetic act in the poem or painting or musical work. Furthermore, as we relate the single feature or act to our total experience of the individual and judge him as a complete personality, so in the art work we may judge the totality created by the relationships of its various qualities. A poem or a picture may lack many of the classic attributes of art, such as unity or balance; yet we may value it highly, even for its aberrant quality, as we value an eccentric personality. The qualities and the relationships will be there where we can point to them, even though we may not be able finally to define their total appeal.

It follows that a work of art cannot be judged wholly on aesthetic considerations. Our total reactions to individuals are appreciative or aesthetic certainly, but factors such as their social outlook, their philosophic or metaphysical beliefs, their taste, will inevitably contribute to their appeal. To ignore similar factors in art, as certain of the Fugitives would have us do, is to distort the actual process of appreciation. As the criteria for friendship, conscious or unconscious, vary for individuals, they must vary in art. However, the human race, at different periods in its development and in different places, has substantially agreed on the traits of character which it has most admired and loved; so, too, it has agreed on its aesthetic standards. As our age differs markedly from earlier ages, our artists, reflecting the age, must differ, and our critical standards, applied to men or art works, must differ also. Not so far, however, that we need mistake a Hitler for a Schweitzer or a Spillane for a Faulkner.

The individual judgments to which I have committed myself in the following pages have often been based on technical considerations, for each formal art has its minimal requirements of technical proficiency growing out of the materials in which it works. (Formal occasions in life have no less their standards in the form of manners, and these, similarly, grow out of the necessities of artificial communication.) Nevertheless, the major conclusions in regard to the creative work of my subjects have, I trust, sprung from such general considerations as I have outlined above. Their value will depend in considerable measure upon the usefulness of my criteria. Still, the considerations are broad enough so that all is not necessarily lost with rejection of the point of view.

I have indicated in the text many debts to modern critics, and I am sure that I have failed to recognize many others. I wish here particularly to express my appreciation to Mr. Austin Warren, whose enormous fund of knowledge, whose critical insights, and whose concrete suggestions have been of great help in my study of the Fugitives.

I regret to report that, at press time, four of the Fugitive group discussed in the following pages as still active are no longer alive: James Marshall Frank, William Frierson, Merrill Moore, Stanley Johnson.

Acknowledgments

I WISH TO THANK the following publishers and authors for permission to quote from books bearing their copyrights: Alfred A. Knopf for John Crowe Ransom, *Two Gentlemen in Bonds*, "Fresco," *Selected Poems*, "Here Lies a Lady," "Bells for John Whiteside's Daughter," "Painted Head," "Of Margaret," "Address to the Scholars of New England," and "Old Mansion"; Charles Scribner's Sons for John Crowe Ransom, *The World's Body*, for Allen Tate, *Reactionary Essays on Poetry and Ideas* and *Poems: 1922-1947* and for Donald Davidson, *Lee in the Mountains and Other Poems, Including The Tall Men;* Henry Regnery Company for Allen Tate, *The Forlorn Demon;* Random House and Robert Penn Warren for Robert Penn Warren, *Night Rider, World Enough and Time, Brother to Dragons,* and *Band of Angels;* Harcourt, Brace and Company for Robert Penn Warren, *At Heaven's Gate, All the King's Men,* and *Circus in the Attic and Other Stories,* for John Crowe Ransom, *God without Thunder: An Unorthodox Defense of Orthodoxy,* for Cleanth Brooks, Jr., *The Well-Wrought Urn,* and for Cleanth Brooks, Jr., and John Edward Hardy, *The Poems of Mr. John Milton;* G. P. Putnam's Sons for Allen Tate, *The Fathers, Reason in Madness, Stonewall Jackson: The Good Soldier,* and *Jefferson Davis: His Rise and Fall;* John Crowe Ransom for his *The New Criticism;* Robert Penn Warren for his *Selected Poems: 1923-1943;* Henry Holt and Company, Inc., and John Crowe Ransom for John Crowe Ransom, *Poems about God* (copyright, 1919, by Henry Holt and Company, Inc., copyright, 1947, by John Crowe Ransom); and Donald Davidson for his *The*

Outland Piper. In abbreviated form, Chapters III and XIII of the present volume have appeared in *Accent Magazine.*

Grateful acknowledgment is made to the Ford Foundation for a grant under its program for assisting American university presses in the publication of works in the humanities and the social sciences.

Table of Contents

THE FUGITIVES

Chapter I

The Beginnings

Allen Tate has written of the Fugitive group to which he belonged as a charter member, "I think that I may disregard the claims of propriety and say quite plainly that, so far as I know, there was never so much talent, knowledge, and character accidentally brought together at one American place in our time."[1]

The unlikely place was Nashville, Tennessee, and the particular time was 1922–26. The talent included more than a dozen writers of poetry, five of whom were quickly recognized in anthologies of American poetry. Four of the group have become leading literary critics and at least three have produced distinguished fiction. As editors of important critical magazines and as teachers of creative writing and criticism, the Fugitive group has effected a near revolution in American letters.

From this handful of men has sprung perhaps the major impetus for what has already become known as the "Southern Literary Renaissance." They have been instrumental in formulating and promulgating the theory and techniques of the "New Criticism," thus far the most fruitful methodology produced in an intensely critic-minded century. As a result of their books and direct influence, the teaching of literature in our colleges has been largely reoriented, literary history revised, and literary reputations extensively reshuffled. Finally, under Fugitive aegis, a formidable body of younger creative writers and critics has grown up in the South, the Midwest, and the East.

1. "The Fugitive—1922–1925," *Princeton University Library Chronicle*, III, 76-83.

This impressive record, unrivaled in American literary history by any cohesive group certainly since Transcendentalist days, has been in large measure the achievement of five men: John Crowe Ransom, Allen Tate, Robert Penn Warren, Donald Davidson, and Cleanth Brooks, Jr. But Tate's "so much talent, knowledge, and character" embraces a considerably wider circle, including all of the then poets associated with *The Fugitive* magazine during the four years of its publication. (Cleanth Brooks, who arrived at Vanderbilt as a Freshman in the year of the magazine's demise, is not technically a "Fugitive," but by every other right he belongs with the group.) Prominent among the associates are Merrill Moore, noted Boston psychiatrist and author of more sonnets than any other poet in recorded literary history; Andrew Lytle, novelist, short story writer, and teacher of creative writing; Walter Clyde Curry, well-known scholar and author of works on Chaucer and Shakespeare; William Frierson, also scholar, teacher, and author of studies on the novel; William Yandell Elliott, again scholar, teacher, and author of books on political science; and Stanley Johnson, novelist and university administrator.

There were others, too: from the town, an invalided man of many parts, chief instigator of the magazine project, Sidney Mttron Hirsch; his brother-in-law, James Marshall Frank, local businessman and chief host for group meetings; local banker Alec Brock Stevenson; and Jesse Wills, "promising young businessman." Finally, there were Ridley Wills, author of two novels; Alfred Starr, a mathematician; and a Louisville housewife, Laura Riding (Gottschalk), who qualifies as a Fugitive only technically.

A phenomenon of such dimensions and such distinction appearing thus suddenly in and about Vanderbilt University, a school previously undistinguished for creative achievements, requires explanation. The first fact that emerges is the curious one that, to quote Tate again, "none of us came there to be writers." He refers here to himself, who came to Vanderbilt to study classical and oriental languages; to Robert Penn Warren, who came for scientific studies; to Merrill Moore, who was a premedical student; and to the other undergraduates with various ambitions. But, in addition, there was Ransom, who had first been a classics scholar and teacher, and Davidson, who had originally envisioned a career in music. It is true that Ransom had already published a wry little volume of *Poems about God*, but neither he nor anyone else had taught a course in creative writing.

What happened at Nashville should be regarded as a slow poetic infection, introduced from distant places, with Ransom as prime carrier, breaking out into a fever among a small group, then becoming rapidly epidemic after the launching of the magazine project. Scholars and businessmen, who were never again to commit a public indiscretion, threw off poetic effusions. Undergraduates intended for discreet callings slighted their courses to turn out verse (the remarkable Merrill Moore, it is recorded, learned shorthand in order to get down more sonnets between class and laboratory). Furthermore, the poetry magazine was adequately supported from the beginning by Nashville citizens.

Despite protestations to the contrary, it must be surmised that regional pride played a considerable role in the poetic excitement of 1922. The magazine itself repudiated "Southern Literature" of the old school and declared itself "quite catholic, and perhaps excessively earnest [only] in literary dogma." But unrecognized pressures were operative in the early twenties, and *The Fugitive* can hardly be conceived as springing to such an abundant life without reference to impulses, both intellectual and social, in the surrounding atmosphere.

The second decade of this century in America had witnessed an extraordinary revival of poetic activity. During the central five years, 1912–16, not only were the first Imagist anthologies published, but along with them the first significant volumes by

Robert Frost, Vachel Lindsay, Edgar Lee Masters, John Gould Fletcher, Conrad Aiken, Robinson Jeffers, Archibald MacLeish, Carl Sandburg, and the Benéts. *Poetry* magazine was launched, and in its wake a fleet of such notable "little magazines" as *The Poetry Journal*, *The Little Review*, *The Globe*, *The Lantern*, *The Midland*, *Others*, *Contemporary Verse*, and *The Seven Arts*. And in these appeared such new names as Edna St. Vincent Millay, Marianne Moore, Elinor Wylie, Wallace Stevens, and William Carlos Williams.

The unprecedented wave of interest in poetry gathered impetus in Amy Lowell's Boston, in Greenwich Village, and in Chicago; it quickly spread as far as San Francisco, with "little magazines" sprouting behind it. By 1920 the South alone of the older sections of the country had failed to participate in the revival. The section had produced no important new literary artists and had attempted no new magazine venture of note. From the pages of *The Smart Set*, H. L. Mencken was periodically sniping at the cultural apathy of the South, "the Sahara of the Bozarts" as he smartly called it. "Down there a poet is as rare as an oboe player, a dry point etcher or a metaphysician."[2]

In January, 1921, *The Double-Dealer*, which was to print the early efforts of Hemingway and Faulkner, as well as many of the Fugitives, broke ground for literary experiment in New Orleans. This iconoclastic venture declared editorially: "The old traditions are no more. . . . The Confederacy has long since been dissolved." *The Double-Dealer* was quickly followed by *The Reviewer*, issued in Richmond, Virginia, a "little magazine" which opened on a high note of encouraging new Southern voices.

Thus, with the Gulf Coast and the Atlantic seaboard represented by new literary outlets at the end of 1921, there remained in the South proper only that middle region known as

2. *Prejudices, 2nd Series*, pp. 136-54.

the "Old West," with Nashville at its geographical center. *The Fugitive* appeared there in April, 1922.

If this account seems somewhat over-deterministic, the emphasis is necessary to correct Tate's accent on the fortuitous element ("accidentally brought together") in the meeting of talent in Nashville. Later (1929) Tate wrote: "These poets started with open minds—that is, with the simple aim of writing poetry. But after five or six years it became clear that quite unconsciously they were fostering a sectional spirit . . . supported by the prejudices, feelings, values into which the poets were born."[3] But even the advertising copy of the early magazine, with its quoting of Mencken, betrays regional self-consciousness. The magazine hastened to repudiate editorially "the high-caste Brahmins of the Old South," and Ransom's introductory poem proclaimed him "an alien" from the "dogmas" and "tall steeples" of the area. Tate himself appended a note to his first contribution to *The Double-Dealer:* "Allen Tate writes that he is 21 and lives in Nashville, Tenn., of which the latter fact is the more damning."[4] Such protestations, aimed as they were at two highly unpalatable aspects of the region, its cultural provincialism and its fast-growing materialism, are in their backhanded way indicative of a "sectional spirit" that would manifest itself positively only after 1925.

Both Warren and Davidson have analyzed the social situation of the South in the early twenties in terms of an intra-Southern civil war. Warren wrote in 1932:

> During the last fifteen years this section has been drawn violently into the national life. This has meant an awakening and an agitation in many respects. But for some this agitation has taken the form of a highly dramatic moral issue: old values implicit in a society have been made explicit, there has been a testing of the old by the new. Some generations back such testing might have taken the form of action, but

3. "American Poetry since 1920," *Bookman,* LXIX, 504.
4. *The Double-Dealer,* III, No. 17, back of cover.

by a peculiar conspiracy of circumstances, the ordinary channels of direct action have been stopped.[5]

At the same time, Davidson found that there had been "civil strife within the South itself," and felt that its effect had been to "dislocate many Southern writers from a proper relation to their own people and their own tradition."[6]

Civil war is a drastic metaphor, perhaps, for what was happening in the twenties, but a considerable dislocation and ferment was evident. Much of the trouble was a direct result of World War I: the wholesale intimate contact of the provincial South's youth with the youth of other sections; the aftermath of disillusion and moral decay, from which the South was not exempt; the insecurity brought on by the immediate postwar depression with its accompanying fears and search for scapegoats. The revival of militant Fundamentalism and of the Klan followed, and with them grew a new romantic sectional patriotism which refurbished the legend of an idyllic ante bellum South.

At the same time, the South was being split by new economic forces. For several decades the "New South" had been advertised in terms of industrialization on the Northern and Eastern pattern, and a considerable development, especially in the rise of new textile mills, had already occurred. It was, in fact, the competition of this industry with the older, larger, and more expensively operated establishments of New England that opened the new phase: that of direct Northern investment in the South and of impersonal absentee ownership in place of the traditional paternalistic system.

The era of "the Golden Glow," as Charles Beard calls it, was in its early flush in these years, with financial and big business interests kindling the bonfires of National Prosperity. Newspapers and magazines took up the torch and soon the New South was alight with dreams of Progress and Profits. The

5. "A Note on Three Southern Poets," *Poetry*, XL, 113.
6. "The Southern Poet and his Tradition," *Poetry*, XL, 101-2.

activities of Rotaries, Kiwanises, and Chambers of Commerce reached a new peak, and the attractions of the South for industrial development were blazoned through the North—with the accent on cheap and docile labor, "99 per cent pure, Anglo-Saxon."[7]

Booms in real estate, especially in and near the expanding cities, but extending to the farms, got quickly under way. Skyscrapers were being built or planned in every city as urban populations soared. A new business tempo invaded even the towns, and the "booster" was in his glory, shouldering aside the Old South dream world and embracing the new "service club" and profit world.

For the Fugitives, neither the militant Fundamentalism, with its anti-intellectual appeal, nor the new boosterism had any attractions at the moment. Their basic reaction, personified chiefly in Ransom, was much that of the Pounds, Steins, Joyces, and Eliots of a few years earlier, a sense of alienation. They tended therefore to shore themselves up in aesthetic-intellectualist preoccupations. They could not, and did not, ignore their immediate surroundings. Nashville, Vanderbilt, and Dr. Edwin Mims were daily realities to most of them, and each of them contributed to the self-consciousness, as well as to the alienation, of the group.

Nashville grew up as the commercial center of the "Old West," an area explored by Long Hunters and developed by gaunt farmers of corn and tobacco, heavy drinkers, horse racers and mule traders, Andrew Jacksons and Sam Houstons—men of slow talk and quick temper, touchy personal pride and, very largely, religious Fundamentalism. In Civil War days, Nashville was occupied by Northern troops and then by carpetbaggers, while native Tennessean Andrew Johnson sat in the statehouse as the Union's military governor. Still, in the early twentieth century it could watch a candidate for governor, defeated in spite of night-rider activities on the part of his

7. Howard Odum, *An American Epoch*, pp. 81 ff.

fanatic Prohibitionist followers, shot on the street for insulting a rival politician—and could condone the prison-gate pardon of his executioner.

Matthew Arnold characteristically called the city "a citadel of Philistinism"; O. Henry saw in it only smoke and dirt. On the other hand, Nashville has long termed itself "the Athens of the South," and backed its claim with the largest concentration of educational institutions, both white and Negro, in the entire region, with a Capitol building combining every possible Grecian motif, and with a full-scale plaster replica of the Parthenon. Furthermore, Robert Nichols once spoke of it as "England and Greece combined."

Nashville, however, was and is not beautiful; it is crowded, narrow, dirty and without plan, and above all commercial-minded, if not heavily industrial. Well within the city stands Vanderbilt University, a monument to the generosity of an ignorant Hudson River boatman. When Ransom first arrived, the school was still reverberating with victory chants over its liberation from Southern Methodist controls. Vanderbilt's government had generally been liberal until, in the early 1890's, a band of militant churchmen opened a campaign to install an all-Methodist faculty. For two decades the battle between educators and churchmen had continued. Then, in 1914, the state Supreme Court ruled the school's Board of Trust free from ecclesiastical interference. Students and numbers of townspeople turned out in gala celebration to cheer the decision.

After 1914, Vanderbilt's growth was steady in all branches except that of religion. Fundamentalism remained strong in the countryside, but William Jennings Bryan was able to condemn Nashville thereafter as "the center of Modernism in the South." The official attitude of the university is best summed up in the statement of the Chancellor following the 1925 Scopes trial: "The answer to the episode at Dayton is the building of new laboratories on the Vanderbilt campus for the teaching of science."[8]

8. Quoted in Edwin Mims, *The Advancing South,* p. 157.

This answer of science to Fundamentalism well may be credited with setting off the chain reaction which resulted in the movement of the Fugitive group out of its literary preoccupations into its social and religious concerns of the late twenties and early thirties. But the basis for those concerns, as I have indicated, long had been laid, and their development undoubtedly had been accelerated by Dr. Mims. As head of the English department, Mims had brought Ransom, a Vanderbilt graduate and Rhodes Scholar, to the department in 1914, and he later added Davidson, whom Ransom had taught, Curry, Elliott, and Johnson. But Mims was decidedly a New South man, given to the genial god of Progress and to boosterism. When the magazine project had matured, Mims invited the Vanderbilt editorial group to luncheon and tried to persuade them to give up the foolhardy venture. When not only Nashville but the nation acclaimed the new poets, he took notice, and finally assumed some modest part in the credit as he discussed books and Progress before women's clubs and Rotaries. Meanwhile he worked on his two volumes of semicultural Babbittry, *The Advancing South* and *Adventurous America*. The Fugitives, who have always preserved their old-school manners, have never publicly accorded to Dr. Mims his full share in developing their attitudes, but they have surely been aware of him as a symbolic nether pole in their accomplishments.

The idea of establishing a magazine of original verse in Nashville must have seemed presumptuous, however, not only to Dr. Mims. Only Ransom of all the prospective contributors had sold a poem, and Ransom's book had fallen off the press into a hush of critical voices. (The notable favorable reviewer in America was Christopher Morley, the book's sponsor, though Robert Graves in England praised it highly.) The seven who formed the original editorial board included besides two English instructors doing graduate work, one undergraduate, two businessmen, and a gentleman of leisure. But the project was not a sudden inspiration, nor was the board unprepared to exercise its critical function.

Even before the war, the nucleus of the group had been meeting with some regularity to discuss philosophy, linguistics, and literature. In the beginning, Davidson and Johnson had been calling together on a Miss Goldie Hirsch of the city; they had soon been drawn into long discussions with her interesting father, Sidney Hirsch, who had been a world traveler, an amateur etymologist and playwright, acquainted with Gertrude Stein, and, according to Tate, a "mystic, and I think a Rosicrucian."[9] Shortly the undergraduates began to bring their professor, Ransom, with them, and soon another undergraduate, William Elliott, was joining them.

Following the hiatus of the war years, the group reconvened, but now usually at the home of the invalided Hirsch's brother-in-law, James M. Frank, with whom Hirsch was now living. Alec Brock Stevenson became a regular addition at the fortnightly meetings, and finally Allen Tate. Others, including scholar Curry, William Frierson, who, like Elliott, soon left on a Rhodes Scholarship, and Alfred Starr and his brother Milton, attended at times.

Mr. Hirsch, Tate recalls, pontificated at the sessions, reclining in a sort of oriental luxury among pillows, but as the tone of the gatherings shifted with an increasing emphasis on literature and aesthetic theory, Ransom was gradually acknowledged as the intellectual leader. Soon everyone was bringing original poems, and an increasing portion of the meetings was devoted to reading of the verse and to criticism. Mr. Hirsch is reported to have suggested a local magazine outlet for the group and funds were forthcoming—"At no time was *The Fugitive* bothered with financial troubles."[10] The editors themselves contributed money, perhaps a good deal of it in the beginning, but backing came also from several prominent Nashville men,

9. "The Fugitive—1922–1925," *op. cit.*, p. 76.
10. *Ibid.*, p. 79.

the Associated Retailers, and Ward-Belmont College. The seven editors selected the contents of the issue by ballot and printed them under pseudonyms.

It was Hirsch again who suggested the name for the magazine, an unfortunate choice for the muscular criticism of the thirties in that it lent itself so readily to charges of escapism of several sorts. But Tate's explanation is: "A Fugitive was quite simply a Poet: the Wanderer, or even the Wandering Jew, the Outcast, the man who carries the secret wisdom of the world."[11] In support of this etymology, Ransom's opening poem, "Ego," speaks of the poet "sentenced from birth/ To love unusual gods beyond all earth." And it continues:

> I have run further, matching your heart and speed
> And tracked the Wary Fugitive with you.

These connotations of pursuit, however, are apparently belied by the Foreword, which states: "*The Fugitive* flees from nothing faster than from the high-caste Brahmins of the Old South." In addition, Donald Davidson has spoken of fleeing "poet-laureating, the cheapness and triviality of public taste, even among those supposed to be cultured; the lack of serious devotion to literature, to the arts, to ideas."[12] And again: "If there is significance in the title of the magazine, it lies perhaps in the sentiment of the editors (on this point I am sure we all agree) to flee from the extremes of conventionalism, whether old or new."[13]

Whether *The Fugitive* primarily fled, pursued, or merely wandered—and it is likely that each staff member carried about his private ambiguities of reference—it is clear that conventional Southern smugness and insensitivity to aesthetic values was a common point of departure and a kind of wisdom the common goal. It is equally clear that these were not a group of "frus-

11. *Ibid.*, pp. 78-79.
12. Quoted in F. J. Hoffman *et al.*, *The Little Magazine*, p. 121.
13. Quoted in *A Vanderbilt Miscellany*, ed. R. C. Beatty, Introduction.

trated Confederate generals," as one critic has made out, fleeing backward to Civil War days.

In the first two issues the poems appeared under the names: Roger Prim (Ransom), Henry Feathertop (Tate), Robin Gallivant (Davidson), Marpha (Curry), Jonathon David (Johnson), Drimbonigher and also King Badger (Stevenson), Dendric (Moore), Philora (Frank), and L. Oafer (a disappointment, for Hirsch). Curry and Moore were quickly editors also.

As a whole, the poetry was not distinguished, though it was immediately greeted and praised on a national scale. There was, however, an uncommonly astringent flavor to much of it, often a deftness of touch and a sensitivity to word values, an air of formality, and above all a complete absence of the stilted and pompous rhetoric for which Southern verse had been long known.

There should have been little question after the first few issues (though there was) that the dominant figure was Ransom. His own poems, though not always fully successful, exhibited a finish and maturity that the others could not match. Tate was still inclined to an immature irony, with sentimental or superficially morbid overtones. In form, mood, and style he suggested a prematurely sophisticated Ransom, though his irregular "Epode" in the third issue already hinted at experiment and new masters. Davidson immediately betrayed a native romanticism, but a romanticism disciplined to look at itself *sub specie Ransomis,* with a wry pull of the mouth. The other poets of these early issues, with the exception of Merrill Moore, whose approach was already clinical, appeared at their best the more nearly they approached Ransom's subject matter and his manner.

CHAPTER II

The Fugitive

IT IS ONLY in the second phase of Fugitive development that we are enabled to define clearly the Ransom influence which had so dominated the first year that two able critics assumed he had written the whole of the two anonymous numbers of the magazine. For only under the challenge of a new model, which Tate's discovery of T. S. Eliot introduced, was Ransom led to define his ideological and aesthetic commitments.

Early Ransomism was both a manner of thinking and a manner of expression. The thinking was eminently rational and sharply realistic, but sensitively alive to human and natural values. Deeply aware of the ineradicable evils of death and decay as the central facts about the human condition, his mind could hold this knowledge at a safe distance while the senses discreetly indulged themselves and the spectacle of human gallantries and human foibles passed before it. His poetic stance was somewhat aloof from the little dramas he preferred to expose in a tone of mild and sympathetic irony. The poetry itself was mannered and often deceptively gay. Constructed in traditional patterns, it relied for its effects on sharp images, neat surprises of diction, and careful modulations of tone. It avoided all pretentiousness, all clichés of phrase and attitude, and all vagueness of structure or of metaphysics. It provided a difficult model to imitate well, if an easy one to follow superficially, but it offered a highly effective humanist discipline for the excesses of young poetic talent.

I have indicated that Ransom's earliest *Fugitive* poems were by no means uniformly successful. There is often an artificiality and strain about them or a mocking irony that fails to come off as planned. His poetry found its proper modulation and ease suddenly, almost coincidentally with the intrusion of Eliot's name into the circle. But the elements of the final style had been present for some time.

Ransom's *Selected Poems* of 1945 includes no poem written before *Fugitive* days, but his slender wartime volume of 1919, *Poems about God*, contained much that is interesting and a great deal that is indicative of later developments.

The author's introduction virtually proclaimed that the conception of the book was a tour de force. Ransom explained that he had been "surprised to notice that each [of his first three or four poetic efforts] made considerable use of the term God." He went on:

> I studied the matter a little and came to the conclusion that this was the most poetic of all terms possible. . . . Wishing to make my poems as poetic as possible, I simply likened myself to a diligent apprentice and went to work to treat rather systematically a number of the occasions on which this term was in use with common American men . . . sincerely and spontaneously.

There is something of the rational ex-classicist in this, but a good deal more of an original flair for irony and ambiguity, amounting almost to quixotism.

As the son of a south-central Tennessee clergyman, Ransom was versed in Fundamentalist piety, "the way of the fathers," as he puts it; and he no more rejects the orthodox intonation of God's name than he forgets a wrestler's "By God, I'll have you down in a minute!" This strange poet can speak "sincerely and spontaneously" of a "crazy God," a God who "still at heart was quite a gentleman"—an epithet also applied to a dog—or a God who "gives an office to my knees." The attitude underlying these ill-consorting usages is not so ingenuous as it would appear. Ransom is simply regarding Deity as a human creation, through whom or which man expresses his sense of "ultimate mystery," joyfully or indignantly or however. From a Fundamentalist point of view, the poems are often blasphemous, but to casual reading they are quite as often orthodoxly humble and God-fearing. Ultimately we must conclude that the poet respects, not the mystery itself, but that quality in man which enables him to accept or to rebel in dignity. In the broader sense of the term, Ransom is revealed as a true humanist. He explicitly rejects only those puritan aspects of religion which would limit and frustrate man's potentialities for full self-realization and joy.

Philosophically Ransom has never abandoned the rational humanism which this volume implies. Similarly, he has only extended the ambiguity, or dualism, which characterizes these poems. What changes essentially is the poet's mastery of his medium, and particularly his tonal control. This early Ransom can write line after line which, despite the sophistication of intent, sounds like the mawkish bucolics of James Whitcomb Riley:

> An extra fork is by my plate,
> I nearly noticed it too late!
>
> Mother, you're keeping a secret back!
> I see the pie-pan through the crack,
> Incrusted thick in gold and black.

Then he comments impudently on the hired man who after dinner has lain down in his vomit to die:

> And God, who had just received full thanks
> For all his kindly daily bread,
> Now called it back again—perhaps
> To see that his birds of the air were fed.

Or his diction will take on a sharper antic air, and an ague

> Will fiddle on his bones.

Again he will inject a flavored archaism into the normal colloquial flow: "Previsal I made"; "so vengeant for his vine and summer song"; "make a soft amend"; "it twitcheth my heart"; or "shrew his splendid features out of shape."

After the opening poem, "The Swimmer," where both subtlety and sharp effect are evident, there is never the slightest question that the author is no crude poetaster. When the homespun appears, and it does immediately, we know it for a costume, worn with an air of mockery, but not without a certain pride at the fit. For a serious poet any pose, particularly a sustained one of naïveté, is perilous; and this early Ransom, like Robert Frost, too often falls victim to his manner. When God helps Mother bake her pie, the effect is not that of, say, Rilke's God showing the "hundred artisans . . . a new skill." Ransom's light flat tone does not sustain the weight of the intimacy. Again, when a Russian pines for snow in Tennessee, or when the poet is gladdened by the sight of "good women" tidying their houses along bad roads, the introduction of God's name does not provide a sufficient connotative richness or emotional excitement to lift the low-keyed preambles into poetry. The occasional Frostian animals, as well as at times the angels and God, incline toward a "cute" archness of behavior. Finally, and most seriously, the poet's pose tempts him often to substitute shock or wit for revelation and dubious taste for realism.

The Ransom of *Poems about God* appears to be driven into his unhappy extremities by two negative impulses. While employing his native material, he wishes chiefly to avoid "those amiable accents" of his Southern predecessors. Furthermore, though he wishes seriously to write of "great moments of the soul," he must shun the banal periods of the staid deacon as well as the emotional excesses of revivalism. Only as a tongue-in-cheek naïf can he see his way clear to manage his avoidances. The more unfortunate aspect of his choice lies, however, not so much in the naïveté itself, as in the rustic garb it generally chooses to wear. In one of the late poems in the volume, Ransom assumes the black of a naïvely hypocritical puritan with marked ironic success:

> Four sisters sitting in one house,
> I said, these roses on a stem
> With bosoms bare. But wayfaring
> I went and ravished one of them.
>
> So one was taken. But the three,
> They spread their petals just the same,
> They turned no decent pale for grief,
> They drew no fragrance back for shame.
>
> The canker is on roses too!
> I cried, and lifted up the rod
> And scourged them bleeding to the ground,
> All, all are sinners unto God.

The poem is slight in several respects, but its frame holds firm throughout. There is never the danger that the poet himself, rather than his protagonist, may become the object of irony.

Poems about God reveals a good deal of the poet without adequately representing him. Despite occasional reminders of Frost and Hardy and Housman, the verse testifies to an original mind and an unusual verbal talent. Furthermore, it speaks with a rare honesty. The poses of which I have been speaking are in large measure cloaks to shield the self-consciousness of the poet from the face of his own honesty. They permit him a raw candor that the more sophisticated masks we are accustomed to wear will not permit us. Every factor in Ransom's background, both literary and personal, as well as the influence of his teaching profession, suggests adherence to conventional standards; yet the poet trusts only his own senses, his vigorous mind, and the ideal of honesty itself. With this spirit, however, comports a solid respect for established forms. The poet may hold up to ironical inspection moral conventions of his time and place; he may even allow himself defiant breaches of good taste; but there is always an air of decorum breathing from the background and escaping through little elegances of speech and gesture, in favored words like "gallant," "valiant," "dainty," "cavalier," "sweet," however ironically they may be employed. The effect is enhanced, furthermore, by the traditional verse forms in which almost all the poems are couched. Already Ransom has established a preference for ballad and other quatrain forms in his more serious poems and for couplets in lighter pieces. Already, too, the polish of his later mannered and salted diction has been exhibited in arresting flashes. The finished poet is in this volume, if the finished poems are not.

When the first *Fugitive* appeared, Ransom was at least five years beyond the poetry of *Poems about God;* yet the opening "Ego" of that issue shows no real advance. There is still a stridency that results from forcing a pose, though the pose here is more congenial than the earlier one. "Ego" is signed with the pseudonym Roger Prim, which may be freely translated as "the fastidious one famed for his prowess with the spear." The name was peculiarly appropriate, for Ransom was writing now in the habit of a precisely accoutered knight-errant of intellectualism and art, with spear leveled, if the anachronism be pardoned, at the balloons of vulgar taste and belief. In "Ego" the spear is brandished somewhat too grandiloquently and too close to the nose. The realism of the poem is still crude and unassimilated into the over-all tonal structure:

> So I take not the vomit where they do
> Comporting downward to the general breed,

which has little but shock value; and the whole is hardly more than a metered expression of prose sentiments, distinguished chiefly by a smug avant-garde intolerance.

If I have borne down rather heavily on this initial poem, it has been for the sake of emphasizing the rapidity with which Ransom's art developed during the first *Fugitive* years. Before the end of the first year of publication, he was printing such brilliantly executed poems as "Epitaph," "Necrological," and "Fall of Leaf." By 1924 he was able to collect a truly distinguished volume of poetry, *Chills and Fever*. (The volume included a mellowed version of "Ego" as "Plea in Mitigation," in which the once topical "Wary Fugitive" has been transformed into the poet's personal "gods," and in which the "Fugitive" pun has been replaced by a reference to the abandoned pseudonym: "And no man's bubble 'scapeth his sharp thorn.")

Ransom's sudden maturation into a major poet probably has no direct relation to Tate's discovery of Eliot, though a kind of precipitation may have occurred. The story runs that Hart Crane, on having read a Tate poem in *The Double-Dealer*, wrote the author mentioning Eliot as the likely source of his style. Tate, who says that he had never read Eliot previously, quickly did so, and shortly thereafter, on his own account, "I began an impertinent campaign in Eliot's behalf in the South."[1] The immediate result was a review, in the fourth issue of *The Fugitive*, of Eliot's *The Waste Land*. It amounted to a declaration of independence.

In the previous issue,[2] reviewing Robert Graves's *On English Poetry*, Ransom had put forward an essentially neoclassical conception of poetry:

> . . . it would seem at least likely that the determinate mathematical regularities of meter which are imposed upon the words have as much to do with the total effect of a poem as, in a sister art, the geometrical

1. "The Fugitive—1922–1925," *Princeton University Library Chronicle*, III, 81.
2. *The Fugitive*, I, No. 3, 68.

regularities of outline which are imposed upon the stones have to do with the total effect of a work of architecture.

In deference to Tate's "Horatian Epode" in the same issue, he did concede that regular meter is not a necessity, but his major contention could hardly admit irregularity.

Tate's reply[3] made its bow back at Ransom's meters with his conclusion that "the old modes are not yet sapped." He allowed that "versification, diction, composition, in a word, mechanics" are the heart of the poet's problem. But shortly he was saying:

> Concede the banality that form and content are one [something that Ransom's dualism of content and "imposed" form had not conceded], and it is clear that the apparently inexplicable framework of T. S. Eliot's *The Waste Land* is inevitable and final; for to imagine that poem in another music would be like thinking of the Iliad . . . in . . . triolets or cinquains.

And he continued categorically:

> I think for all time—so important is *The Waste Land*—Mr. Eliot has demonstrated the necessity, in special cases, of an aberrant versification, for doubtless none assails the authenticity of his impersonal and increasingly abstract art, though some may not care for it.

Some indeed! Ransom not only, as it was soon evident, did not care for it; he violently assailed its authenticity.

Ransom's essay on *The Waste Land* did not appear until six months later, in Henry Seidel Canby's supplement to the New York *Evening Post, The Literary Review.*[4] It was his first full-length critical piece and, I think, his one example of intemperate writing. Not only did Ransom attack the poem and certain of Eliot's critical statements, but he issued a warning to the "young artist . . . not to think that his synthesis of experience is worth as much as an old one's." On the poem he is merciless; it "seems to bring to a head all the specifically modern errors,"

3. *Ibid.*, I, No. 4, 99-100.
4. "Waste Lands," *Literary Review*, III, 825-26.

it is guilty of "extreme disconnection," written in "an extremely free verse which we know as the medium of a half-hearted and disillusioned art." Eliot "debases" by his distortions "lovely borrowed lines" and lacks any true "organization of experience." Finally: "*The Waste Land* is one of the most insubordinate poems in the language, and perhaps it is the most unequal." Eliot's fundamental difficulty, Ransom finds, is "typically an American one," the pursuit of novelty, in the belief that "each age must have its own 'form.' "

I do not wish to imply that any more than a temporary and exclusively aesthetic cleavage occurred within the group as the result of Tate's importation of Eliot. The poets already disagreed on many points of doctrine, and Ransom certainly had made no attempt to force unanimity in any degree. By 1924, however, a new spirit of independence was manifesting itself among the Fugitives. Ransom developed his dualism and his defense of the traditional. In the Eliot essay he had set up his larger frame: science, with its abstractionist skeletal tendency, as opposed to the full body and flesh of art. Now he defines the dual role of poetry: "to conduct a logical sequence with their meanings on the one hand, and to realize an objective pattern with their sounds on the other." He insists that there is no correspondence generally between meanings and sounds, and extends the dualism to a definition of poetry as an "adaptation of the free inner life to the outward necessity of things."[5]

But Tate, as a monist following Eliot's conception of "fusion," dissents.[6] Ransom's dualism assumes that poetry "is exclusively concerned with rational exposition, rather than with pure presentation, of intuitions or ideas." Poetry, by Ransom's thesis, becomes only prose uttered with virtuosity; its content "would be identical with that of prose." For Tate there is a "radical difference between a vocabulary of exposition and an idiom flexible enough to accommodate a presentation of the

5. *The Fugitive,* III, No. 1, 2.
6. *Ibid.*, III, No. 2, 34-36.

entire fantasy of sensation." Free verse is as old as *Les Fleurs du Mal* and "in a very real sense more traditional than" revived older forms. "Repetition . . . isn't tradition."

In the next issue[7] Davidson enters to dissent from both of his philosophically minded confreres. It is a fallacy to demand "that a good poet must be possessed of an aesthetic." "Poets need above all things to be perfectly unsystematic." And, "Aesthetics is a trap for poets, the resource of weak imagination, the frumpery of the philosopher." This was, of course, such heresy as even the heretical Tate could not commit. Davidson, whose recent volume, *An Outland Piper*, had given him new authority, was reverting now to his original romantic colors, repudiating the whole rational platform on which the Fugitives had been recognized as standing.

Attentive reading of the final volume of *The Fugitive* reveals a complex situation among the theorists. A complicating factor was the introduction of young Robert Penn Warren, who caught the Eliot infection in virulent form. He had been elected to the staff the previous year and was already, with Ransom, sharing chief editorial duties. In many ways Warren combined the Tate-Eliot and Ransom positions, though he evidenced it chiefly in his own poetry. However, in his one review[8] for the magazine, he scored Auslander's poetry for its lack of "cerebration" and exclaimed: "one cries out for something tough and bitter."

Ransom, in this first 1924 issue,[9] immediately disposed of the romantics and simple effusiveness, without directly censuring Davidson's romantic thesis. Byron, Keats, and Shelley never grew up. In fact: "Nobody in the whole century knew how to put his whole mind and experience to work in poetry, as had Chaucer, Spenser, Shakespeare, and Milton." Now, having defined the true enemy, Ransom could make concessions in the other direction. Without defining, he referred to certain

7. *Ibid.*, III, No. 3, 66-68.
8. *Ibid.*, IV, No. 1, 29-30.
9. *Ibid.*, IV, No. 1, 28-29.

modern poets who, "from a trifling generation . . . will have to bear the charge of being wilful and obscure." This shifting of the full onus to the public is only momentary, however, for he continues: "So they are; but may it not be a sin on the nobler side?" Only in the penultimate issue[10] of *The Fugitive* does Ransom bid for a full armistice: "but to dogmatize our own poetic likings into a standard for others," he agrees in reviewing Graves's *Poetic Unreason*, "is to subtract fatally from the conception of poetry as a spontaneous and expressive art." He can offer no "universal standard"; instead he projects a new dualism. "Poetry is saved from being utterly licentious and chaotic by having a form and content based closely (as a general thing) upon the tradition." He has by no means, therefore, given up his positions; but he has, with whatever reservations, allowed Tate his.

In the meantime, Tate himself has moved to New York and begun a free-lance career as poet, critic, and reviewer, and he contributes no more to *The Fugitive*. Following Eliot steadily, he is applying the theme of the loss of a "racial myth," together with that of the poet's need to be "aware of his own age," which is the "Age of the Sophist." And he lands, finally, rather far from home and Ransom's accent on tradition in "empiricism" as "the only alternative to intellectual suicide" for the Southerner.

Only Davidson remains to carry on the critical discussion in the magazine, and it is a chastened, open-minded Davidson who appears. He tackles Eliot's essays and the poetry of Eliot's disciple, Archibald MacLeish. "A better *apologia* for a great part of modern poetry, and especially a character of poetry in which *The Fugitive* has been most interested could hardly be devised," he says of Eliot's *Homage to John Dryden*. Furthermore, "Eliot has come nearer than any other critic to justifying the modern dislike for the 19th century poets and to defending on valid grounds the complexity, or obscurity, or

10. *Ibid.*, IV, No. 3, 93-94.

difficulty of much modern poetry."[11] And he has only praise for MacLeish's achievement in "the very difficult modern technique," suggesting even that "Mr. MacLeish may go T. S. Eliot one better, purge out the grosser elements that afflicted *The Waste Land* and evolve something of his own."[12]

This set of bows in the directions of his two colleagues does not constitute a conversion; rather it projects his ultimate dilemma. In the next issue,[13] discussing Cummings and Allen, Davidson defines the dilemma himself: "one wishes to be new, but encounters a risk of being tedious in affectation; or one wishes to revivify the old, but discovers that the task requires a philosopher as well as a poet." The alternatives leave no place for "outland pipers."

The Fugitive passed quietly away with 1925, bestowing as it went the accolade of editorship on youthful Andrew Lytle and mathematician Starr. The enthusiastic unanimity of its beginning had been dissipated, but the confraternity of its editors had never been broken. Ideologically and artistically they were taking different directions, asserting individualities which generally had been submerged in the group effort. However, unlike many a similar project, *The Fugitive* never had developed serious animosities within its unwieldy board, and the cordial relations among the leading members have continued since. In 1928 eleven of the group appeared together again in *Fugitives: An Anthology of Verse,* and two years later Ransom, Tate, Davidson, Warren, and Lytle joined in the group publication, *I'll Take My Stand,* while Brooks was an additional collaborator on the second Agrarian volume, *Who Owns America?*

The *Fugitive* period ended with Warren in California as a graduate student and instructor, Tate in New York free-lancing, Davidson editing a book page for the Nashville *Tennessean,*

11. *Ibid.,* IV, No. 2, 61-62.
12. *Ibid.,* IV, No. 2, 62-63.
13. *Ibid.,* IV, No. 3, 94-95.

and Moore in medical school. But all of the central group continued to be active poets. Ransom had published another volume of poetry, Davidson one, and each had an additional book well on the way. Tate had already been called "the White Hope of the South"[14] in poetry, and was shortly to be recognized as "the only critic worth reading in the United States."[15] Ridley Wills had two novels off the press, Johnson one, and Hirsch a poetic drama. Soon scholarly volumes by Curry and Frierson were to appear as well. It had been an amazingly fruitful spring for the central "Sahara of the Bozarts."

14. Quoted in Tate, "The Fugitive—1922–1925," *op. cit.*, p. 81.
15. Yvor Winters, "Fugitives," *Poetry*, XXXII, 102.

Chapter III

Ransom as Poet

Ransom emerged from the *Fugitive* era matured as a poet and possessed of a clearly defined, if not a fully integrated and developed, view of life. His humanist training imposed on a traditional Methodist substratum had developed a habitually dualistic mode of thought. In his most characteristic utterances he opposes human reason to a nonrational natural order, which he accepts empirically. His recognition of Nature's indifference and mystery, however, is tempered with a sensuous appreciation of her careless bounties and beauties. As a true humanist, he insists upon cultivation of both body and mind, senses and reason; he sets himself equally against puritan asceticism and irrational indulgence.

Ransom's early attempts to order his intellectual position appear in the *Waste Land* essay and in the later issues of *The Fugitive*. In particular, his "Thoughts on the Poetic Discontent" (IV, 2), later rewritten for *The Calendar of Modern Letters*, establishes a general theory and provides it with a genealogy. His final position he calls simply "irony," but this is a special irony arrived at as the mature product of a series of abandoned formulations. Ransom begins with the "dualism" of the unsophisticated practical man who "sees himself as one, and the objective world as another," a world against which he applies what force he can muster "where it will do most good." Eventual recognition of the world's intractability and his own impotence leads man "to surrender the idea of his own dominating personality" for a share in a "mystical community" with God or Nature. But this transcendental romanticism must face "the sober observation of his science," before which it frequently capitulates. The result is a new disillusioned dualism, critical but still "romantic and poetical," like that which afflicted the Victorians. The tough mind, however, is not content with self-indulgent disillusion. The final attitude is that in which "the earlier and greater poets (Chaucer, Shakespeare, Spenser, Donne, Milton) . . . turned back to the stubborn fact of dualism with a mellow wisdom which we may call irony."

It is evident that Ransom is describing not only a historic development in poetic philosophy but a generic process in individual intellectual growth (a process often to be illustrated later in Warren's novels). The ultimate "mature" position is further defined in roughly contemporary articles as "stoic" and as "tragic irony." Most illuminating is a review of Freud's work for *The Saturday Review*.[1] Here he discovers "the spirit of tragic irony" in the Viennese analyst; then he defines more fully: "To be a tragic ironist is to be aware sharply and grimly, but not too painfully, of the constant involvement of life with death." This statement provides an excellent description of the spirit which animates and the mind which orders Ransom's poetry of this period.

Two volumes of poetry, *Chills and Fever* (1924) and *Two Gentlemen in Bonds* (1927), represent Ransom's major work as a poet during the *Fugitive* years. Except for five later poems included in the *Selected Poems* (1945), these two books contain all the poetry which the author has wished to preserve.

The two volumes are of a piece, and together they place Ransom as one of the very limited number of original poetic voices in our century. The poetry is modest in the sense that it attempts no grand syntheses in the manner of Hart Crane or Pound, and makes no dramatic break with the main line of formal tradition in the manner of Hopkins or Eliot. The memorable poems in these volumes are brief dramas or dramatic lyrics, "having," to quote the author in a late *Fugitive*

1. "Freud and Literature," *Saturday Review of Literature*, X, No. 1, 161-62.

article,[2] "a form and content based closely (as a general thing) on the tradition." For poetry is to Ransom "a familiar art, and we all know what to expect"; hence "its conventionality, its formality." However, it also "expresses that which needs expression from our private deeps." The discipline of traditional form operates to limit the "licentious and chaotic," as well as the private.

The primary originality of Ransom's poetry is a product of his philosophic "irony" certainly; it is not, however, an originality *in* philosophy. The balanced dualistic view enables Ransom to create a special world of his own. This world has mythic aspects, aspects of an old and a new South, and of a fabulous nursery world inhabited by monsters and articulate animals. In the main, it is a surprisingly blue, airy place to hold so much death and promise of death. It is peopled with a great many birdlike females—fluttering girls and twittering ladies—and tall girls walking proud in the doom of their beauty, or broken. It contains gay children and dead children, animals knowing and perverse. Then there are gallant gentlemen, real or mythic, lost or "stoic"; old men wise and frustrate; and an occasional merchant, corrupt inevitably. Finally, there are couples straining both together and apart, or "orbited nice" in a painful equilibrium. In Ransom's own words, this is a "perilous and beautiful" world, through which chilled and feverish beings walk in dignity, poised at any moment to break into screams.

On one level, the poetry of these volumes must be read as an extended allegory, or symbolic version, of a dying way of life, stricken in the midst of its charm. The sense of loss or "declension" is best defined in "Old Mansion" of the first volume and "Antique Harvesters" of the second. "Old Mansion" describes a decayed "Southern manor" which has "expired sweetly as Nature." Not at all "ignoble," "if its peacock *was* a pigeon," it retains beauty, but can endure little longer

2. *The Fugitive,* IV, No. 3, 93-94.

even as an exhibit. The poet, "on retreating," sees in the house the image of himself:

> . . . and I went with courage shaken
> To dip, alas, into some unseemlier world.

Ransom portrays himself as already a foreigner to the ante bellum version of Southern culture, an observer depressed at his exclusion but inevitably committed to a less congenial world, where, as "Philomela" puts it, "It goes not liquidly for us."

"Antique Harvesters," the scene of which is punningly located on the "bank sinister" of the Mississippi and Ohio rivers, exploits an image of autumn yellowness. The pattern is already familiar from "The School" of *Poems about God*, where the poet speaks of himself as "in a wilderness of autumn" and "Sealed in a yellow tomb." Here, however, the yellow is itself fugitive:

> But grey will quench it shortly—the field,
> men, stones.

The dominant color tone of these volumes is blue. The progression, therefore, is from clear Hellenic blue, symbolic of the ante bellum cultural ideal of the South, through the yellow decline of its present autumn, to the grey winter of its foreseen death.

But the domination of blue does not make an idyll of life in Ransom's world at any stage. On a second level, the implied allegory is one of modern life as a whole. The theme here is that which, since Pound and Eliot, at least, has largely set the spirit and tone of twentieth-century Anglo-American poetry and criticism. Through the increasing scientism and mercantilism of our age (and especially for Ransom the accompanying tendency toward abstraction), man is losing his once simple and direct relation to nature, to other men, and finally to life's ultimate values. America, "this other Thrace," as Ransom sees it, is farthest gone from the "Attic" ideal. A number of Ransom's poems project this dilemma in terms of ironic dualism—that balance of the contending impulses he has discovered at the heart of his own creative processes. "Man without Sense of Direction" dramatizes the situation in a protagonist who "cannot fathom nor perform his nature." His "curse-hung head" is filled with abstract "perfect forms," and "uncouth/ Demonstrations of joy" in nature offend "the ear of the fervorless youth." "His doom is upon him," and even the passion of "the loveliest," his bride, cannot "kiss that harried one/ To peace," for he has no "cause, time, nor country."

A number of the poems deal with this dilemma at one stage or another, but the title sonnet sequence of *Two Gentlemen in Bonds* treats it in full detail. The active man, Paul of the poem, delights in nature and physical sensation; but, as his times demand, he plays the mercenary game and accepts the ruinous conventional standards by which the active man must live. Meanwhile, his counterpart, the philosophic idealist, keeps to his rat-infested tower, defies the world, and is able to retain only his bleak integrity and hopes for death. These two men, like the Christ and Antichrist of the earlier "Armageddon," represent the two equally untenable positions into which modern man is forced. In Eliot's language, they illustrate "dissociation of sensibility," or call it the disjunction of feeling and thought (see Tate's account of *Jefferson Davis*), or of fact and idea (see Warren's *All the King's Men*).[3]

Even this second, however, is not the topmost level of Ransom's reading of earth. For the duality of thought and feeling in man reflects for the poet a basic duality in the constitution of things. Thus, even the blue world where most of Ransom's characters dwell in some pride and dignity is a precarious one. Its Edenic atmosphere is subtly poisoned, and

3. This theme of Ransom's, with the accent on abstractionism, has dominated all Fugitive writing, including the Agrarian tracts. Warren was the first to comment on it in relation to Ransom's poetry in a fine essay, "John Crowe Ransom: A Study in Irony," *Virginia Quarterly Review*, II, 93-112.

all of its inhabitants are driven inevitably to taste of the forbidden fruit. Even the gayest of the "blue girls" in her innocent unconsciousness is making directly for the fateful tree. There she will learn knowledge, not of "good" and "evil," for these are empty abstractions, but the harsh realities of her human condition. She will learn that she, a creature avid of life, is faced with death; that she, beautiful in her twirling skirts, must look forward to the inevitable decay of beauty. Further, loving, she will learn of love's equivocations and its "chasms," and of nature's luring indifference. Being a woman, she may not fully understand how "desperate our cases" are, or conclude with John Black that "We are one part love/ And nine parts bitter thought"; but she will send off venomous letters to her lover and stand to watch them go, "hot as fever/ And cold as any icicle," or "in terror [flee] from the marriage chamber," "dream unlawful dreams" and "waken full of [her] own screams."

Ransom's characters are exhibited to us for the most part in the precarious stage of innocence or of experience still unabsorbed; none of them has, like Mithridates, developed tolerance for the ubiquitous poison. In Ransom's terms, they all lack a developed ironic philosophy which could make them "aware sharply and grimly, but not too painfully, of the constant involvement of life with death."[4] Herein lies the poet's advantage, and he makes shrewd and telling use of it. Despite the dramatic quality of these poems, the Ransomic personality envelops them all. Various critics have described the peculiar attitude or tone which constitutes the essential Ransom as "wrinkled laughter" (Morley), "acid gayety" (Van Doren), "detached, mock-pedantic, wittily complicated" (Jarrell), "ambiguous and unhappy" (Winters), "suave," "mixed," or simply "ironic." However we may choose to describe it, the success of the attitude depends primarily upon its detachment, both from protagonists and from self. Warren puts it that "the

4. "Freud and Literature," *op. cit.*, p. 162.

poem itself is a commentary on the situation," delivered "from the security of his position."[5] From this position, *sub specie Dei* (in Whom all antitheses are contained), Ransom is able to achieve a magnificent aloofness which is still intimately aware of the sharpness and grimness of the situation, shared always by the poet himself.

Ransom's particular flavor is a product of much more than detachment, of course. Detachment is the enabling act, as it were, which liberates the personality of the poet above the sort of immediate desperation which Tate and sometimes Warren are likely to exhibit. This personal quality in Ransom's poetry is a complex product of diction, formal structure, and what is best described as modulation. The familiar "Here Lies a Lady" will serve to illustrate where definition is all but impossible:

> Here lies a lady of beauty and high degree.
> Of chills and fever she died, of fever and chills,
> The delight of her husband, her aunts, an infant
>   of three,
> And of medicos marvelling sweetly on her ills.
>
> For either she burned, and her confident eyes
>   would blaze,
> And her fingers fly in a manner to puzzle their
>   heads—
> What was she making? Why, nothing; she sat
>   in a maze
> Of old scraps of lace, snipped into curious shreds—
>
> Or this would pass, and the light of her fire decline
> Till she lay discouraged and cold, like a stalk
>   white and blown,
> And would not open her eyes, to kisses, to wine;

5. "John Crowe Ransom: A Study in Irony," *op. cit.*, p. 103.

The sixth of these states was her last; the cold
settled down.

Sweet ladies, long may ye bloom, and toughly I
hope ye may thole,
But was she not lucky? In flowers and lace and
mourning,
In love and great honor we bade God rest her soul
After six little spaces of chill, and six of
burning.

The prevailing tone of this elegy is close to that of Gray's "Ode on the Death of a Favorite Cat," scandalously close, the pious may find. However, once we accept the poet's remove from too human concern, the lady-cat parallel is justified—both pets (well pedigreed), favorites, decorative, and ineffectual. In both cases the poets combine a certain raciness of rhythm with elaboration of diction to produce an effect of light mockery. But here the similarity ends, for Gray turns his poem into a moral fable, while Ransom preserves his aesthetic and moral distance absolutely. That is to say, whereas Gray steps out of his narrative to appear in person, smiling and wagging his finger at his audience, Ransom's commentary preserves his separation from the human concern, and he leaves it only to step anonymously into the ceremony. To neither poet is the protagonist of real concern; to Ransom, however, the ritual is important, the preservation of forms, the tribute to nonutilitarian values of beauty and innocence. (Note the deliberately excessive piling-up of formal tribute, far beyond any conceivable desert, in the final lines.) For Ransom, ceremony transcends its frail object, for it protects vital human values; in saying as much, the poet preserves his own kind of ceremonious transcendence above mortality itself.

Critics have commonly commended, and in rare cases deplored, the "elegance" of Ransom's style. The distinguished contributors to the special Ransom issue of *The Sewanee Review* (July, 1948) find themselves fascinated largely by this aspect of his work. Brooks traces parallels to Miltonic diction, Matthiessen to Biblical and to "the old-fashioned country expression" of the South; Stauffer speaks of "medieval diction," and Lowell of "the language of Henry James." Evidently the sources of Ransom's peculiar style are too various for profitable exploration. There is, however, a sort of basic idiom, or rather there are two idioms which constantly invade one another's precincts to produce tonal shifts and contrasts. Both of these languages have on them a patina of formality, or even artificiality, which the invocation of a mannered culture demands. This "elegant" surface effect ensures the poet's detachment and guards him against the excesses of personal passion—"a self-protective rhetoric," Jarrell calls it.

The two strains are essentially those which T. S. Eliot has described as splitting apart in the seventeenth century, toward Milton on the one hand, and toward Dryden on the other—the poetry of "magniloquence" and that of "wit." With Ransom, however, the magniloquence, harking back to Spenser primarily, is always mocking, or, to use Brooks's phrase, a "parody of the grand style." In general, the lighter the mood, the more nearly does Ransom's style approach the pure mock-magniloquent. "Armageddon," for example, immediately asserts a Spenserian rhetoric:

> Antichrist, playing his lissome flute and merry
> As was his wont, debouched upon the plain.

The witty Caroline strain is adequately illustrated in "Here Lies." But neither style is ever completely pure. Not only do they borrow from one another, as "Here Lies" borrows the archaic "thole"; but each is spiced with various sorts of modernisms from the street slang of "let 'em have it" to nursery "moo's" and "clack clack's," or to fine neologisms, like the proud young bosoms "poutering by."

The last stanza of "Here Lies" exhibits not only Ransom's diction under perfect control, but also the subtler effects achieved by what I have called modulation. The Elizabethan courtliness of address and the conventionality of the succeeding courtesy are in one of the regular variants of the basic wit idiom, just as the flower metaphor implied in "bloom" is a regular variant of Ransom's basic woman-bird comparison, with its implications of beauty and shy innocence. ("The Innocent Doves" is the subtitle for the feminine section of *Two Gentlemen in Bonds*.) The harshness of the world which awaits innocence might have been suggested by a sharp change of tone (Eliot's "'Jug Jug' to dirty ears"), but Ransom manages a much subtler effect by a careful preservation of tone and rhythm, even of alliteration and assonance. "Toughly" and "thole," following the sound pattern of "long" and "bloom," slip by, as it were, over the heads of the listeners, as a discourtesy may pass in a formal receiving line with the preservation of polite tone. The very pedantry of the Old English word aids in the tonal disguise, and the poet immediately blocks any fatal inquiry by the brightly colloquial question. The question is, of course, tipped with the same barb, but this time the easy geniality is the disguise. One imagines the pretty listeners murmuring polite "Wasn't she's?" before full comprehension occurs. The whole flavor of this passage, and Ransom manages many like it, is that of an aloof and perfectly mannered gentleman playing the social game on his own sophisticated level, above the heads of his character-auditors. There follows a shift of author position and tone as Ransom builds up the ceremony, complete with pious cliché, before the return to the lightly tripping rhythm, as well as the idiom, of the poem's main body.

The sprightliness of this verse, characteristic of a number of the poems in these volumes, does not invalidate Matthiessen's comment that Ransom's poetry is keyed to "a speaking rather than a singing voice"; or Lowell's, that it has the "distinction of good conversation." However gay the rhythm, the poet is always speaking (when his characters are not), never carolling. A "singing voice" (even at times an "organ voice") can be a dubious asset for a poet who is not patently writing songs, where the import of the words is not of major concern. One need only witness the more "musical" verses of Lanier, Swinburne, or Poe. Ransom possesses a "poetic voice," more dramatic, perhaps, than lyrical, but still capable of producing a rich variety of metrical effects while never straying far from traditional poetic patterns.

Ransom often, like Donne, fails of "keeping of accent" and the established number of accents. The first two stanzas of "Here Lies" set up a pentameter norm, predominantly anapestic; the "Sweet ladies" line deliberately breaks over into hexameter. To preserve the perfect balance between the address and courtesy on the one hand and the ironic addition on the other, Ransom adds a third accent following the caesura. Again, in the next to last line, the flow of the anapests is interrupted by a spondaic series for the solemn cliché of the service. Similarly in other poems, stanza patterns and rhyme schemes are varied or interrupted as confidently as the meter. "Conrad Sits in Twilight" builds to a swinging "Miniver Cheevy" rhythm, only to shift, not alone rhythm, but rhyme scheme and tone, for one of the finest passages of meditative description in modern poetry.

Ransom's rhyming can be as loose as the sequence in "Miriam Tazewell": flowers, courses, bridals, poplars, dependent entirely on the final "s" and the unfixed "r" and "l" sounds. But despite such radical variations, the total effect of any single poem is one of traditional formality and control. Like Auden, Ransom is a master of such neglected forms as Skeltonic short line verse, used for the comic-satiric effects traditionally associated with the form. He retains all of Skelton's freedom, shifting from dipodic nursery line patterns, like:

Kneaded it and caked it
And buttered it and baked it,
("Our Two Worthies")

to an abrupt:

And they quarreled,
Not carolled. ("In Mr. Minnit's House")

With equal ease he can swing into a double dipodic meter like that popularized by Tennyson, Morris, and Masefield, as in "Emily Hardcastle, Spinster":

We shall come tomorrow morning, who were not
to have her love.

For his lighter fables, he may deviate into a colloquial blank verse or into eccentric closed couplets:

But swarthy and blotched was simpering Jezebel,
So late with the worms, so soon to be bride of Hell.

Then Cleopatra enacted every wile
That had ensnared the antique world at Nile.
("Fresco")

Ransom's favorite forms, however, are still ballad variations, and his particular mastery in these volumes is the final short line. The abrupt stanza ending is perfectly adapted for the sort of ironic understatement in which the poet delights. In "Judith of Bethulia," a penultimate long line question is followed by a cryptic answer:

Might she walk in the market, sit in the council
of soldiers?
Only of the extreme elders.

In "Tom, Tom," "To a Lady," "Eclogue," and others, the device is employed effectively, but its triumph is "Bells for

John Whiteside's Daughter," where its unexpectedness, its faint disappointment and jar, sharpen the pathos to an extremely delicate poignance:

> There was such speed in her little body,
> And such lightness in her footfall,
> It is no wonder her brown study
> Astonishes us all.

If, as T. S. Eliot among others has come to believe, the final value of a literary accomplishment must depend on essentially extra-aesthetic values, the initial test of the poet must still be his command of language, as the painter's must be the command of line and color. By this test, no writer of our time better deserves the name of poet than Ransom. His effects in these volumes are limited by the limitations of the ironic mode, and this, despite Brooks and others, is limitation; but within his range he achieves an extraordinary variety of shadings. Consider, for example, the variations through which he rings a favorite, and once almost discredited, word like "sweet" and its adverb. The courtly "Sweet ladies" slides off into a contemptuously sarcastic "sweet sirs" when a mountebank coaxes his audience to challenge his savage hound. The "sweet tongue" of birds becomes in a woman the "sweet monotone she twitters." There are normally "sweet wines," but William Blake "foundered on" a more cloying "sweet cake." Sin is also sweet, so sweet that men curse the last trumpet which has "sundered them" from it. Cleopatra's breasts are sweet to the sucking asp, who, in his turn, is "too sweet to hiss." The poet is lured by "female tissue sweetly shaped," but a rat's "sweet features" have their place as well in another setting. Almost always Ransom's use of the word contains an ambiguous element, suggesting the dual and equivocal nature of this special world, where medicos marvel "sweetly" on one's ills and fictitious girls make "sweet disport," where soldiers' oaths are as sweet as "love's exchange." In such modulations, through which he implies the beautiful and perilous balance of a world at once unique and recognizably universal, Ransom's special grace as a poet lies.

After the close of the *Fugitive* period, Ransom writes poetry only occasionally, but there is no least sign of diminution in his poetic powers. Whatever personal reasons may have influenced his practice, it is clear that the immediate stimulation of the magazine project was removed, and that a new excitement in the form of socio-economic and general aesthetic theory tempted him away from creative activity. If, as Tate has it, the fate of the creative Southern mind has been diversion from its natural tendency by the inveterate need of the South for practical thinkers to fight its losing political battles, Ransom's course in the late twenties was a continuation of regional tradition. But Ransom's major battle in the twenties and since has been one for the rehabilitation of art as the way to fuller life.

Ransom has chosen to represent his poetic activity since 1927 with only four short pieces, all of them products of the thirties. ("What Ducks Require," an early Agrarian fable included in the *Selected Poems,* was first printed in 1927.) Three other uncollected poems appeared in 1929, two of them in an experimental extended sonnet form, called by Ransom "English sonnet of Italian parts" (8-8-8-6), and the third an annotated verse essay. None of these efforts displays the poet at his best, though the language is often highly distinguished. For five years thereafter, the period of major Agrarian activity, Ransom printed no verse at all. Then, in 1934, with Agrarianism a rapidly failing cause, Ransom produced three fine poems, two of them relating back in matter and manner to the *Fugitive* period. The third, "Painted Head," is a brilliant metaphysical "conceit" poem, a mode in which Ransom was taking increasing interest at this time (see especially his essay of this year, "Poetry: A Note in Ontology"; here the "Metaphysical" becomes the ultimate mode of the greatest poetry, distinguished from the "Physical" and the "Platonic"). The final poem, an occasional piece written after another lapse of five years for the June, 1939, convocation of the Harvard chapter of Phi Beta Kappa, is an extraordinarily fine poetic essay.

Surprisingly, the three finest of these poems—"Prelude to Evening," "Painted Head," and the "Address"—are written in unrhymed stanzas, all nominally regular in metrics, but very free for the most part. "Prelude" substitutes for rhyme, patterns of internal alliteration and assonance, while the other two rely largely on the repetition of key words. The experimental nature of these patterns, and further of syntax, indicates that Ransom is here working with new standards. Impressed certainly by Donne and Marvell, and perhaps by the dense verse of Tate and Warren, he strives in these later poems for a new intellectual compression. His imagery becomes tighter, the grammar severely economical. No word is wasted, no epithet admitted that will not bear its full weight in concrete evocation and connotative aptness. There is some sacrifice of flavor words, archaisms, colloquialisms, and such old favorites as "sweet," but in their places appear freighted metaphysical puns and sharp physical detail.

Such losses as the new density entails become obvious only as the poems are read in sequence, but the gains are even more evident. "Of Margaret" lacks the bright ironic finish of the earlier woman poems, but it achieves a new and moving intimacy, compounded of deep affection and regret, for a woman and a way of life, for devotion and unfulfillment. Furthermore, Ransom's old mastery of sound and overtone is richly demonstrated. Margaret watches, mourning, as the first leaf falls, knowing that all must descend,

> and the blind land be filled
> With dead, and a mere windiness unchild
> Her of the sons of all her mothering.

"Painted Head" is a perfect textbook example of the extended "conceit" poem. The controlling metaphor is built out of Ransom's obsessive concern: his war against abstraction in behalf of a recovered "world's body." In a smiling portrait head he sees a strikingly apt image of the "dark severance" of mind and body enforced by modern life. The head is "a capital on no/ Column," a flower cut off from its "body bush" or "faithful stem," a widower, an "iron acropolis," and a "Platonic perhaps head/ On a canvas sky depending from nothing." (Plato, with the windy abstractionism of his realm of ideas, is Ransom's original villain from far back.) "Beauty is of body," Ransom insists, and the body bears the head "Not to the glory of tyrant head but to/ The increase of body." The poem ends with a series of bold metaphorical extensions: eyes as "big blue birds," ears as "sea-shell flats/ And caves," and for the brain itself, one judges, an "olive garden for the nightingales." Though these final flights are climactic, there is no change of key. From the opening, "By dark severance the apparition head/ Smiles," the extravagant baroque tone is sounded, and the poem builds with a firm augmenting logic of fantastic accumulation. The theme word, "head," is sounded again and again, and even the sentences are decapitated—the second, third, fourth, and sixth stanzas omit the subject, in the first three cases the body of the sentence being severed from the understood "head."

"Painted Head" abounds in metaphysical wit also, plays on the head theme. Research scholars appear as "historian headhunters"; the ordering of the portrait was "capital irony"; the flesh having been "vinegarly traduced," the head becomes a "hard egg . . . shrunken to its own deathlike surface"; and there are notable plays on the historic custom of head-rolling for treason. Structurally and tonally, this poem is wholly admirable, a brilliant intellectual feat. If finally it lacks the moving warmth of such similar "conceit" poems as those of Donne, Herbert, Traherne, or Edward Taylor, it is the very abstraction of the theme that determines the effect. The instructive paradox in this case is one that applies to others of the Fugitive group influenced by Ransom's controlling idea to the extent of using it as a major theme. "Painted Head" is a poem completely of the head, a wit poem dominated by the abstract idea of anti-abstractionism. (Note that the "conceit" poems of Donne and the others commonly have their basis in passion, love physical or love religious.) A similar development occurs, for example, in Tate's novel, *The Fathers*, where the overdomination of the abstractionism theme tends to rob the characters of free life and convert them, too, into pale abstractions.

In the poetic essay form of "The Address to the Scholars of New England," Ransom has adopted a genre admirably suited to the abstraction theme, as well as to his own later manner. Here wit has full play, with the intensity slacked off. The wit is sometimes metaphysical: the New England fathers "fetched the Pure Idea in a bound box/ And fastened him in a steeple," whence "raffish sons" may one time come and

> With positive steel they'll pry into the steeple,
> And blinking through the cracked ribs at the void
> A judgment laughter rakes the cynic sons.

Or it may be lightly ironic: Plato's "scandal-mongering," the Pilgrims as "rich Heirs traveling incognito . . ./ And but affecting that dog's life of pilgrims." And somewhere between, the fine ironic stanza:

> But they reared their heads into the always clouds
> And stooped to the event of war and bread,
> The secular perforces and short speech
> Being labors surlily done with the left hand,
> The chief strength giddying with transcendent clouds.

As a whole, this poem is a brilliantly sustained bit of polemics, achieved on a high level of metaphorical irony. Only the best of Wyatt's, Donne's, or Dryden's "satires" and passages of

Auden, Eliot, and Shapiro can bear comparison with Ransom's brilliantly unified achievement here.

"Prelude to an Evening," in many ways the finest poem that Ransom has written, is a small drama of domestic crisis. The theme recalls that of several earlier poems, notably "Eclogue," "Two in August," and "Man without Sense of Direction." The situation of the thought-haunted husband and the distracted wife is treated here, however, with increased intimacy and intensity. As Cleanth Brooks has pointed out, Ransom does not discard his habitual formal distance from his subject; the distraction of the wife is seen through the poet-husband's "perverse supposal," not directly, and the poem is a "prelude," rather than the evening itself. Still, the distance is noticeably lessened in comparison with that prevailing in the earlier poems. The result is that the wife's "gallant fear" comes to us with a new poignancy, though the communication is almost wholly through objective detail, evoked with sure and masterful economy. It is the clock which "metronome's" the "gallant fear"; crying has twice "unbeautied" her mouth "against the pillow"; we see her "needles clicking" mechanically, hear her "heels detonating the stair's cavern," watch her "Freshening the water in the blue bowls/ For the buckberries with not all [her] love," listening for "the low wind," saying "Noes but wanderingly/ Smoothing the heads of the hungry children." Not only are such details precise and directly evocative, but they catch unerringly the pulse of her expectant fear and the suspenseful abstraction of her calm. Like the Jane Sneed of "Eclogue," this wife is one of the "innocent doves," suffering at second hand from the "too banded Eumenides" who pursue her husband. But we do not, as in "Eclogue," hear her discuss the problem with him who is "one part love/ And nine parts bitter thought"; here she is presented, seen, and felt in direct images which tranfer her and her predicament with new immediacy. The poet-husband is seen only as a hounded "tired wolf," dragging his "infected wound," but the very objectivity with which he depicts her plight leads us to sense the poignance of his helpless pity.

If Ransom's poetic abilities have suffered no attenuation as the result of his absorption in theoretical problems, the nature of his talents provides its own explanation. Ransom has stated that he turned to poetry in reaction against scientific studies; in his criticism, therefore, he has insisted upon the "irrelevant tissue," or suprarational "texture," which distinguishes poetry, and upon the "love of nature" and other "romantic" elements as well. However, his early development of an "ironic" philosophy indicates that he had already essentially rejected the typical romantic syntheses, and romantic disillusion in its turn, to reach a system of balance. Balance is the distinguishing mark of the "classical" mind, and it is characterized precisely by its "not too painful" acceptance of the human condition, its accent on man's dignity, its pride in his intellectual capacity. However the true classical mind may argue for the necessity of myth or religion, his faith remains rooted in his reason. Ransom did not, like A. E. Housman, remain a classical scholar, but he has remained a fundamental "classicist."

Ransom's poetry has always been notable for its lucid and highly sophisticated intellectualism. Despite his theoretical accent on the irrelevant, there are no logical irrelevancies in the poems. The imagery is always under strict control; it knows the effects it intends to create and goes directly for them. There is no strain to imply more than words can reasonably convey, no vagueness, nothing slipshod or loose. It is characteristic of the method that the metaphors are most often "conversions downward" to the lesser and more concrete: death is "a gentleman in a dustcoat," the traveled scholar an "amphibious crocodile," women birds, a mortal wound a "puncture," Christ a Diomede. The overtones, however subtle or fantastic, are always logically coherent.

Poetry of this sort, with its consciousness of intention and its tight control of emotional effects, entails some loss in suggestibility. One of Ransom's latest theoretical formulations speaks of the "id" element in poetry through which imagery of the irrational unconscious is tapped. It is precisely this ingredient, a "romantic" ingredient certainly, which Ransom's poetry lacks. His poems at no moment create the illusion of taking charge of themselves. There is no drawing on a reservoir of half-submerged ambiguous images that seem to carry the mind beyond its conscious limits. It is arguable that only the essentially "religious" or "metaphysical" mentality produces such imagery. In our century, Yeats, Eliot, Auden, and of the Fugitives, Robert Penn Warren, all endowed with a sense of the suprarational, pre-eminently induce this sort of rich, unplumbable ambiguity. In contrast, Ransom's ambiguities are balances of carefully weighted alternatives. The irony that results in Ransom's case is likely, therefore, to be less complex than that, say, of Eliot. It will lack a final, if perhaps nebulous, level of reference. It will operate on the moral plane, but hardly on the metaphysical.

Whether or not we regard this absence of a "religious" plane as a serious defect will depend largely on the personal orientation of the critic. Aestheticians in the romantic or German metaphysical tradition generally, and this will include many of the psychoanalytic aestheticians influenced by Jung and Otto Rank, must find the omission all but fatal. But this attitude, which emphasizes a conception of the poet as *vates* rather than as *faber*, will virtually deny the name of "poet" to the greatest classical writers. Ransom as a poet has never broken in any fundamental way with his classical, rationalist prepossessions as they appeared in his earliest essay. He has remained a poet of the conscious mind, of traditionist, even aristocratic, taste; but with these qualities he has brought to his poetry a rich sensibility which operates directly on his natural and human environment.

Ransom has not, therefore, produced the grandest poetry of our period. But within the limits prescribed in his stricter structure-texture theory, his achievement is brilliant. His logically and subtly balanced structures, filled out with the eloquently counterpointed language, the sensitive observations, and the wit of his remarkable textures, have given us many of our most distinguished poems.

CHAPTER IV

Apprentice Tate

THE ALLEN TATE whom we meet first as Henry Feathertop in the pages of *The Fugitive* is a brash, precociously ironic young intellectual, adept with words, flip with postures, but withal seriously dedicated to poetry, ambitious, and quick to learn. He begins as a poet under the direct influence of Ransom, with some excursion into the Davidson manner, but he is soon lured away by his momentous discovery of T. S. Eliot. Once he commits himself to the authority of Eliot's poetry and his critical ideas, Tate never wavers in his allegiance.

His first published poem, a sonnet "To Intellectual Detachment," echoes Ransom in manner and diction while it exhibits a sly portrait of his mentor. A dramatized sketch of the kind at which Ransom excelled, it fails of Ransom's subtlety and control, but it carries a sharpness of its own. A line like "God give him peace! He gave none other peace," rings a clear echo of Ransom's courtly phrasing, but the poem provides no tonal setting for the language. The final quatrain reads:

> And his art, disjected from his mind,
> Was utterly a tool, so it possessed him;
> A passionate devil, informed in humankind,
> It turned on him—he's dead. Shall we detest him?

The phrasing, the light feminine rhyme, the broken quality and the twist of the final line, the irresolution, are all good Ransomic devices, but nothing is quite right. The Ransomic sounding "so it possessed him" can hardly be construed with the implications of "art disjected" and "tool." The ultimate question comes not as a vital indecision growing out of the complication of attitudes expressed in the body of the poem, but simply as a sprightly afterthought, without consequence.

So it is with a number of Tate's early ventures in the Ransom manner. "Cul de Sac," which the author early marked "Cancel!" in the Vanderbilt library copy of the magazine, contains such stanzas as:

> His classic taint of otherness,
> Changing his human blood to wine,
> Smirked at the doorway of her soul,
> Which he had told her was a shrine.

The poet is clearly striving for unusual images and ironic effects, but achieving only a series of gestures in language, with a "taint" smirking and blood changing to wine evidently only for the sake of the rhyme.

There is a great deal of sophisticated pose in the verse of this apprentice Tate. As he strives toward Ransom's attitude of "tragic irony," he arrives at a flippant insouciance:

> Brazen the horn of death and loud its blowing:
> Give me, Lady, your heart; then I'll be going.

or theatricality:

> Somewhere I heard the clang of a hearse.
> You are very far away, dear Lady—
> As I light this cigarette—and under an inscrutable
> curse.

Tate is least felicitous at this period, however, when he takes his cue from his other teacher-colleague, Donald Davidson. In such poems as "In Secret Valley" and "Call on, Deep Voice," both marked with the author's cancellation, the romantic pall is thick:

> I sicken of this beauty as mountains of their snow,

or

> Now darkness over all, but darkness most in me,

or

> Yet ere You come I will kiss this child and rock her
> To sleep, so young, so white, whom I adore.

Three times, however, in the first year of the magazine's publication, Tate produced poems which he has seen fit to reprint and then again include in his *Poems: 1922–1947*. One of these is a free translation from Sappho, "Farewell to Anactoria"; another, "To Oenia in Wintertime," in a Latin mode. Both of these poems gain from the compression and restrained passion of their models. They are the first manifestation of a classic strain which will re-enter Tate's poetry to modify the influence of Eliot. The third of these poems, a "Horatian Epode to the Duchess of Malfi," is the most interesting in view of Tate's development. Here the form, much of the vocabulary, and some of the imagery derive again from the classic, but the sharp ironic juxtapositions and especially the final modern contrast and dying fall inevitably suggest Eliot:

> It is moot whether there be divinities
> As I finish this play by Webster:
> The street-cars are still running however
> And the catharsis fades in the warm water
> of a yawn.

When we recall Eliot's "Whispers of Immortality," beginning "Webster was much possessed by death," the resemblance is striking.

The "Horatian Epode" appeared some months following the publication in *The Double-Dealer* of a Tate poem entitled "Euthanasia." In his account of the *Fugitive* years, Tate speaks of a letter he received from Hart Crane following the printing[1]

1. Tate says he received it in May, 1922 or 1923. "Euthanasia" appeared in the May, 1922, issue of *The Double-Dealer*.

of this *Double-Dealer* poem. Crane remarked that the poem indicated that Tate had been reading Eliot. Tate was surprised, he says, because he had not then discovered Eliot. It is reasonably certain, then, that the "Horatian Epode" is the first poem written by Tate under the influence of Eliot. The next issue of *The Fugitive* (December, 1922) contained the critical essay eulogizing *The Waste Land.*

For some time the mood and imagery of the Stuart tragedians cling to Tate's work, and with them the Eliotic device of throwing into sudden opposition past and present. The irony, however, is more often Ransomic, and the formal patterns persist. Conceptually, these poems are immature; dominated by the imagery of death and weariness, they come to no adult terms with the experience they present. The poet is still, fundamentally, lighting his cigarette under an inscrutable curse. Or he is mourning, like Davidson, the "contemporary irrelevancy of myth" by comparing Leda with the prostitute who "lives in Redkey, Indiana." Or, finally, he is merely a too young and world-weary Eliot:

> And we are weary infants
> In a palsied age. ("Calidus Juventa")

As in the early Ransom, the tendency to pose in Tate's first poems destroys the validity of his insights. There are, however, considerable differences between the situations and accomplishments of the two apprentice poets. From his beginnings, Ransom was an original. The conception of his *Poems about God,* the ambiguous attitude which prompted it, as well as the mannered diction, were almost uninfluenced by any contemporary poetry. On the other hand, Tate, for better or for worse, was inevitably derivative. He had directly before him both Ransom and Davidson as older, more polished practitioners; and he discovered a still more congenial model in Eliot before he had progressed far in his apprenticeship. His verbal talents were undeniable, but he had reached no synthesis of experience that could be called his own, and his taste was still unsure. His poses were necessary disguises to cover his lack of an attitude. When the editors of *The Double-Dealer* called him the "White Hope of the South,"[2] they were counting on an eclectic talent which had as yet produced no true poetry of its own. Not until the close of the *Fugitive* period did Tate begin to develop his own voice.

At the same time, his critical faculties were being sharpened rapidly in his tilts with Ransom and Davidson. He begins as a critic under the stimulus of *The Waste Land*, and his conceptions originate in Eliot's essays from this time on. He evidently studies not only Eliot but the earlier critics to whom Eliot refers. His second critical article[3] reflects the reading. His theoretic formulation recalls Eliot's conception of the poetic tradition and of "fusion"; he refers to Rémy de Gourmont, whom Eliot had called "a real master of fact—sometimes, I am afraid . . . a master illusionist of fact," as "the shifty Remy de Gourmont." Baudelaire, one of Eliot's acknowledged masters, is mentioned by Tate as the source of "modern poetic diction" and of "modern free verse."

The bulk of this essay is an application of one of Eliot's major theses, expounded in his article on Blake and elsewhere, that the great poet requires "a framework of accepted and traditional ideas which [prevents] him from indulging in a philosophy of his own," a "framework of mythology and theology and philosophy." Tate's version is that the lack of "a harmonious firmament of stage-properties and sentiments" has produced "the age of the Sophist." "Our times cleaves to no racial myth, its myth is the apotheosis of machinery." Then he adds a further note from Eliot, one calculated to ruffle Ransom: "at least our poet is aware of his own age."

2. Allen Tate, "The Fugitive—1922–1925," *Princeton University Library Chronicle*, III, 81.

3. *The Fugitive*, III, No. 2, 34-36.

The thesis of the loss of a "racial myth" and the consequent "sort of Decadence" quickly becomes the central theme of Tate's criticism—and to an extent of his poetry. In a *Nation* review[4] of Cabell's works, he applies it to the Southern poet. "The sensitive person from the South in this age," he says, "approaches literature with few or none of the prepossessions, or benefits, derived from the interdependency of a religion and a society. His mind is open for experiment in form, for curiosity." He allows "empiricism" as the Southerner's "only alternative to intellectual suicide." Eliot, he says, left St. Louis "in the state of knowing oneself to be a foreigner at home." Tate now had left the South for New York.

From this point, with only an experimental empiricism left him, Tate's proper development begins. It begins away from home and essentially away from his earliest masters. Both physically and spiritually he has chosen to follow Eliot in a search for new values in a mythless age. Through 1925 and 1926 Tate does an immense amount of reading in aesthetic theory and social philosophy, as well as in literature proper. His philosophic position, however, remains a clear reflection of Eliot's. In this age of "dissociated intelligences," he says in an article on Edwin Muir, "our mythology is dead and we have not achieved a substitute for it out of the world picture of modern science." Muir, fully comprehending the dilemma, asks for "the construction of new myths which 'idealize man's goal.' " But, says Tate, the "intellectual integrity of optimism doesn't exist"; Muir "ignores the hopeless breach between the abstractionism of science . . . and the object itself . . . to which it is the business of the poet to return."[5] This last is directly out of Ransom, but it is also a logical derivation from the T. E. Hulme-Eliot position.

By the beginning of 1927 Tate has formulated a full-fledged neo-Aristotelian aesthetic theory. Writing in *The*

4. "Last Days of a Charming Lady," *Nation*, CXXI, 485-86.
5. "Tiresias," *Nation*, CXXIII, 509.

Sewanee Review[6] in answer to Ransom's theory of "tragic irony," Tate defines an aesthetic absolutism which leaves Ransom's thesis irrelevant to the primary issue. Tate had already objected to sociological criticism and, by implication, to moralistic criteria. Now he finds that Ransom, in dealing only with the general metaphysical position proper to the poetic mind, omits the essential "specific poetic intelligence," which applies not between "the poet and his world," but between the poet or reader and the poem. "This relation," he continues, "as poetry tends toward purity, conduces to an absolutism the problem of which lies outside the metaphysical enquiry into the nature of reality. To understand this relation is doubtless the chief end of criticism."

In developing his theory, Tate explicitly pays his respects to Eliot and to an undefined "school of criticism headed by Mr. T. S. Eliot"; and indeed Eliot's presence is everywhere. Tate is simply pushing Eliot's doctrines a step farther in the direction of poetic autonomy. He insists that "the ultimate value of experience [is] its ordered intensification; and this is the sole value and meaning of poetry." (Eliot's less drastic version is that "it is not the . . . intensity, of the emotions . . . but the intensity of the artistic process . . . that counts.")[7] Tate says that it is likely, through "exclusive attention to the perceptions which [the poem] concentrates—through the 'more than usual order' given them—that the disturbance . . . is absolved." (Eliot: "Poetry is not a turning loose of emotion, but an escape from emotion.")[8] The world of the poem "is a section of the known world," but "unlike the portion of the knowable world for which it stands as a portion it is complete, it is finite." (Eliot: "But the difference between art and the event is always absolute.")[9]

Tate grounds his theory in an unargued hypothesis, "the irresistible need of the mind for absolute experience," over

6. "Poetry and the Absolute," *Sewanee Review,* XXXV, 41-52.
7. T. S. Eliot, *Selected Essays,* p. 8. 8. *Ibid.,* p. 10. 9. *Ibid.,* p. 9.

and above the sentimental desire for an "absolute metaphysics." The existence of this need, which cannot "be adequately satisfied in ordinary cursory experience," "immediately explains the necessity for art." This is the first instance of many when the logic of their arguments on aesthetics forces the Fugitive critics into the field of psychology, where I. A. Richards with much better grounding had preceded them. Eliot avoids the dilemma by refusing to construct a systematic theory, but both Ransom and Tate are propelled by more rigorously rationalistic impulses. Their theories, therefore, which originate in bold assumptions, are constantly being reworked in terms of new evidence from fields of knowledge into which they find themselves pushed. And it is finally psychology which lures them, for only in the indeterminateness of psychological knowledge can they find a refuge against positivism broad enough to admit the logic of the illogical demanded by art.

Thus Tate in 1927 has set up a purely formal aesthetic creed. He has eliminated moral, sociological, philosophical, and historical criteria, and has called for a new school of critics "attending exclusively to the properties of poetry as a fine art." This call will be repeated later by Ransom when he writes "Wanted: An Ontological Critic," and the cry will be heeded by the younger "New Critics" everywhere.

In this argument there is little room for Tate's "racial myth" thesis. But he does not abandon it for all its sociological nature. Tate the poet, lost with his generation in empiricism, feels acutely the need for an integrating philosophy which will orient his "specific poetic intelligence." He repeats his earlier argument in more direct terms for *The New Republic*,[10] again paraphrasing Eliot and quoting Eliot's favorite, "la sua voluntade e nostra pace" from Dante. "The advantage of the poet in Dante's time" was that he could "focus on method," while "the modern poet has to construct, besides his personal vision, the scheme itself."

10. "The Revolt against Literature," *New Republic*, XLIX, 329-30.

The next step for Tate as a practicing poet is an attempt to reorient his own personal vision in terms of a "scheme" that has the proper validity. There is no doubt that Eliot's acceptance of Anglo-Catholicism prodded Tate's search. It is likely that Hart Crane's adoption of the Whitman mythos added incentive. At all events, in this setting Tate rediscovers the Southern heritage which he has repudiated as a "strictly political and economic aristocracy."

Tate writes in his recollections of this period: "And then one day—I cannot be sure of the year, I think 1926—I wrote John Ransom a new sort of letter. I told him we must do something about Southern history and the culture of the South. John had written on the same day, the same message to me."[11] What Tate was seeking, perhaps to some extent creating, was what he called a "common historical myth," only historical because it evidently lacked any adequate religious foundation that could appeal to either Ransom or Tate. I think it important, in Tate's case at least, to insist that the theory demanded the myth, and that the integration which unified Tate's poetic vision was primarily an intellectual process. It is perhaps only a coincidence that Faulkner found his myth of the South at much the same time.

Tate published his first volume of poetry, *Mr. Pope and Other Poems,* in 1928, shortly after his concern with the Southern historical myth had developed. The very divisions of this collection are indications of the new orientation: "Space," "Time," and "History"; and many of the more important poems in the volume date from 1926 and 1927. In general, these are more compact, more intellectually wrought than the earlier poems. They attempt a synthesis of experience from the perspective of a continuing historical tradition, of what Tate will later call a "temporal past," as distinguished from the "spatial," or logical, past of the scientist.

11. "The Fugitive—1922–1925," *op. cit.*, p. 84.

The poet's imagination is set free, his past experience is made "available," to use I. A. Richards' term, not by any new moral or metaphysical conclusions reached, but by his discovery of a subject and of an attitude toward that subject. Tate's subject is the relationship between past and present from the point of view of the spiritual "exile." The attitude is that defined in "Poetry and the Absolute," a purely aesthetic one, concerned only with the "ordered intensification" of the experiences. Thus he may, and usually does, present a moral dilemma, but he presents it as ordered experience, resolved only in the sense that the creative act is itself a resolution. This attitude emphatically does not imply that intellectual action will be excluded from the poetry; on the contrary, for Tate, as for Eliot and Donne, intellection is an integral part of every complete experience.

This aesthetic attitude governs all the more mature poems in *Mr. Pope,* as indeed it governs most of Tate's later verse as well. Once subject and attitude are fully grasped, a considerable amount of the noted "obscurity" of the individual poems is clarified. There remain, however, many difficulties caused by the intellectual density and complexity of image and symbol. A central poem of the "Space" section illustrates both types of obscurity. It is called "The Idiot," and presents a picture of a Southern yard at evening, with the idiot lolling in his hammock; his sister beside him mends lace and Negroes people the background. The poem is unintelligible until we realize that Tate is presenting a concentration of experience as apprehended through the limited faculties of the protagonist, who has been construed as symbolic of modern man's dissociated sensibility. Sense impressions occur to him as discrete and unintegrated phenomena:

> A dog barks, the hammock swings, he lies.
> One two three the cows bulge on the hill.

His own physical impulses start up, and as suddenly die away, with no discriminatory concepts operating to give them continuity:

> Till now his arteries lag and now they start
> Reverence with the frigid gusts of sin.

"Motion, that is not time," determines his world; values are lacking, so that "magnolias drench the ground/ with Appomattox"; with a fan he "lifts/ The Ozarks"; a lightning-bug suggests "Diving. 'I am the captain of new wars!'" Finally and formlessly, "the towering weak and pale/ Covers his eyes with memory like a sheet." The image is one of death, from which the idiot, who can substitute only motion for the continuity that is life, has never emerged. The death image has been prepared in the lines:

> Now in the idiot's heart a chamber stinks
> Of dead asters, as the potter's field of May.

Compare Eliot's opening of *The Waste Land:*

> April is the cruellest month, breeding
> Lilacs out of the dead land,

and note that Tate's asters carry an additional connotation since, dead, they smell (to Tate, at least) like carrion. They reappear in this poem as springing "from the important picnic of a fool"—ironically the "dead" past?—and as a single only "peeled aster" in "Death of Little Boys." (It might further be noted that the "sheet" which covers the sight of the idiot is that of "memory," and that Eliot's *Waste Land* lines continue with "mixing/ Memory with desire," all that modern man has left for his spiritual and physical sustenance.)

The interpretation of the idiot symbol, which is vital, of course, for any reading of the poem, depends, perhaps, on more than appears in the poem. Like Eliot, and even more like Yeats, Tate builds his symbols incrementally, so that they tend to progress from the status of images to that of more and more heavily freighted symbols. The idiot image appears explicitly in "Subway," where the world of mechanism is characterized in terms of "the cold revery of an idiot." In the "Epistle (To E. W.)" the rule of urban civilization is personified as "the idiot king of a savage court"; and the "idiots in the street" of "Art" are clearly his subjects. Finally, since Tate evidently means to include himself in the "modern" category, we may without offense quote an autobiographical note written for *Twentieth Century Authors*. Referring to the somewhat enlarged head he possessed in childhood, he says, "The family belief that I was an imbecile redoubled my secret efforts to prove them wrong."[12]

Through all of these references we are enabled to carry to the reading of "The Idiot" a considerable freight of symbolic extension. The Southern setting, the "frigid gusts of sin," the "panther's heart" image of savagery are elucidated. And the symbol central to this poem is, with the related madman concept, at least peripheral in most of the more important poems of this volume.

"The Idiot" remains a portrait, or filling out of a symbol. Other poems project specific problems, but their resolutions are uniformly aesthetic, rather than philosophic or practical. The much discussed "The Death of Little Boys" is a case in point. Ransom has used this poem to illustrate a distinction between "pure" and "obscure" poetry. It is "as if," Ransom says, "the obscure poet [here Tate] presented a subject in order to play with a great deal of important predication without ever completing any." Yvor Winters has rightly, if overharshly, taken Ransom to task for this statement—for him the poem is not obscure but simply bad. Actually Tate's poem is obscure only in the sense that it makes no overt predication about the experience itself. In the manner of "A Pauper" and of "Ode to the Confederate Dead," it presents in ostensibly objective terms,

12. Stanley J. Kunitz and Howard Haycraft, *Twentieth Century Authors*, p. 1386.

which nevertheless imply emotional upset, an intellectual dilemma. The problem is the death of a child, but the dilemma faced is the impossibility of dealing with death at all in a world which provides no system of belief and no ritual within whose framework death can be given meaning. The concluding irony does not resolve the dilemma:

> There is a calm for you where men and women
> Unroll the chill precision of moving feet.

Absorbing oneself in a mechanistic world where men and women are automata, cogs in an ever-moving machine, will make of the death a statistic, and there need therefore be no emotional concern.

"Subway," another of the mature poems, does not quite admit of Mr. Winters' comment, "that the poet has faced and defined the possibility of . . . madness . . . and has arrived at a moral attitude toward it, . . . a feeling of dignity and self-control in the face of a situation of major difficulty." The poem is overcharged, I feel, but the poet professes himself only "dazed," transformed temporarily by his experience in the hell of mechanism from a human being living in time into a spatial entity—"I am become geometries"—a part of mechanism itself, governed by "idiot" abstraction.

Most of the other late poems in *Mr. Pope* deal with related subjects and are resolved in the same fashion. "Ditty," the most explicit, offers the symbol of night, "now the easy peer of day" (a symbol to be much exploited), and the moon, with its lunatic extension. Here night stands for the evil of man's lot, once accepted along with the day good, presented in a rural setting. In contrast, the modern city setting sees men violently escaping the fact of natural evil, plunging in crowds, and finally managing to

> Tuck in their eyes, and cover
> The flying dark with sleep like falling leaves.

These final lines are as reminiscent of the close of "The Idiot" as the previous ones are of "Subway."

"Ode to the Confederate Dead" and "Obituary" are still further treatments of the problem of death's meaning, but now deaths in the past of one's tradition. "The Pauper" brings the series up to the poet's immediate parents. The Confederate war dead, despite the "furious murmur of their chivalry," the "sunlit" memory of the long-dead grandmother, and the unacceptable heritage of the father, "deaf to the pathos" of the mother's death, are presented as equally useless since they "Define no attitude to the present winter." In each case, there remains the unanswered question: How can we accept the past dead, death itself, our own foreseen deaths? But the question itself supplies the poet with subject and attitude.

Once Tate's apprenticeship is over, as it is in this volume, it becomes possible to examine the materials from which his personal poetic synthesis has been constructed and to assess its early effectiveness. The influences of Ransom and Eliot remain dominant. Much of the Ransomic irony and balance, as well as the concern with modern "dissociation" and with death, are reflected in the developed Tate. More importantly, Eliot and Ransom reinforce each other on many points: the concern with tradition, the anti-mechanistic, anti-relativistic bias, the insistence on concrete detail. Technically, Tate's chief debt is to Eliot, but Ransom's formal patterns, with their calculated irregularities, occur as often as the freer *Waste Land* and "Gerontion" forms. The special Ransomic diction appears in many scattered lines and sometimes in whole stanzas:

> When Alexander Pope strolled in the city
> Strict was the glint of pearl and gold sedans.
> Ladies leaned out more out of fear than pity
> For Pope's tight back was rather a goat's than man's.

This is pure Ransom in almost every particular. One suspects, however, that Ransom would not have allowed the inaccurately hard "glint" for pearl.

On the other hand, practically the whole of "Retroduction to American History" and much of "The Pauper" echo Eliot in word and manner. Many of Tate's special devices stem directly from Eliot: the use of both learned and private reference; the omission of logical connectives—"qualitative progression," in Winters' phrase; the emphasis on the "objective correlative"; the abrupt juxtaposition of scenes from the past and the present; and even what Morton Zabel condemned in his review[13] of *Mr. Pope,* "plotted obscurities," a means, it would seem, of forcing intensive reading.

The most characteristic of Tate's devices, however, is his continuous metaphorical animation of abstractions, a device that will come more and more to distinguish Tate's style. Much of this practice, certainly, had its origin in passages like the central one in Eliot's "Gerontion," beginning:

> Think now
> History has many cunning passages, contrived
> corridors
> And issues, deceives with whispering ambitions. . . .

In Tate, the practice is more constant and more tortured:

> And abnegation folds hands, crossed like the knees
> Of the complacent tailor, stitches cloaks of mercy
> To the backs of obsessions.

This passage (from "Retroduction") illustrates not only Tate's extension of this device, but his further practice of building metaphor within metaphor, or in and out of metaphor.

It is evident that Tate is attempting by these means to increase the animation and visual force of his intellectually propelled verse. And it is further evident that he is increasing

13. "A Critic's Poetry," *Poetry*, XXXIII, 282.

the density and complexity. This tendency, together with the use of a richer and sometimes more strained vocabulary, came into prominence during the period when Tate was in closest relation with Hart Crane. The similarities of diction and imagery between Crane's "Paraphrase" and Tate's "Death of Little Boys" is striking, though Eliot is in the shadows behind both poems.

Tate's language develops an extraordinary density. Cleanth Brooks has remarked: "Almost every adjective in his poetry challenges the reader's imagination to follow it off at a tangent."[14] Brooks instances from the "Ode" such epithets as the "brute curiosity" of a marble angel's stare, and "Ambitious November with the humors of the year." But these are neither so typical nor so provocative of tangential associations as others from the same poem. The poet speaks of the "immodest circumstance/ Of those who fall," and the shock effect leads the mind into unfortunate associations. (Tate later changed this adjective to "arrogant.") Epithets like "immitigable pines" and "inscrutable infantry rising" force an arrest in the reading to inquire, to whom immitigable? to whom inscrutable? This short passage also contains "the immoderate past" and "the unimportant shrift of death."

Tate's fondness for Latinity and for negative involution is amply demonstrated in this passage. In eschewing the direct epithet, he achieves a somewhat specious complexity. At the same time, he is often accomplishing an economical elision of concepts and percepts. The "inscrutable infantry" combines some sense of their hiddenness from an observer, with an inability on our part, perhaps also on their own part, to fathom their motives. A more extreme instance comes from "Retroduction," where a passage begins, "Narcissus is vocabulary." In the context, the paraphrase would read something like this: myth has become unreal in the modern world—has become simply words, or even Freudian talk. Furthermore, the choice

14. *Modern Poetry and the Tradition*, pp. 95-96.

of Narcissus adds the concept of self-concentration or solipsism, as characteristic of the modern.

The strain for this sort of density often leads to a violent mixing of metaphors:

> Her tousled eyes no longer rinse the haze
> Of winter sprawled like a carcass by the door.

The effect here is one of fragmentation; the concept is shattered rather than elucidated by the involvement of the imagery. Eyes become hair, then hands to rinse out an insubstantial haze which emanates from a very substantial body.

Strain appears also in Tate's use of the "objective correlative," or concrete image which will convey precisely a complex of feeling. The aster of "The Death of Little Boys" is a controverted example:

> As the window pane extends a fear to you
> From one peeled aster drenched with the wind all day.

Winters censures the endeavor "to achieve a concrete image where a concrete image is improper."[15] Why a concrete image ever should be improper is difficult to see, but the strain is evident. My assumption of a death-smell in dead asters could explain Tate's choice, but not its relevance here, since odor is excluded by its position outside and especially by its "drenching" in the wind.

Speaking only of the poems by Tate which appeared in *Fugitives: An Anthology of Verse* (1928), Edmund Wilson noted "a strange originality, a special vein of *macabre* imagination, a deeply stained color";[16] while Yvor Winters marked an "almost sullen and decidedly powerful sense of tragedy."[17] These observations are noteworthy among the first considered

15. Yvor Winters, *In Defense of Reason*, pp. 529-30.
16. "Tennessee Poets," *New Republic*, LIV, 103-4.
17. "Fugitives," *Poetry*, XXXII, 106.

attempts to define the peculiar tone which pervades Tate's poetry. Tone is always elusive, but since it is ultimately a quality attaching to words, its source must be sought in vocabulary, and particularly in the image-making vocabulary of the poet. Much of the early Tate's special flavor, which Wilson finally calls "heavy," attaches to the multisyllabled epithets of Latin origin (often negative inversions like those of the "Ode"). These, however, are not image-forming. Hovering over the whole of *Mr. Pope* are the concepts of the "idiot," used overtly in five poems and implied in many more; the "curse," of mortality or of the age; "broken" and "fractured"; "stricken" and "blind"; "iron," "stone," and "bone"; "winter," "cold," "dark," and "night," all heavily accented in rhyme and other positions of emphasis; and especially "death," "dead," "corpse," or "carcass." These last four words appear some forty-six times in thirty-six short poems.

There are, of course, contrasting images ("gold" and "sun," for example), but they serve only to lend stress or relief to the dark foreground. Tate's world is therefore a far cry from Ransom's perilously beautiful one, though the two share many common aspects. The difference is accounted for largely by the difference in perspective. Tate is almost never the detached observer; he is himself a desperate part of the world he creates. His world, in turn, becomes a nightmarish projection of his own harried sensibilities. Where "every son-of-a-bitch is Christ, at least Rousseau," and "a corpse is your bedfellow" (to quote "Retroduction"), there is little possibility for detachment. Whatever corpses appear in Ransom, and there are many, the poet himself does not lie with; he gazes at them, reflects, and is disturbed, but "not too painfully." With bodies thick in his bed, with idiots, fools, and mummies, cursed and broken, swarming about him in a dark winter atmosphere, Tate's voice can only be desperate.

Mr. Pope and Other Poems was pilloried by Morton Zabel and praised by Yvor Winters at its appearance. Later, the critics' positions were to be exactly reversed. That such competent critics should disagree so thoroughly, and later substantially alter their judgments, is less a commentary on Tate's own development, which is not startling, than on a shift in critical attachments which was forced in large measure by Tate and the other Fugitives in their own critical formulations. Tate's poetry, as we shall see, has not changed substantially, either in its preoccupations or in its tone and manner, since the later poems in this volume. It remains an "obscure" poetry, not because it lacks rational structure or logically analyzable imagery, but because it is compressed to the straining point and makes such constant intellectual demands upon the reader that the unifying feeling comes through in overwrought distortion.

CHAPTER V

Other Apprentices

THE FIRST considerable poet to feel the influence of John Crowe Ransom was his later colleague on the Vanderbilt faculty, Donald Davidson. Like Ransom himself, Davidson came rather late to a preoccupation with poetry and, similarly, he abandoned his creative efforts early. Although he was born a few miles from Ransom's home, the son of a rural school teacher, Davidson's attitude toward his cultural background betrays almost none of the critical spirit which distinguished Ransom's early poems. Proud of a pioneer ancestry, devoted to the Middle Tennessee countryside, he has reserved his criticism for the "foreign" influences which he feels are destroying the "manliness" of the "tall men," the beauty of the country, and the spirit of poetry in life. When his own teaching career brought him back to Vanderbilt in 1920, his frustrate romantic tendencies found their antithetic image in the city of Nashville itself, a stone and steel "Leviathan."

"Robin Gallivant," as Davidson appropriately called himself in the first issues of *The Fugitive,* immediately revealed a romantic pastoral spirit reminiscent of early Keats. His first *Fugitive* piece, later printed as the title poem of *An Outland Piper* (1924), described the lure of an "alien piper, so like me," whom the poet insists on following, despite his warning:

> Though I be of thy father bred,
> And though I speak from thine own blood,
> Yet I am not of mortal brood;
> And follow not my piping sweet
> To find the walking world a cheat. . . .

Deserted, the poet learns "to know a world's deceit," and seeks

an unknown kin
Through all the streets I travel in.

This self-definition Davidson is later to expand upon. In *The Tall Men* he discovers three men in himself: a pagan and lover of chivalry, a Methodist, and an "observant friend of the world as it looks to be." Of these, however, only the first is strongly evident in the early verse of *An Outland Piper.* It is hardly the Methodist, for example, who engages in the Ransomic attack on "Ecclesiasticus," the preacher who resigns himself to calling his flock sinners and eating roast chicken; and on "Ecclesiasticus II," who "Sanctifieth Boosters' Clubs." Neither is it an "observant friend" who describes the store-keeper as "The Wolf" drooling over his money, or the "Iconoclast" who "loathed his personal condition," or the several social butterflies, male and female. On the other hand, the dream-haunted romanticist is everywhere. The earlier section of this volume is peopled with "demon brothers," magic "amulets" for "white necks," "slim enchanted mandolin's," strange women "riding/ A tiger's velvet back," another "Tiger Woman," the "Faery," and fair Rosabelles. The poet himself, when not piping, goes "with a rose and a lute"; or, after seeing "too many faces/ Hardening in the mould," he finds "a certain magic/ For those who walk in woe," and is content to put even the raven in his song.

In the later section of the book, Davidson turns to little vignettes from life and allegories, all in the Ransom manner but generally without the Ransom distinction. Davidson, as R. P. Warren noted in 1932, "is not an ironist."[1] In terms of Ransom's early analysis of philosophic irony, Davidson remains in the Byronic stage of romantic disillusion, unable to pass from there into the wise balance of a mature "dualism." Many of Davidson's sketches recall the more overt pieces of

1. "A Note on Three Southern Poets," *Poetry,* XL, 109.

Poems about God, without Ransom's ambiguous attitude: Ecclesiasticus,

> girding up his bishoply paunch,
> Assailed nineteen heretic cults,

and the "ardent Cecile" of "Prie Dieu" is told to pray

> For warm juvescence of those ichored limbs. . .
> For lips unblanched by pattering of hymns.

The method generally is that of satire, rather than of irony. The poet is concerned only to attack certain aspects of modern society through representative characters or through allegorical figures, and to contrast with them pagan ideals of freedom and joy in love and nature.

In these poems Davidson's diction achieves distinction only as it reflects Ransom's manner. The lush romantic vocabulary of the earlier section—the "golden hair" and "white necks," the "enchanted bays" below "blue cliffs," the "wistful me," the "nigh's" and the exhortations: "Up, Dust, into the Sun, and sing!"—is never wholly abandoned. In the later pages, however, both a homelier and an archly pedantic speech, clearly influenced by Ransom, add variety and a sharper flavor. The final longer poem, "The Man Who Would Not Die," reveals still another mode of Davidson's. Here the model for the conversational but often sharply phrased blank verse would appear to be E. A. Robinson. This final poem is transitional in form and manner to the verse of *The Tall Men*. The favorite ballad and short-line quatrain forms of *An Outland Piper* are to be virtually discarded in Davidson's later poetry, for, unlike Ransom, he has no genius for form and tight organization. Once he gives up the simple lyric effusion, he requires a freer medium. As his fellow poets move toward a stricter intellectual control, Davidson begins to find his congenial verse form in a loose blank verse that allows his narrative and descriptive abilities rein and demands no restraint upon his expressionistic progressions.

In his final year as editor of *The Fugitive*, Davidson, as I have noted, had to some extent foresworn his original inspirationalist position in criticism so far as to admit the necessity of coordinated thought in poetry. In the practice that follows, this admission of the intellect takes the form for Davidson of a conscious effort to "revivify the old" in terms of his own heritage. Like Tate, Davidson rediscovers his past. But his discovery is that of a "romantic traditionalist," to use Tate's term, for he finds a glamorized tradition that contrasts strikingly with a decadent industrial-financial present.

The Tall Men appeared in 1927, and though in most respects it reflects a post-*Fugitive* development, the seeds of it were clearly planted in "The Man Who Would Not Die" and the later *Fugitive* reviews. In the meantime, Davidson had accepted an extramural position as literary editor for the Nashville *Tennessean*. Davidson's book page soon distinguished not only the *Tennessean* but the Knoxville *Journal* and the Memphis *Commercial Appeal*, all of them tied to the rising star of the fabulous Colonel Luke Lea. (Davidson's continued loyalty to Lea, after the collapse of the Caldwell and Co.–Lea enterprise in 1930, and even after Lea's conviction on various charges involving intent to defraud, is perhaps symptomatic of his uncritical attachment to the pioneer spirit of his home country, though its modern form involves financial buccaneering.) While teaching his classes and editing his weekly page, Davidson found time for considerable study in the history of his section. *The Tall Men* was conceived as an excursion into the past, an attempt to reassess the Tennessee heritage, the men of Tennessee, and the poet himself as a representative Tennessean of today's world.

The volume is a loose series of compositions, half narrative, half lyric and reflective. The Prologue, "A Long Street," sets the mood with macabre images among the "steel thews of houses" and on "the baked curve of asphalt":

Steel answers steel. Dust whirls.
Skulls hurry past with the pale flesh still clinging
And a little hair. Fevered bones under clean
Linen. Aimless knuckles of bones
Within buttoned gloves waving to eyeless sockets.

The poet, "across the portals of an iron age," reaches back to "take leave/ Of dead men under a pall." His memory summons the pioneer "tall men" themselves, the long riflemen, John Sevier, Andrew Jackson, Davy Crockett, celebrating through them a lost courage, honor, devotion, and joy in living. Later sections glorify the Confederate battles and their leaders, contrasting their high ideals to those of "America Now," with its

constitution of, by, for the pig—
Meanwhile pushing his trotters well in the trough.

The sections following go on to detail the poet's childhood recollections of the countryside and the Negroes—the poet asks the "black man," "Let us not bruise our foreheads on the wall" between us—; to celebrate the role of the "tall men" in World War I; to describe the poet's painful efforts at reintegration in post-War Nashville; to chant an "Epithalamion" for the poet's marriage to an Ohio girl; and to conclude with a symbolic "Fire in Belmont Street," Nashville.

It should be evident, even in such a summary, that what unity is inherent in the conception of the "tall men" and the time sequence does not serve to integrate the material which Davidson introduces into a single whole. There are too many traditions, and too much variety within the traditions, to be integrated, and Davidson is not selective. He adopts a wholly uncritical attitude toward a past which includes "silk gowns . . . ruffled shirts . . . rifles,"

Hunting-shirts, Bibles, looms, and desperate
Flags uncrowned;

and an equally antipathetic attitude toward the entire catalogue of modern possibilities. The Walpurgis Night scene called "Conversation in a Bedroom" is for the most part a compendium of satires on the modern artist and intellectual in his search for viable values. The section is climaxed by a parody of T. S. Eliot:

> Out of the broken gospels, out of the desert,
> The parched, the shattered temples I heard a voice
> Chanting to a strident harp: *Oh, come, come in,*
> *Come in under the shadow of this red rock . . .*
> For all is said
> And will not bear repeating . . . at the world's end.

The poem is alternatively angry and rhapsodic, and this alternation brings with it lapses both of judgment and of good taste.

The attitude is singularly inappropriate for an epic-scale piece. Treating a theme almost as broad as Hart Crane attempted in *The Bridge,* Davidson lacks both a unifying metaphorical concept and a range of sympathy and acceptance. The feeling remains provincial, except as it is broken for the extraordinarily unintegrated break occasioned by the wife's Northern origin. The World War in these pages is fought exclusively by Tennesseans, and no Tennessean here can do other than curse the "damn Yankees"—this despite the number of descendants of "long rifles" from East Tennessee who fought for Union. Davidson's sympathy is broad enough to include one representative from the North and none from a foreign country. The result is a kind of cramping that consorts badly with the broad pattern of the poem's form. The "tall men" shrink disproportionately as the poem progresses; at the end they have left only a surly and belligerent pettiness.

While the large conception of the poem fails, there remains considerable local excitement in the verse. The narrative sequences, in particular, have vigor and a sharp visual quality. Descriptions of individuals and types, though done in black and white, are often boldly effective; and Davidson is at his best in colorful evocations of his native fields and hills, and of the companions of his childhood. Still, the achievement is never a completely poetic one; it is basically a rhetorical one. For in no single division of the poem does the poet manage to synthesize the experience recorded; no maturely artistic attitude governs the choice of image or epithet. The whole and the individual units as well fragment into series of pictures, praises and curses, cries into the past. Davidson, on the eve of his Agrarian commitment, remains a bitterly disillusioned romantic, unable either technically or philosophically to integrate his memories with his present experiences.

Robert Penn Warren, whom Tate has called "the most gifted person I have ever known," came to Vanderbilt from the hill country of Southern Kentucky so sharply recalled in his "Kentucky Mountain Farm" and in his first novel, *Night Rider*. When he was invited into the ranks of the Fugitives, at eighteen,[2] he had already published two poems in the magazine, both of them vaguely recalling Archibald MacLeish. Neither of these first efforts is a polished poem; they are exercises in a new medium, competent metrically and sharp in imagery. Before his *Fugitive* career is over, however, Warren takes large strides as a poet.

By the time he is twenty, it has become evident that Warren, like Tate, has bitten fiercely into the fruit of knowledge of good and evil which Ransom offered his protégés. Evident, too, is the debt he owes to Eliot, introduced to him by Tate, and to Tate himself as a poet. Tate has recalled the scenes from *The Waste Land* with which young Warren decorated the walls of the room he shared with Tate and Ridley Wills, "the rat creeping softly through the vegetation, and the typist putting a

2. The error persists (see F. J. Hoffman *et al.*, *The Little Magazine*) that Warren was sixteen when he was elected to the staff. His birthdate is April, 1905; he first appears as editor in Vol. III, No. 1 (1924).

record on the gramophone."[3] Then, there are strikingly Eliotic lines, for which Warren has a natural affinity:

> The drift of dust along the vacant hall
> Is stilled by the rat's breath only or the wind;

or

> Ever in the hot street one walks unseen
> Beside you;

or

> Your face is blown, an apparition, past.

There is perhaps an addition from Tate in the constant brain and blood and bone images:

> the coat that lies
> Crumpled like a brain upon the chair;
>
> And know how black and turbulent the blood
> Will beat through iron chambers of the brain.

The combination of influences, with Warren's own touch added, appears in a typical passage such as this, from "To a Face in the Crowd":

> Where among rocks the faint lascivious grass
> Fingers in lust the arrogant bones of men.

The "fingers" is Ransom, the "arrogant" more typically Tate. Both "lascivious" and "in lust" are toned up from Ransom and Eliot, but in the Tate range. The adjective "faint" provides a modulation which is not early Tate, and the rock setting, derived from Eliot, is still a hallmark of the early Warren as it couples with the thin grass of his native landscapes.

John L. Stewart has characterized[4] Warren's early poetry

3. "The Fugitive—1922–1925," *Princeton University Library Chronicle*, III, 82.

4. "The Achievement of Robert Penn Warren," *South Atlantic Quarterly*, XLVII, 563.

as strings of images of decay and death. Certainly he has caught from his mentors a fascination with "bone and blood and sweat and agony," with the night, the "weary dream," and the "chill daylight." Much sooner and more completely, however, than Tate, Warren has absorbed the Judaistic aspect of Ransom's thought, the aspect which will dominate *God without Thunder*.[5] At times he writes simple death lyrics recalling the Hardy of "Forget Not Me" or the Housman of "Alter Quies," and sometimes he does Davidson-like character pieces, such as "Portrait of Three Ladies." But more typically he faces up to the hard realities of man's condition with brutal directness:

> The thews that through the tortured years have
> striven
> To breach the flesh so sure to spill when broken,
> The only breath, a cry, and the dark blood
> That forever we would keep if but we could!
> ("The Wrestling Match")

In the final section of "Images on the Tomb," called "Night: But a Sultry Wind," he cries out for the violent, for "the loud thunder" to contort "the craggy dark" and tear "terribly/ The fabrics of the firmament asunder" in order that he may face head-on the full calamity of the mortal situation. But for our time there is only a "sultry wind" and "white faces turned to the wall" in sleep. If we turn away and "renounce the night," there remains for us, he says in "To a Face in the Crowd," only "the lost procession of these feet"—the same procession which a little later will offer the protagonist of Tate's "Death of Little Boys" an ironic relief in a similar predicament.

Warren's is certainly a precocious advocacy of a "God of thunder." But Ransom's hard reading of earth appeals immediately to a mind conditioned, as the poet himself states, "in

5. W. P. Southard, in "The Religious Poetry of Robert Penn Warren," *Kenyon Review*, VII, has stressed the Judaism of Warren's poetry. His insights are highly perceptive and valuable, though his Look-I-can-do-it-with-one-hand style is at least unfortunate.

kinship to the savage stone" and teeming with rocky images. For, as "Croesus in Autumn" puts it, in a tone recalling first Ransom, then Tate:

> The seasons down our country have a way
> To stir the bald and metaphysic skull,
> Fuddling the stout cortex so mortally
> That it cries no more, Proud heart, be still,
> be still.

But the early Warren is unable, again like Tate, to accept the brutal realities with Ransom's equanimity. With Roman stoicism certainly, for there is no other choice; the rock, as Southard has it, is the "constant inanimate preceptor":[6]

> Instruct the heart, lean men, of a rocky place
> That even the little flesh and fevered bone
> May keep the sweet sterility of stone.
> ("Rebuke of the Rocks")

But even the rocks are fractured and

> borne
> Down shifting waters to the tall, profound
> Shadow of the absolute deeps. ("At the Hour of the
> Breaking of the Rocks")

Accepting the predicament, Warren, like Tate, begins to probe into the past. There is not in Warren, however, the nightmare desperation which Tate often exhibits in his search. There is no idiot image of the modern mechanical world, no feeling of absolute isolation and distraction, for it is chiefly the irremediable evils with which Warren is concerned. Warren has, furthermore, Ransom's intimate feeling for the natural world, and a profound human sympathy. His thinking is directly figurative and his language, when it does not borrow—

6. *Ibid.*, p. 657.

"the escheat heart is quick estopped"—is naturally concrete, earthy, and vivid.

Up to 1928, when Warren's first selection from his poetry appeared in *Fugitives: An Anthology of Verse*, the poet's probing has yielded little positive result. In "Pro Sua Vita" and "Letter of a Mother," he explores the parental relation. The former poem reaches the conclusion that both man and nature are waste products, God's and man's own, out of their prodigal creativity. In the latter, the severance of mother and son is found irrevocable; the dissolution of the grave will possess "the tired child" as the "mother flesh" cannot. The exploration of history, done later the same year in the fine "History Among the Rocks," unearths no more. Of those, both blue and gray, who fought in the Civil War, he can only say: "Their reason is hard to guess and a long time past." There are still "many ways to die": the "natural" ways of freezing in the rocks, going down with atoms of fractured rock "To ocean where the blind tides flow," or the copperhead's poison in the fields. History suggests purposes, ideals; but for the poet the reality of death itself is the reality still, and he implies no choice of manner or means.

Warren's verse forms during this period are thoroughly traditional—sonnets, quatrains, couplets—and he employs them with considerably less freedom than Ransom is using. At moments there are indications that he is uncomfortable in strict meters—a "did go" for a "went," and well-worn rhymes—but he gradually begins to loosen his rhythms and to relax his standard of rhyme, permitting such near- or half-rhymes as "striven-broken" and "pens-tins." Despite the influence of Eliot operating on diction and manner, Warren's interest in freer verse forms does not develop until "The Return: An Elegy," which did not receive its final form until after the publication of the anthology. On the other hand, Warren has no hesitation about mixing his manners. His poetry from very early is "impure," to use his own word. The "Dawn" sonnet, beginning:

> Too late returns the measured sun and slow,

is broken by:

> 'Get up, get up, wash the face, comb the hair.'

And "The Wrestling Match," opening colloquially:

> 'Here in this corner, ladies and gentlemen,
> I now presents "Mug" Hill, weight two-hundred-ten,'

moves into language involving:

> as in an absurd vision
> The truculent dull spirit.

This mixed or "impure" aspect of Warren's poetry continues to develop—and it becomes prominent in his prose later—as he moves toward increasing complexity. At this stage, it is sufficient to note that the particular brand of honesty toward his own experience which Ransom exhibited and taught, leads directly to this sort of expression. Warren cannot reject any relevant part of an experience, no matter how its tone clashes with the dominant mood.

The *Fugitive* period produced a number of other poets whose best work was collected in the *Fugitives* anthology. Of these, Laura Riding (Gottschalk) has no connection with the group except through the appearance of her poems in the magazine, and through the fact that her name was added to the editorial list after she won a poetry prize contest conducted by *The Fugitive.* During the entire period she remained in Louisville as the wife of Dr. Louis Gottschalk of the University of Louisville faculty, and neither influenced nor was influenced by the Fugitives proper. In 1928 she appears already herself, shrewd, avant-gardist, brittle, and more than a little superficial. Of the other editors, William Yandell Elliott and James Marshall Frank make no real pretense at serious poetry. Stanley Johnson, Alec Brock Stevenson, and Jesse Wills suffer the fate of imitators. Only Merrill Moore is an original voice.

Johnson's poetry at its worst is almost a parody of Ransom's; at its best it is directly derivative. In the atmosphere of Vanderbilt's little renaissance, it was inevitable that a number of language-conscious men should try their hands at verse, and it was equally inevitable that most of them would not turn out to be poets. Johnson, English instructor and author of a novel stemming from the *Fugitive* experience, was one who could catch the manner, though his ear constantly betrayed him. He writes on themes familiar from Ransom. There is the wife and husband argument, ending:

> So lie, my love, that odd will be as even—
> I'll love you so, that hell will be as heaven,

a conclusion growing, not out of the experience recorded in the poem, but out of the necessity for a Ransomic ironic twist, of a sort. There is a modern swan in a modern park cramming "peanuts and the white popcorn" to be compared with mythic "storied" birds. There is a downward-toward-disillusion love sonnet sequence recalling Tate's "Oenone" series. Only in "An Intellectual's Funeral," which takes a leaf directly out of Ransom's book, does Johnson write a relatively successful poem. But even here he has lapses. It begins:

> On such a day we put him in a box
> And carried him to that last house, the grave.

This is somewhat paled and over-explicit Ransom. Then:

> All round the people walked upon the streets
> Without once thinking that he had gone.

The language goes completely flat with none of Ransom's dramatic shift in tone to sustain the flatness; and the rhythm breaks for no conceivable reason except that Ransom often breaks his. The poem achieves its success in the final lines:

> and we went pitiful,
> Our clacking heels upon the pavement stones
> Did knock and knock for death to let us in.

These lines are Ransom in every overt particular. They are impressive, but by a borrowed radiance. Once Ransom's light is removed and the lines are contemplated in their own right as part of a complete poetic statement, they begin to fall apart. The death-feeling of the mourners has not been implemented in the body of the poem. They have looked on with "grave wonder," feeling that the dead man "knew all at last"; but nothing suggests the final pity and knocking for Death. Both of these aspects of the final attitude seem to grow out of characteristic Ransom attitudes, not out of the poem.

Alec Brock Stevenson, the only businessman-poet on the staff, owes more to early Davidson and a native romanticism than to the pervasive themes and ironies of the major Fugitives. Preoccupied, like Davidson, with the chivalric past and with nature—"A rock, a river, a tree and a star"—he never reaches Davidson's bitterness of disillusion. His tonal range is limited to a melancholic joy or a more poignant regret. The romantic quality of his imagination constantly recalls Davidson, but he lacks the lyric grace to redeem a "pure" poetry, not submitted to the discipline of intellectual processes. His purely lyric "In the County of Davidson" (Nashville's county), for example, works into a varied refrain in Elizabethan style:

> Sang reveille in England . . .
> That breathed the heart of England . . .
> The primrose skies of England,

and works out of it again without establishing a pattern, with rhythmic bumps and jolts that have no place in such verse. Like Johnson, he seems to feel that such variation, since it was employed by the major Fugitives for their effects, is a mark of poetic maturity. He employs it haphazardly where tone and theme require a melodious flow. "In the County" ends:

> God keep the streams of my own land
> 	And let them still run
> When April's come to all the hills
> 	And I to Davidson.

The second line simply cannot be read in relation to the others. Stevenson deliberately avoids the obvious rhythm of "always," but the variation makes a wreck of the lines.

The sonnet "To a Wise Man" marks Stevenson's peak. The quatrains, descriptive of the unsmiling man and of nature, are somewhat pedestrian, but the couplet rings true with a light warm grace:

> The rustling path, the lonely woodland clover,
> The stream, and his brown hand to help me over.

Stevenson has the makings of a slight but charming poet, anachronistic certainly, but melodious and sprightly. His failures are functions of his imitative efforts.

"That sly parody of the devil" was Tate's description, in the original version of "Causerie," of Jesse Wills, cousin of the Ridley Wills who roomed for a year with Tate and Warren. (Tate later changed the name in "Causerie" to that of Edmund Wilson.) The verse by which Jesse Wills is represented in *Fugitives* does possess its minor aspects of diabolism—particularly "Trinity," which identifies in not too ambiguous order "an ape, a man, and God" as "Father, son, and paraclete." Actually, however, Wills more nearly resembles a sly parody of Ransom and Tate. He does not, like Johnson, imitate the mannerisms of his mentors (except in "Trinity"), but he adopts the mocking tone, the anti-urbanism and anti-industrialism of his colleagues. What Wills chiefly misses is an underlying serious concern for humanity. He is generally content to describe, and often he does it in sharp, fresh imagery, flavoring the descriptions with Ransomic acid. So the pretty typist in "Primavera":

> You laugh beneath the mazda suns;
> Your voice is like a windy bell;
> In a white dance each finger runs
> A naiad on the stairs of hell.

In "Night Windows," on the moonlit road's "glacier way,"

> dragon motors hiss by, softly ranging,
> Or on some quest off darting through the gray
> Night that spins out to silver yapping horns.

"To a Tired Clerk" offers the addressed sufferer hope in the form of the city's eventual decay, when

> Nomads, bronze-armed, shall note where mystery
> carves
> Your firm's worn name, and dread their wizard
> sires,
> Curbing their foam-necked horses, while their
> scarves
> And ruddy hair are strung upon the wind.

These are the high points in Wills's verse. He offers no original vision, and he does not exhibit either a real commitment in the point of view he adopts or any dedication to his art. The result is that his poems sag badly when his rhetoric slips off its highest pitch. He cannot afford simplicity since he fails to provide sufficient tension to sustain it. His semi-colloquial pieces, therefore, are flat failures, and no single poem is a wholly sustained performance.

Merrill Moore is a different matter. Possessed, happily, of a mind of his own at an early age, he sets his own course and sails it serenely, undisturbed by the commotion which his more intense colleagues are stirring. As a premedical student, Moore submitted his first poems to Tate shortly after the initial issue of *The Fugitive* appeared. Forthwith, he was elected to the staff, and thereafter, Tate says, never appeared at the group meetings without ten or more of his sonnets. His amazing fecundity since that time has given rise to a whole body of legend. Louis Untermeyer, one of his early admirers, vouches for the fact that "Moore learned shorthand in order to get more of his fourteen-liners done between classroom and laboratory."[7] Moore has himself stated recently that his three volumes, one called *M* for the thousand sonnets it contains, plus "a number of pamphlets . . . don't represent one per cent of my output."[8] Beyond any reasonable doubt, he holds the modern record, not only for sonnet production, but for poetic output generally—and this while concentrating his major energies on study and practice as a psychiatrist.

Moore's background is thoroughly Southern. Son of the Tennessee historian John Trotwood Moore, brought up in Columbia, Tennessee, and graduated from Vanderbilt, he might have been expected to follow the traditionalist Fugitive pattern. But even his earliest poetry evidences a different orientation. In the poem "And to the Young Men," he addresses a preceptor:

> And to the young men awaiting their sacrifice
> You brought water in an invisible pail . . .
> And sang to some at night and fanned by day
> Those who were fevering into paradise.
>
> But even then you did not do enough.

7. Louis Untermeyer (ed.), *Modern American Poetry* (5th rev. ed.; New York: Harcourt, Brace and Co., 1936), p. 615.
8. *New York Times Book Review*, January 23, 1949, p. 8.

He recalls a silent boy who felt the winter wind too keenly, and adds:

> Well, you should have brought him cresses from a
> far stream
> Over which nymphs and under which naiads dream.

Already the young poet accents the individual disease and the individual remedy. Ransom's bitter diet will not digest in every stomach, and Dr. Moore's attention will not be diverted from the single body and mind to the body social or body politic.

Moore is not a philosopher and not, despite his output, a committed poet. He takes his poetry as he finds it, on the run, out of a stray observation or a stray fancy. "It is Winter, I Know" is an instance of the type, a group of observations and a mood, set off with sharp descriptive phrases: "small birds peppering the sky," the "birds' indeclinable twitter." "I Saw You First" consists of two contrasted scenes from modern suburban life. "Shot Who? Jim Lane!" is contained largely in the opening lines:

> When he was shot he toppled to the ground
> As if the toughened posts that were his thighs
> Had felt that all that held him up were lies.

There is no extension of the observation beyond the obvious one of mortal pride and weakness. "Abschied" records an after-dance scene, "How She Resolved to Act" a small love scene, "Why He Stroked the Cat" a bit of fear reaction. The quality of such poems resides entirely in the acuteness of the eye and the psychological penetration, never in evoked emotion. None of them probes deeply, but each reveals a foible or a disguised motive. Most often the exposure is amusing as well as mildly illuminating. The high spirits of the young man in "Enthusiasm" cause him to magnify

the gutter into a roaring chasm
That he must leap across successfully,
A thing anyone could do. He did it well
And strode up the walk after easily conquering Hell,
Lucifer, Peter, Heaven, and Chaos as well!

In addition to his observations, Moore has his fancies, again likely to turn out amusing rather than profound. The "Two Idle Dolphins" note the guilty and glutted actions of young sharks leaving a shipwreck where a group of handsome young sailors has been drowned. This, with its little Ransom touch, is often Moore's level, but "The Book of How" is better, on a plane nearer Ransom's wit pieces. God, "After the stars were all hung separately out," sits down, to angelic applause, to write a book on the manner of His creation. But the devils laugh,

For somehow He managed entirely to omit
The most important facts in accomplishing it,
Where He got the ladder to reach the stars
And how He lighted them, especially Mars,
And what He hung them on when He got them there
Eternally distant, luminous in the air.

William Carlos Williams once credited Moore with rescuing the essence of the sonnet and reforming it in "magnificent" poems, and Louis Untermeyer highly praised his natural or spontaneous "American sonnets." Despite these authoritative judgments, it is difficult to grant Moore any creative originality in form. Apparently he simply seized on the pattern held in highest repute by the traditionalists as offering the greatest challenge to his ingenuity and versatility. He conquered the form immediately, filling it with his natural conversational language made piquant and shaped to eight lines of presentation, six of response. Since he was animated by no theory of expressive form and by no experimental fervor, and since both the sonnet's length and its restraining discipline were congenial, he has had no incentive to venture further afield. Moore has a gift for word and phrase, if not a startling one, but none for music. His free variations in meter are evidently expedient, dictated by the thought or the attraction of a phrasing, never by subtler expressive considerations. He is not innovating in his irregularities; he is simply improvising freely and easily on a normative pattern.

At one time or another, Moore is a victim of all the hazards to which a single pattern and an improvising spirit expose him. He pads his verse unconscionably at times, spinning out an observation into fourteen thin lines and repeating unfunctionally. Images seem sometimes suggested rather by the exigencies of rhyme than by an over-all conception or attitude; or a set of controlling images, as in "Naked and Drenched"—thunder, lightning, hail, rain—leads to considerable straining to fit the human situation for which they stand as metaphors. Such faults as these are major ones by the standards which Moore's colleagues are to set up as criteria for genuine poetry. By more liberal standards, they still reduce Moore's stature to something less than Poet in the Shelleyan sense. But the Boston psychiatrist clearly makes no such grand pretensions. As Ransom has indicated, poetry for him is a sort of regularly indulged holiday activity, perhaps even a psychological release. So, too, for his reader. His acute eye, his sprightly fancy, and his undemanding wit offer a pleasant relief from the sometimes overintense soul-searching of Tate and Warren.

CHAPTER VI

Critics and Agrarians

THE DAY ON WHICH Tate's and Ransom's letters crossed, each suggesting that they "do something about Southern history and the culture of the South," was a fateful one. It heralded a new burst of excitement comparable to that of the first days of the magazine project some five or six years earlier.[1] In the later twenties and early thirties all of the major group are brought back into close relation, despite a geographic distribution which at times covers two continents. The new enthusiasm is not primarily literary, but for Ransom, Tate, and Warren, at least, the religio-agrarian surface movement is animated from beneath by aesthetic concerns. Tate's phrase, to "do something," is vague enough, but it can be glossed by reference to his own poetic dilemma of the period, as I already have indicated. The "something," then, was to be an attempt to establish, or re-establish, a native tradition or a *mythos* which could serve as a valid framework for poetry, and to offer a countermovement against the "positivistic" and materialistic forces which a boom economy was encouraging. The agrarian program itself, as well as the reanimation of the Southern historical myth and even the new emphasis on religion, was at bottom a rather desperate effort to set up the preconditions for an integrated life in which poetry might naturally assume a vital role. The impulse originated in an aesthetic dilemma, brought on, as theory had it, by a social situation, but it demanded a philosophic solution which would embrace both aesthetic and social aspects of the problem.

1. Tate's tentative date, 1926, seems too early on the evidence of his critical articles and his poetry.

Both Ransom and T. S. Eliot, seconded by Tate, already had pointed the direction in which the synthesis could be reached. Each had insisted on the stabilizing value of a continuing tradition. For both, the root difficulty in modern life could be diagnosed as "dissociation of sensibility," the divorce between thought and feeling which prevents integrated and purposeful action. Both prescribed a code of values derived from the past as a guide for living and a basis for artistic creation. There were areas of disagreement, such as those which were leading Eliot toward Anglo-Catholicism, Ransom to a "God with thunder," and Tate to Southern history; but the agreement was extremely important. It not only determined the artistic and critical bearings of the group involved; it also foreshadowed, if indeed it did not directly beget, the literary development of the forties dubbed by *Partisan Review* critics, the "Failure of Nerve."

Biographies by Tate and Warren were the first overt manifestation of the new preoccupations, if we except the poems of Tate and Warren discussed elsewhere. Tate, first in the field, goes directly to the heart of the Confederate cause with *Stonewall Jackson: The Good Soldier* (1928) and *Jefferson Davis* (1929). These books explore positive and negative aspects of the Southern tradition as they appear in the colorless soldier, whose virtues are presented simply as those of his society, and in the unstable politician, who suggests a "modern" weakness at the center of the Southern cause. Tate, at least, does not stack his cards in his choices.

The Jackson biography is a rapid, vivid narrative for the most part, making no apologies for its heavy Confederate bias, its near worship of Lee, and its undisguised contempt for Lincoln. At the same time, Tate stresses Jackson's simple-mindedness and unimaginative piety. The surface picture is one of a routinely "good," but dull and uninspired, soldier. But Jackson represents much more than that for the author; he becomes a symbol for the integrity and redeeming purposefulness of a life made possible by a society organized on the principle of strict adherence to an established code of conduct. Jackson, of course, cannot be an ideal for Tate—Lee and Calhoun are that[2]—but is an average product of the society, "practical, materialistic," but "socially and economically secure," capable therefore of courage, devotion to a cause, and sacrifice.

The core of Tate's book is to be found, not in his delineation of personalities, but in his contrasts between Northern and Southern ways of life. He justifies slavery on Calhoun's grounds, that "it had become a necessary element in a stable society" and that "only in a society of fixed classes can men be free." The "historical sense of obligation implied a certain freedom to do right," and "took the form of benevolent protection: the White man was in every sense responsible for the Black. The Black man, 'free,' would have been exploited." (Tate has said earlier: "Without possessions a man did not morally exist." Benevolent protection may have seemed a poor substitute in the Black man's case for moral nonexistence. But Tate is never concerned with the Negro as man.) In the North, on the other hand, the feeling of obligation was wanting. Lacking the "historical sense," the North "had come to believe in abstract right. Where abstract right supplants obligation, interest begins to supplant loyalty. . . . Its freedom is the freedom to do wrong"; and, since "no external order exists . . . too much . . . is left to the individual."

All this is a kind of secular rationalization deriving from the Eliotic doctrine of a traditional framework of authority and from Ransom's anti-abstractionism. Religion, too, inevitably figures prominently in this book, since Jackson's simple Protestant piety was notorious; but in Tate's treatment the Church becomes only another "symbol of order" in the society. The North is characterized as "mystical, religious" at one point

2. Andrew Jackson, Tate says, "hated wealth, if it brought leisure, and he hated institutions, by means of which a society devoted its leisure to culture. . . . It is just possible to see Calhoun and Andrew Jackson as the Christ and Antichrist of political order in the United States."

where it is opposed to Southern "materialism"—here evidently not equivalent to pragmatic positivism, but perhaps to agrarian realism. Tate's difficulty in handling the religious element of the Southern tradition, and he runs into difficulties whenever it appears in these years, reflects his uncertain position between Ransom and Eliot. He is from old attached to Ransom's thunderous and mythic God to the extent that he cannot pursue Eliot's brand of traditionalism to its logical conclusion.

Jefferson Davis is a less perplexing problem from Tate's point of view. In his second biographical venture, he is able to utilize a concept developed independently by Ransom and Eliot. The President of the Confederacy is regarded simply as an anachronistic example of dissociated sensibility, "the curious separation of his intellect and his feelings," as Tate expresses it. The book offers a clear and dramatic interpretation of Davis and his responsibility for the failure of Southern arms. But the book is chiefly notable, from our point of view, for the distinction between Southern traditions necessitated by the thesis of Davis' inadequacy to his function, where Jackson was adequate. Tate, in the early chapters, describes Davis' "Lower South" plantation heritage and contrasts it unfavorably with the "pioneer nationalism" of the Kentucky-Tennessee area of the author's own provenance. The effete *nouveau riche* character of the lower Mississippi Valley culture—a character later to be ascribed in Tate's fiction to the Tidewater element also which moved into Tate's own territory—thus becomes the villain of the piece. More and more, Tate is forced to eliminate and define in his attempt to establish a tradition which can sustain his version of a historical, rather than a religious, heritage.

Robert Penn Warren, whose career in the later twenties takes him for graduate work to California, New Haven, and Oxford, rejoins the main current of Fugitive activity in 1929 with a biography, not this time of a Southerner, but of John Brown, the North's martyr. Warren's book is an animated interpretation which derives its major thesis from Ransom's theories, and it forecasts the ideational patterns of his later novels. Brown is presented both as a rare individual and as an extreme personification of Puritan-Transcendental abstract man. He exemplifies for Warren the typical New England failing, the attempt to live by an idea without reference to the human environment in which it must operate. Brown "could not understand the philosophy that one must live in an imperfect world and should try to do what one can with the imperfect institutions devised by other imperfect men." Acting on the idea alone, with little human knowledge or sympathy, he was always "alone, for his egotism would permit nothing else," and his acts were inevitably violent. Finally, "If John Brown had no scruples at deception it was because the end justified the means," and, as the terms of the end, or idea, grew larger and more abstract, the easier it became to justify the means.

John Brown is thus a typical Warren character, at least one of whom appears in each of his novels, and whose position each of his protagonists shares at one stage in his tragic career. Jeremiah Beaumont of *World Enough and Time*, for example, in his final moments of self-analysis discovers the romantic errors of the position and gives them their classic expression: "I had thought that the idea in and of itself might redeem the world, and in that thought had scorned the world"; and then the attempt follows "to use the means of the natural world, and its dark ways, to gain that end he names holy by the idea." Warren is no less critical of his protagonist in this biography than Tate of Jefferson Davis, but is less biased, more philosophical, and more broadly sympathetic. We need only cite his treatment of Lincoln in contrast to Tate's contemptuous references: "Lincoln, humane, wise, and fallible, but learning from his own failings." The book, in its attempt to re-create history in terms of a set of coherent ideas, may be thought of as a rehearsal for Warren's later fiction. And its color, its drama, its human insights and evocation of character are promising testaments to his talent for the novel.

By far the most important Fugitive book of this period, for its clarification of the central doctrines of the group and for its lasting influence, was Ransom's *God without Thunder: An Unorthodox Defense of Orthodoxy* (1930). This volume contains little that was actually new for anyone who had followed Ransom's poetry and essays, but it goes more extensively and directly into the central issues and comes out with a firm set of theological, philosophical, and aesthetic conclusions.

There seems little doubt that Ransom was urged into the production of this book by a number of pressures, most of them stemming from the renewed intimacy with Tate, and thus with Eliot's ideas and commitments. The religious issue had been made crucial by Eliot's conversion and by the challenge of the newly influential Humanist school of criticism. None of the Fugitives publicly discussed Eliot's action, but for Tate, whose critical positions and interests were so closely paralleling Eliot's, the logic of the step was evidently compelling. Furthermore, the argument against the new Humanists seemed to require the security of a defined religious position.

In essence the Humanists, despite founder Irving Babbitt's unadvertized mystical leanings and Paul Elmer More's eclectic Christianity, represented a compromise between the strict authoritarianism of a hierarchical religious system and the modern scientific spirit, a sort of critical unitarianism. In the place of ecclesiastical authority, they substituted the human authority of the "great minds." The classic principles of restraint, or proportion, or the "inner check" were to curb romantic individualism; and submission to external control, no longer acceptable to reason, was to be replaced by the internal control of the reason itself, guided by moral philosophers and by great artists, who must be studied therefore largely for their moral precepts. Eliot attacked the Humanist position at some length in 1927 and again in 1929, and he centered his argument on the failure of the Humanists to admit the necessary support of an external authority for the moral system they projected. Babbitt, he said, tried to "make humanism . . . work without religion," imagining "that the 'outer' restraints of an orthodox religion, as they weaken, can be supplied by the inner restraint of the individual over himself." Eliot deplored these "positivistic tendencies," insisting that morals must be attached to a system with supernatural sanctions: "you must be a naturalist or a supernaturalist."[3]

This last was an underscoring of Tate's dilemma. However, before Eliot's second article had appeared, Tate rushed in to support the entire Eliot argument in an article printed first in Eliot's review, *The Criterion*, and subsequently, with additions, in *Hound and Horn* (January, 1930). As Tate expressed it, the new Humanism suffered from the lack of a technique for "validating values." "The whole fallacy," he diagnosed, "comes directly out of the attempt to isolate the moral technique from its traditional supports." "A moral system not responsible to any other system is bound to be naturalistic." "Religion," he concludes, "is the sole technique for validating values." So far, the spirit, tone, and even much of the terminology has echoed Eliot. However, Tate proceeds to define religion as, in essence, "experience, immediately and traditionally fused," the virtue of which lies in its "successful representation of the problem of evil." This is Ransomic language, and it clearly points the need for a full Ransomic treatment. Tate's note appended to the *Hound and Horn* essay states, as the *Criterion* essay did not: "It must be understood that this essay urges the claim of no particular Western church, and it is in no sense a confession of faith." This kind of statement understandably baffled and irritated new Humanist

3. *Selected Essays*, pp. 387, 397.

Robert Shafer, who could see in the article nothing but impudence.[4] He, too, required Ransom's volume.

God without Thunder has its eccentric aspects as a treatise in theology—an Agrarian Eden, an Agrarian Milton, a Satan who appears at various times in guises of Christ, of Shelley, and of the positivistic scientist—but its perversities are neither new with Ransom nor iconoclastic. *Poems about God* and such later poems as "Armegeddon" are an adequate preparation for the apparent heresies of this volume. The emphasis here is on the necessity for an adequate religious myth to provide a realistic and fully human, hence an aesthetic as well as a scientific, way of looking at life and enduring its frustrations. The ancient Hebrews, says Ransom, accomplished the "successful representation of evil" by creating a God totally irresponsible to man's sense of justice, a God of thunder who subsumed in Himself the principles of both good and evil. Western Christianity, by introducing a loving Christ as the "Man-God," and accenting the benevolence of Deity toward man, reduced the old myth religion to the "closest approach to pure secularism that a religion has ever made." Christ Himself Ransom defends as "the Demigod who refused to set up as God." But his followers "have disobeyed his admonition, forgotten his limits, and made him assume the throne after all," where, as God only of good and love, "he sits quite incompetent to rule over the dominions of" the God of thunder He replaced. Finally, the evangelist John, speaking of the God as the Logos (an abstract conception), was the prophet of the new "naturalistic, scientific God"; and Shelley, unbinding Prometheus-man by the agencies of science and love, was His truest apostle.

Ransom's realistic reading of experience lays heavy emphasis on evil as the root fact of the human condition, for evil is

4. "Humanism and Impudence," *American Bookman*, LXX, 489-98. Mr. Shafer's intemperance in this article seems strangely at odds with the doctrines of restraint and inner check which he defends.

simply that which thwarts man in his pursuit of satisfactions, ultimately death. He praises the Eastern religions for "realism" which recognizes the ascendency of evil, ignoring the tendency of a Hinayana Buddhism to develop into a softer, love-dominated Mahayana. He notes the excess of lamentations in the Bible, and remarks in a somewhat masochistic parenthesis: "(Our own opportunities in this respect have been nothing like so rich.)"

Ransom contends that the Hebrew and the Eastern religions generally not only represent the experience of life truly, but do it in terms "of the inexhaustible fullness and particularity that exceeds formulation." They provide, therefore, true aesthetic experience for the worshipper. Their myths are, on a grander scale, the myths of poetry. Ransom describes the process of creating a religion in these terms: "The myth-maker sets him up a God" Who is concrete and "will furnish us with esthetic experience." But does one, should one, then believe in Him? We must guard against looking upon our "God as an actuality" and treating our "supernatural fictions as natural objects." That is magic. But, he proceeds, "all first-class religionists are Fundamentalists," and the Fundamentalist who "has *legislated* [Ransom's italics] his god into being," now literally believes in Him. He avoids magic only if he prays, " 'Not my will, but Thine.' " "In fact, [prayer's] purpose is opposite to that usually ascribed to it: it reconciles him to his impending defeat." This is hard doctrine, if good psychiatric procedure; but still we must ask how and to what extent does one believe in this creation of his to whom he prays?

Ultimately, I think the answer for Ransom lies in the phrase, "furnish us with esthetic experience." Belief becomes Coleridge's "willing suspension of disbelief for the moment, which constitutes poetic faith." Ransom rejects dogma of every sort, but he insists on a *poetic* faith in religions, myths, and finally, of course, poems themselves. It is this faith which will lead Ransom eventually to announce, like Coleridge's intimate, Wordsworth, that poetry is knowledge.

This also must be taken as substantially Tate's position during this period. A few years later, speaking of religious authority, he can insist: "I do not believe in it, and . . . none . . . of the Agrarians has written a single sentence setting forth belief in it. *Neither the Agrarian economics nor religious authority is a legitimate object of belief, nor can it be.*" (Tate's italics.) These are matters of "historical fact," and only the unprovable is subject to belief. "The absolutes of religion . . . are not imperatives of belief; they are rather imperatives of reference." There is certainly some evasionism in this, but Tate, like Ransom, wants his religious sanctions for authority, if not his religions themselves. Tate's difficulty lies in what he calls "the anomaly that produced in the Old South a feudal society without a feudal religion."[5] In other words, the particular tradition to which he is committed did not enjoin belief in an authoritative religion; the authority on which it depended was secular. The "revivalist" religions which others may accept fail, for Tate as well as for Ransom, to take adequate recognition of radical evil. Thus Tate, too, accepts his religion in a metaphorical sense only. There is a difference, however, for Ransom's approach is essentially humanistic, Tate's ministerial. Ransom is interested in sanctions for a full life of the "sensibility," the faculty by which "*Man not only lives his animal life but enjoys it*" (Ransom's italics); Tate is interested in the authority it confers.

Ransom's objection to the new Humanism, therefore, is that they build a "cult of reason," which leads inevitably to a "cult of science." They are lacking in the true humanism of the "sensibility, a faculty as exclusively human as the reason." Hence, they cannot accept myth, which insists on irrational particularity as opposed to abstraction. The trouble with More's Christianity, as Ransom sees it, is that More wants a

5. *Reason in Madness*, pp. 200-3.

"rational and benevolent world, and therefore so decrees it." Ransom, in his decadent environment, finds an irrational and at best indifferent world, and therefore sanctions certain myths about it and an aesthetic attitude toward it.

The Agrarian movement, formally launched at the moment of the Great Depression, brought the Fugitives together in the unfamiliar role of economists, a role which many an amateur adopted in 1930 and thereafter. Beginning in the reassessment of the older Southern tradition and in deep-seated opposition to the mechanization and commercialization of modern life, it found itself, at the time of financial collapse, in possession of a full-blown critique of finance capitalism and a program for reform. During the early Depression period, it made its impression and won followers, but its emphasis on the past—on return rather than progress—and on cultural values rather than material ones doomed it to a position inferior to Marxism in general, and even in intellectual, appeal.[6]

T. S. Eliot's interest in "Distributism," the English counterpart of Agrarianism, may be granted some influence, at least, on the American program, certainly in its development. Both movements had had a long history, stemming chiefly from Jefferson on this side of the water and from William Cobbett, once a violent Tory journalist in Philadelphia, on the other. In both cases, a substantial radical history had been reversed in the twentieth century. In England, the new Distributism was largely in the hands of Catholic littérateurs, Hilaire Belloc and Gilbert Keith Chesterton, and it was from them or their followers that Eliot derived his interest, following his conversion. Tate, who expressly repudiated the Jeffersonian tradition of "scientific" agrarianism, was likely to have felt the influence of Distributism through Eliot. Certainly the Fugitive program,

6. John L. Stewart has noted the importance of the British volume by Christopher Hollis, *The American Heresy* (1927), on the new view of the Civil War South adopted by the Fugitives (unpublished dissertation). The Scopes trial as well was not without influence.

though it drew almost entirely on the example of the American South, derived many of its ideas and much of its dialectic from British sources.

As signers of the Agrarian manifesto and contributors to *I'll Take My Stand* (1930) appear not only Ransom and Tate, but Davidson and Warren, the latter just returned from Oxford. Another late Fugitive, Andrew Lytle, who as an undergraduate had only just begun his writing career when the magazine expired, added his name and his essay to the Agrarian volume. Lytle and Warren concern themselves with extra-literary problems in *I'll Take My Stand,* as do Ransom and Tate for the most part. Davidson, however, deals directly with literature in relation to the social and religious concerns of the Agrarian platform. He has his fling at industrialism and at the Humanists. His major thesis is the by now familiar one that art flourishes best in a "stable, religious, and agrarian" society, though he cannot adduce an argument from the South's literary poverty. Davidson's personal note is still romanticism, and he insists "that if there is to be any art at all under the conditions of modern life, it must probably be Romantic art"—that is to say, art which is individualistic and in "fundamental contradiction with the dominant social forces of the age." The artist may choose "the spiritual solace of retreating to a refuge secure against the doubtful implications of his position in contemporary society"—the refuge of the past. Or he may assert his individuality and sing "for himself" in the " 'unique' style demanded of modern poets, highly idiomatic, perhaps obscure." Or he may in one way or another surrender his integrity. *The Tall Men* and *Lee in the Mountains,* the latter not published until 1938, make it sufficiently clear that Davidson has solved his own problem by "retreating." It is equally clear, however, that none of the choices could fully satisfy him, though he remarks a further possibility: "Left undisturbed, the Southern tradition would undoubtedly register effectively in art." He explains this only in a conclusion reminiscent of the dark warning at the end of *The Tall Men.* The remedy, he says, lies in the "rise to power of a body of Southern writers, economists, politicians, and clergy who will fight to a finish the new order of carpet-baggers and scalawags—or else assimilate them."[7] Davidson remains not only the least critical but the most bellicose of the defenders of the Southern historical myth.

The Agrarian movement can best be justified as a plea for a social and economic organization which could allow a simpler and more satisfying relation between the individual and his environment. In so far as the movement was backward-looking, though hardly "primitivistic" as John L. Stewart has it, it was unrealistic as a practical program—so unrealistic that it was not able to produce even an abortive Brook Farm experiment (though anything collective was out of the question). Without the total condition, of course, no true experiment was possible, but the major Fugitives were, like the Transcendentalists, committed intellectuals who must have found the routine of farm life stultifying, a "punishment," as Ransom was to admit in 1945. The Agrarian ideal, as it existed in the minds of some of its more rabid supporters—Tate certainly—was by no means the direct tiller-soil relationship which the program appeared to envisage. As his *Stonewall Jackson* implied, Tate's conception was oligarchic, stemming directly from Calhoun. His Agrarianism required "the historical sense of obligation" dependent on a hierarchy of "fixed classes"; his ideal farmer was the owner-manager, with responsibility and leisure.

Considered simply as a plea for a direct appreciative approach to life, in contrast to the pragmatic approach which modern city life enjoins, Agrarianism has considerable appeal. Doctrinally, the concept depends on Ransom's distinction between "abstraction" and "particularity." Ransom never denies the necessity for scientific abstractionism to manage our practical lives, but he insists that the scientific revolution of our times has heavily overbalanced the scale to its side, until we are

7. "The Southern Poet and his Tradition," *Poetry*, XL, 101, 102.

in immanent danger of crushing out of our lives the vital aesthetic responses. He says in *God without Thunder:*

> The esthetic attitude is the most objective and the most innocent in which we can look upon the world, and it is possible only when we neither desire the world nor pretend to control it. Our pleasure in this attitude probably lies in the feeling of communion or *rapport* with environment which is fundamental in our human requirements—but which is sternly discouraged in the mind that has the scientific habit.
>
> I should say that the esthetic attitude is definable with a fair accuracy in the simple and almost sentimental terms: the love of nature.[8]

This attitude, of course, involves no Emersonian transcendentalism; it is rather the complement of the recognition of nature's indifference, therefore her "evil." Ransom's disinterested joy in nature is post-Edenic innocence, and his joy in human nature is of the same "ironic" kind. It will be this aspect of Ransom's thought that Warren will develop in his poetry and his novels. Tate, as we shall see, is less concerned with making his peace with nature or man.

8. P. 173.

CHAPTER VII

Aesthetic Formalism

AT THE CLOSE of his essay "Poetry and the Absolute," published in 1927, Tate had issued what amounted to a call for a new school of critics, who, "by attending exclusively to the properties of poetry as a fine art," could develop "an elaborate aesthetic attitude . . . enabling [them] to isolate explicitly the absolute quality of particular poets and to reject a poetry from which the quality is missing." Tate acknowledged in a final note that his formulation here owed a debt to "the tendency of ideas in the *Metaphysics* and the *Poetics* of Aristotle." However, the group of American critics who were to develop the techniques for which Tate called were not to be Neo-Aristotelians. In the thirties and forties a body of critics answering substantially to Tate's specifications rose to a prominence challenged only by the Marxist group centering about the *Partisan Review* and *The New Masses.* These aesthetically minded critics, who first found a major organ in *Hound and Horn* and later in *The Southern Review,* were never so tightly knit a group that they earned from their contemporaries a distinguishing designation. After the publication of Ransom's *The New Criticism* in 1941, that book's title came to be applied to the Fugitives themselves among others. Since Ransom had referred specifically to Eliot, Richards, Empson, Winters, and Charles Morris, only three of whom could be considered to fit Tate's definition even approximately, and since the term "New Criticism" had been employed by Joel Spingarn for his type of impressionistic "adventures," the title seems particularly unfortunate. At this late date, it is presumptuous to suggest an alternative for general adoption; however, to distinguish the

Fugitive practitioners and those chiefly indebted to Eliot, Ransom, and Tate, I shall use the clumsy but more descriptive compound, "aesthetic formalist" critics. Aesthetic formalism, then, owing much to I. A. Richards' linguistic analysis also, made its first collective impression in the pages of *Hound and Horn*, "A Harvard Miscellany" in its early years, 1927-30, but an independent quarterly thereafter until its demise in September, 1934. R. P. Blackmur had been an editor in 1929 and remained one of the important contributors. In 1931 Tate accepted a regional editorship and Yvor Winters another, under Lincoln Kirstein, and the policy of judging art from a "technical" point of view was announced.

The *Hound and Horn* was in no sense a Fugitive venture. Of the other Fugitives, only Davidson was represented in its pages, and he with a single essay on "Sectionalism in America." Even Tate's contributions were largely in the form of book reviews, though an occasional poem of his appeared and, as has been noted, his essay on "The Fallacy of Humanism" was reprinted in revision. The reviews, however, contain some of Tate's best writing of the period. A discussion of Crane's *The Bridge* and a later tribute to Crane after his death, reviews of Eliot's *Ash Wednesday* and of Wilson's *Axel's Castle* are important pieces. At the same time, Tate's criticism was appearing in *Outlook*, *This Quarter*, and *Poetry*. All of this work is represented in the selection of *Reactionary Essays*, published in 1936.

Meanwhile, the *Hound and Horn* ceased publication with the summer issue of 1934, leaving no organ in America with critical standards approximating those it had advocated. In this situation, it was the enterprise of two Fugitives in an unlikely spot which produced almost immediately a journal which was to be in every way worthy of its predecessor in the field. The history of little magazines and critical quarterlies had clearly demonstrated the necessity of solid and stable financial backing, beyond the hazards of individual caprice. The oldest literary quarterly in the United States, *The Sewanee Review,* had survived in distinguished fashion from 1892 through its connection with the University of the South. During the boom era of the "little magazine," several sound quarterlies had been established on the solid ground of university support. It seemed not unreasonable, therefore, to young Professors Robert Penn Warren and Cleanth Brooks, Jr., that Louisiana State University, then basking in the golden favor of Huey P. Long, should increase its prestige intellectually through the establishment of a literary quarterly which would provide an outlet for the group of Southern critics and the aesthetic formalists in general.

The Southern Review was established in 1935, and its first issue appeared only two months before Senator Long's assassination. If the grant which made it possible carried a certain taint, the money was spent better certainly than the larger amount set aside each year for the support of the tiger which served as mascot for the football team. As might have been anticipated, the magazine outshone its rivals by a large margin in the quality of its paper and its printing. In addition, it surpassed them in the quality of its contents, for it could pay its contributors and it had the discerning editorship, under Charles W. Pipkin, of Warren and Brooks.

Warren had arrived at Baton Rouge by a roundabout route. After Vanderbilt, the University of California, and Yale, he had been selected as a Rhodes Scholar in 1928, taken a Litt.B. at Oxford, and returned to teach first at Southwestern University, then at Vanderbilt, before being appointed at L.S.U. in 1934. Cleanth Brooks, a year younger, had followed Warren as a Rhodes Scholar to Oxford and, with his Litt.B., had gone directly to L.S.U. in 1932. Technically, Brooks is not a Fugitive since, as a Freshman in the year when the magazine ceased publication, he had not appeared in *The Fugitive.* He had, however, printed a poem in the 1928 *Facets,* a little project of Vanderbilt English students. His close association from college days with Ransom and then with Warren and the similarity of his critical approach to those of his colleagues make it inevitable that he be thought of and treated as a true Fugitive. In the pages of *The Southern Review,* he immediately exhibited a formalist bias, as well as a trained sensibility, that linked him closely with Ransom, Tate, and Warren.

The Southern Review quickly reached a position of almost unparalleled distinction and authority in the area of modern letters and critical theory. It published all the Fugitives in essays and in poetry and fiction. Brooks did numerous reviews, but made his major contribution in a series of critical pieces which later formed chapters in his first book, *Modern Poetry and the Tradition.* Warren soon gave up reviewing to concentrate on poetry and on a series of short stories later to be included in his collection *Circus in the Attic* and, in one case, in his first novel, *Night Rider.* Ransom, Tate, Davidson, and Lytle appeared with some regularity; and the newer group of Southern women writers, especially Katherine Anne Porter, Eudora Welty, and Caroline Gordon (Mrs. Allen Tate), found an important outlet in the magazine. Of non-Fugitive critics, R. P. Blackmur, Kenneth Burke, John Peale Bishop, Delmore Schwartz, F. O. Matthiessen, Arthur Mizener, and Howard Baker were perhaps the most important to be printed fairly regularly. Not all, by any means, of those published were sympathetic to the aesthetic formalist point of view, but the tone of the magazine was set by what may be called the Eliot-Tate, Ransom-Warren-Brooks, and Richards-Empson successions.

Tate's discussion of "The Present Function of the Critical Quarterly" in 1936[1] insisted that the duty of such a magazine was to "supply its readers with coherent standards of taste, . . . A sound critical program . . . *allows to the reader no choice in the standards of judgment.*" (Tate's italics.) *The Southern Review* was by no means so rigidly programmatic as Tate would

1. In *Reason in Madness,* p. 186.

have had it, but the book reviews in particular applied such rigorous standards as to incur considerable protest. Reviewers had no patience with unskilled craftsmanship, with any compromise toward the "popular," with any species of "propaganda" literature, with anything smacking of pragmatism or positivism—though it published essays by John Dewey. At their narrowest, they pilloried critical theories which approached literature from any extrinsic standard. At their broadest, they printed direct attacks on their own positions and those of their Fugitive colleagues.

On the whole the tenor of *The Southern Review* reflected Allen Tate. Neither Warren nor Brooks can be considered a direct disciple of Tate, for both, starting from Ransom's influence and gathering doctrines from several sources, developed their individual lines. But the magazine evidently was conceived as a sort of *Hound and Horn* with a Southern accent, and Tate, as a former editor, must have seemed the logical authority for reference. Whether or not Tate was actually consulted in policy matters, his influence was apparent before he printed his prescription for the critical quarterly. The almost religious devotion to literature as such, the accent on close textual analysis, and the tendency toward dogmatism were so characteristic of Tate as to conjure up a vision of his image occupying the chair nominally held by Editor Pipkin.

The career of *The Southern Review* coincides almost exactly with the "golden era" of Fugitive criticism. Ransom's two volumes of the period on literary problems, *The World's Body* (1938) and *The New Criticism* (1941), contain almost all of his more important contributions to critical theory and practice to date. Tate's *Reactionary Essays* (1936) and *Reason in Madness* (1941) similarly include the most important body of criticism yet produced by the author. Cleanth Brooks in 1939 published his brilliant synthesis of aesthetic formalist doctrine, *Modern Poetry and the Tradition*, a book which includes also his best single pieces of practical criticism thus far.

Together Brooks and Warren issued their highly influential *Understanding Poetry* (1938), and their almost equally important *Understanding Fiction* (1943). By the end of 1942 Davidson had done almost all of the literary criticism he was to do. His *The Attack on Leviathan* marked, as well, the last large-scale Agrarian-inspired maneuver, following *Who Owns America?*, a joint product edited by Tate and Herbert Agar, including once more essays by the entire group of major Fugitives. But Agrarianism was already a dead issue in 1936; aesthetic formalism was only beginning a remarkably fecund existence.

Chapter VIII

Tate as Critic

Allen Tate was the first of the Fugitive writers to collect a volume of criticism, and he has remained their leading producer of critical essays. He has printed an imposing number of articles and reviews, published five books of criticism, and reprinted, under his own editorship or in anthologies edited by others, a number of his essays a number of times.

Despite this imposing record, Tate has not proved an original, seminal critic for his generation, as have Eliot, Richards, Edmund Wilson, and Kenneth Burke. His earlier work, both in the *Fugitive* articles and in his free-lance period in New York, was directly dependent on Eliot. When Eliot's influence waned, the original stimulus of Ransom reasserted itself, now strongly aided by that of Brooks and Warren, who were synthesizing the new critical doctrines. Finally, when he became a convert to Roman Catholicism, Tate moved back toward Eliot, while his further debt to M. Jacques Maritain was both evident and acknowledged.

What has characterized Tate's criticism from the first has been an apostolic fervor; and the firmness, often the dogmatic assurance, of his missionary zeal has inspired a large discipleship. He has, like no other American critic of his time, compelled attention. In an era gone largely over on its intellectual side to Marxist and militantly progressive ideals, he defiantly entitled his first critical volume *Reactionary Essays on Poetry and Ideas* (1936). The belligerence of this opening attack set a tone that has only gradually been modified in the following volumes. The new personal modesty that marks the late work offers a radically different surface effect, but an authoritative core remains. The critic is no longer dogmatic in his own right, but dogma is still the basis of his argument.

The major themes of Tate's critical work are few, and their derivations clear; his ultimate value as a critic, therefore, must rest on the cogency and relevance of his applications. However, his firm championship of the principles he has espoused has largely determined his influence. Most importantly, Tate has stood for the autonomy of art and for the "new critical," or aesthetic formalist, basis of critical analysis. He has not, however, held this position consistently. Under the influence of Eliot and Agrarian doctrines in the late twenties and early thirties, he deviated into a kind of cultural determinism to account for the larger values and limitations in a poet's work. Again in the late forties, now under the sway of Catholic tradition, he adopted extraliterary criteria. Still, his period of greatest effect as a critic was coincident with his single-minded advocacy of literary autotelism.

Tate's second major emphasis has been tradition; at times chiefly historical, at others religious, but always social. It is true that his traditionalism did not for some time extend to literary form, except in the sense defined in Eliot's "Tradition and the Individual Talent." On the other hand, he has consistently supported a militant Southern traditionalism historically derived from Calhoun, and he has always used religious tradition as an "imperative of reference," if not always as an imperative of belief.

Tate's most insistent and persistent motif has been his appeal to authority, though the seat of his authority has shifted more than once. In fact, we may view his progress as a theoretical critic in terms of an extended search for an adequate base of authority on which to support his literary and social positions. However, while his search has continued, he has treated each of his provisional bases as if it were final. As a result, his statements of judgment have often sounded with the ring of cathedral pronouncements. Tate has severely attacked other modern poets and critics; he has scored public education and modern intellectual apathy for the "obscurity" attributed to contemporary literature; he has derogated modern science and particularly scientific positivism; and he has finally deprecated the whole tradition of Western liberalism. Seldom has he sounded like one who has "conducted his education in public," as he described his activities in a recent book, but like one who has, like a taskmaster, unpleasant public duties to perform.

Tate's prepossessions, like those of the other major Fugitives, were essentially rationalistic. His original conceptions were those of Ransom; and when he broke with Ransom's philosophic dualism, it was in the interest of establishing a rational monistic system in which literary expression and religious as well as social imperatives were to be integrated into a hierarchical order. Through the years, Tate has been forced by the logic of his positions farther and farther beyond his original commitments into the area of metaphysical speculation. His theory of literature as "knowledge," annunciated in *Reason in Madness,* led to an invocation of myth and "mythic knowledge"; and from this resort he was induced to assume a highly subjective "power within us, the imaginative power of the relation of things" as the source of art's special insights. In his latest Catholic pronouncements, Tate has invoked "a higher unity of truth," or "Truth," which literature must ultimately reflect, or consent to be regarded as "only illusion." It would appear that Tate's relentless pursuit of a rational justification of the art to which he has dedicated his life has pressed him finally into suprarationalism.

On the level of practical criticism, Tate has proved himself from the start a highly perceptive reader with a sensitivity that guides him directly to the source of a writer's quality. His knowledge of the writer's problems and his own technical proficiency in verse and prose constantly enrich his insights. Often his strictures, under the promptings of theory, are harsh, but they are based as a rule on rigorous analyses. His generalizations, when they are not strained by the impositions of theory, are telling, despite their dogmatic tone and their persistent bias. Tate's range of appreciation is narrow, but within his provinces of metaphysical poetry and symbolic naturalism, he always illuminates the texts and broadens understanding. Outside this area, he is quick to discover local flaws and general limitations; yet his judgments here, with all their special weighting, are never impertinent nor imperceptive. When he speaks in purely literary terms, Tate is lucid and compelling. His natural propensities, however, are those of a moralist, even of a public censor. His criticism, therefore, is heavily burdened with the theories and pronouncements of the philosopher, the sociologist, the historian of ideas, and the public moralist. In these roles, Tate has exerted much influence and stimulated much controversy, but the critic in him has often been forced into the position of a supporting actor.

As he appears in his first critical book, *Reactionary Essays*, Tate is not at all the purely formal critic he had called for in 1927, "attending exclusively to the properties of poetry as a fine art." There are fine passages of formal criticism in the book, but Tate's characteristic method is to move from aesthetic analysis into a theoretical account of the poet's achievements and limitations in terms of the intellectual, social, and religious heritage out of which he writes. Alternatively, he begins directly with a theoretic formulation and buttresses his argument with reference and quotation. Both of these procedures are typical of Eliot in his *Selected Essays, 1917–1932*. Furthermore, Tate's analyses in this book, like those of Eliot, are closely related to the concerns of his own poetry at the period. If they are not quite what Eliot has called his own essays, "a prolongation of the thinking that went into the formation of my own verse,"[1] they are always pertinent to the validation of Tate's kind of poetry in Tate's kind of modern dilemma.

1. T. S. Eliot, "The Frontiers of Criticism," *Sewanee Review*, LXIV, 529.

In probing his own heritage, Tate, again like Eliot, had found a crumbling tradition with values chaotic. As he elucidates this situation in *Reactionary Essays*, his antecedents are John Donne and Emily Dickinson, poets writing out of similar transitional periods without fixed values. The relevant foils are Dante and Milton, both of whom inherited absolute systems of value. Tate's problem, therefore, is to establish the legitimacy of transitional poetry, to which he is committed in taste and necessarily in practice, without vitiating Eliot's thesis that the greatest poetry proceeds from fixed and accepted values. In his Donne essay, Tate remarks that, like Dante, "Milton stood for the historical absolute, which is the myth. And unless it will again be possible for men to give themselves up to a self-contained, objective system of truths, the principles of Donne . . . will continue to be our own."

But he has stated that Donne's verse "presents the problem of personal poetry in its simplest terms," and that his vocabulary "lacks the ultimate, symbolic character of myth." In the same category he places Dickinson's poetry of "personal revelation," which proceeds from her questioning of the value system into which she was born.

The implications of such verdicts as these, and they are impressively documented, would appear to relegate the poetry of Donne and Dickinson, as also that of Eliot and Tate, to a low "personal" level. And these implications are extended later in this volume by a series of negative verdicts on modern poets. Crane, MacLeish, Pound, Bishop, Robinson, Millay, and Cummings are all judged as lacking an "implicit body of ideas," and capable therefore of only "personal poetry," or the "quest of pure sensation and its ordering symbolism." Eliot, himself, is called a "personal" poet, but he escapes the censure attached to the other verdicts.

At this point it becomes evident that Tate's "personal" label need not be wholly derogatory. And in fact Tate has already been at considerable pains to rescue Donne and Dickinson, and with them presumably the modern Southern poet. The Dickinson essay sets up rather unobtrusively the prior conditions of great poetry as "the thoroughness of the poet's discipline in an objective system of truth, and his lack of consciousness of such a discipline," so that his "sense of the natural world is not blunted by a too rigid system of ideas." The "personal" poet, therefore, the inevitable product of a transitional situation, is saved if he possesses an unconscious heritage of values. He attempts to "live apart from a cultural tradition that no longer sustains him," and develops an "egoism grown irresponsible in religion, and decadent in morals . . . the perfect literary situation," for "poetry probes the deficiencies of a tradition."

In this context Dante and Milton do not appear, and Dante in particular seems to be left lacking a proper cultural situation. The dangers of a too rigid system of ideas are later illustrated in an essay on "Three Types of Poetry," where Tate advances Spenserian allegory as the natural result. Dante would appear to escape this dilemma by virtue of his vital sense of the natural world, induced perhaps by his exile. But Tate nowhere argues such points, and we are left at the end of *Reactionary Essays* with two incompatible accounts of literary determinism, each of them based on a thesis of Eliot's.

Throughout this book, the acute literary insights, of which there are many, become submerged in the cultural theories to which his reliance on Eliot has committed the critic. By the time of *Reason in Madness* (1941), however, Tate's ties to Eliot have been considerably loosened, and he is drawn into a new intellectual solidarity with Ransom and the other Fugitives. A major result of the renewed alliance appears in Tate's abandonment of determinism. The literary and the socio-moral sections of *Reason in Madness* are rigidly separated. Even in his discussion of "Nine Poets: 1937," no mention is made of systems of belief or of social determinants. In the two sociological essays, Tate avoids literary references while rejecting the concept of a "religious myth" as irrelevant to the Southern tradition. In its place he substitutes a Ransomic "lower myth," historic rather than religious, essentially a moral code which enabled the members of the society to "form a definite conception of their human role." Tate cannot abandon his attachment to codes and authority, but he does abandon the attempt to relate them directly to the creative problem.

The opening essay in *Reason in Madness* makes it clear that Tate has committed himself whole mindedly to aesthetic formalism. He blames positivism, pragmatism, instrumentalism, scientism, totalitarianism, and high pressure groups for deplorable conditions in which spiritual values have been corrupted. But this wholesale indictment of modern culture becomes the pretext only for discarding all cultural referents for the critic. He is to attend now only to the work itself.

The promise of a book of practical criticism implied in this introductory essay is quickly belied, since only three of the pieces, all appearing late in the book, attend closely to literary texts: one a sweeping review of "Nine Poets," another an exposition of one of his own poems, and the third on "Hardy's Philosophical Metaphors." The main body of the book, stemming from Ransom's thesis that art should be granted a status commensurate with that of religion and of science as a form of knowledge, becomes an extended theoretic discussion of a philosophic thesis. Tate's version, which, like Ransom's, has many Arnoldian overtones, is stated with an unprecedented boldness. The introductory essay announces that "the higher forms of literature offer the only complete, thus the most responsible, version of experience"; and again, that there is a "special, unique and complete knowledge which the great forms of literature afford us."

Tate's "knowledge" involves more than Ransom's representation of the world in its particularity; this Tate grants the scientist equally. The key term for Tate is "cognition," the act of knowing by a mind, "the expression of an interaction among certain elements of a 'situation.'" The exposition of this mind-external world interaction prepares the arguments to follow and elucidates the broad definition which appears at the end of the essay on I. A. Richards: "Literature is the complete knowledge of man's experience, and by knowledge I mean that unique and formed intelligence of the world of which man alone is capable."

From the heights of this theory, Tate examines such critics as Richards, Arnold, Coleridge, and Charles Morris. All of these, he finds, have omitted one or the other of his essential elements, the perceiving mind or the perceived object. With the later point of view of I. A. Richards, however, he is able finally to agree, and the agreement is in terms of Ransom's "myth." Tate's version is that literature offers "neither the world of verifiable science nor a projection of ourselves; yet it is complete [with] the completeness . . . not of the experimental order, but of the experienced order; it is, in short, of the mythical order." The definition of myths is quoted from Richards: "They are [the] hard realities [of life] in projection, their symbolic recognition, coordination and acceptance. . . . The opposite and discordant qualities in things in them acquire a form."

The argument here, whether we wish to credit it essentially to Ransom or Richards or Tate himself, is tautological. Literature has been defined as "the complete knowledge of man's experience," and this knowledge is expressed in terms of the "completeness . . . of the experienced order," which is "mythical," which in turn is an expression of the "hard realities" of experience. The circularity of the argument results, as F. X. Roellinger quickly pointed out,[2] from Tate's failure to supply any external referent for his "knowledge." To place his knowledge "*in* the poem," rather than in the object or in the knowing mind, is to deny it any verification out-

2. "Two Theories of Poetry as Knowledge," *Southern Review*, VII, 690-701.

side itself, and furthermore to allow no criteria for distinguishing true from false knowledge.

Whatever the ultimate philosophic value of the literature-as-knowledge thesis—and, with modifications, it has remained a cardinal Fugitive tenet—the commitment to artistic values per se which it assumes was soon to become the one common denominator of the "new criticism." *Reason in Madness*, together with Ransom's earlier *The World's Body* and later *The New Criticism*, and Brooks's *Modern Poetry and the Tradition*, to which Tate pays high tribute, effectively became the bibles of "new critical" theory in America.

Reason in Madness is notable as well for its whole-hearted defense of modern poets and their experimental techniques. Along with this discussion, it is possible to include the brilliant exposition, in "Narcissus as Narcissus," of the author's own "Ode to the Confederate Dead." This essay demonstrates better than any theoretical argument the value of the formalist criticism advocated in the volume as a whole. Although Tate feels that such detailed exegesis should not be necessary for a properly educated public, he provides it impersonally and effectively. As a document in intentional criticism, at the least, this essay remains one of the most valuable so far produced in the English language.

A further interesting theoretical formulation of Tate's appears in the essay on "Tension in Poetry." One critic has found in it Tate's major contribution to modern critical theory.[3] The thesis here derives from Ransom's earlier application of the terms "extension" and "intension," as well as from Ransom's discussion of "metaphysical" poetry in *The World's Body* and Tate's own earlier treatment of allegory. Tate finds that the "meaning of poetry is its 'tension,' the full organized body of all the extension and intension that we can find in it." Extension is roughly equivalent to denotation, the rational or

3. Clifford Amyx, "The Aesthetics of Allen Tate," *Western Review*, XIII, 135-44.

logical element; intension to connotation, or the affective factor. He explains:

> The metaphysical poet as a rationalist begins at or near the extensive . . . end of the line; the romantic or Symbolist poet at the other, intensive end; and each by a straining feat of the imagination tries to push his meaning as far as he can toward the opposite end, so as to occupy the entire scale.

As an analysis of poetic strategies, though exceptions crowd into the mind, this distinction is useful. However, Tate leaves his reader his full-scale tension as an ultimate criterion of value and provides no means for its identification. Recognition of tension, he says, is a "gift of experience, of culture, or, if you will, our humanism." He proceeds, then, to the Arnoldian resort of providing touchstones. Like Arnold's, these touchstones of "tension," taken thus out of context, provide nothing more than a sample of Tate's excellent taste in rhetoric. Tension has proved an extremely useful concept in the analysis of the plastic arts, but Tate has not here demonstrated a similar value for it in application to linguistic media.

Tate's later critical works have not inspired the enthusiasm or produced the following which his first two volumes elicited. His third and fourth books of criticism appeared almost simultaneously, though only one of these was altogether new. *On the Limits of Poetry* was the author's selection from the whole corpus of his critical writing to 1948, and no attempt was made to update or modify the judgments contained in the earlier essays. The other volume, *The Hovering Fly*, was completely new in material and new also in tone. Furthermore, it called attention to a broadening of the critic's range to include fiction as well as poetry. Although the excellent essay on Hardy's metaphors, basically approaching the novel in terms of poetics, had appeared in *Reason in Madness*, Tate's special interest in the criticism of fiction developed in the late forties and culminated in 1951 with his critical anthology (co-edited by his wife, Caroline Gordon), *The House of Fiction.*

Both this new subject and the new tone are evident in the title essay of the 1949 volume. Originally titled "Dostoevsky's Hovering Fly," this discussion hovers and buzzes about its major concerns, the "imagination and the actual world," with all the tantalizing uncertainty of the fly's own flight. With excessive self-deprecation, Tate professes an ignorance of "what poetry is, or even how it functions," of philosophy generally, and of "the actual world" itself. What finally develops is a modification of the *Reason in Madness* thesis: that "we can to a degree *know* the actual world" through the imaginative projection offered by literature, as "we shall not know [it] by looking at it," or by science's abstractions from it.

The other major essay dealing with the novel, "Techniques of Fiction," takes off from Henry James, Percy Lubbock's discussion of James and Flaubert, and Virginia Woolf's provocative "Mr. Bennett and Mrs. Brown." Tate does not argue the epistemological problem here; he is concerned chiefly to explicate James's dictum that good fiction must offer primarily "the direct impression of life," and to locate the center of the artist's problem in attempting to produce this impression. He finds his center, through the medium of an *exemplum* from *Madame Bovary,* in the author's forcing himself to do "the complete imaginative job himself"; that is, presenting and dramatizing everything, leaving none of the crucial actualization to the reader. But Tate is no longer content with crediting a rational process on the author's part, the sort of process which, as a matter of fact, Flaubert has described with painful detail in his account of the writing of *Madame Bovary;* he insists on a suprarational principle, which he calls "animal tact," in addition to certain "tricks of the trade" passed on from writer to writer but not to critics. Once we add this "tact" to the "obscure power within us, the imaginative power of the relation of things," which was invoked in "The Hovering Fly," we begin to sense something of the new compulsion that is pushing Tate beyond his rationalistic preconceptions toward the Kierkegaardian "leap" which he shortly takes.

Another important development in Tate's critical thinking is evidenced in his essay on Keats. As in the somewhat aberrant (for its period) discussion of Hardy in *Reason in Madness*, the limitations of the art are explicated in part, at least, by reference to the intellectual biography of the poet. A less rigid conception of the formal approach to criticism is implied in this provocative study; furthermore, Tate has evidently done more of the critic-scholar's homework for this essay than he has commonly done. His first concern, as in the treatments of fiction, is that the poet "realize" his symbols and abstract constructions. Keats, he finds, exhibits a "space"-dominated sensibility, and fails to realize "an ordered symbolism through which he may *know* the common and ideal reality [specifically that of the "Ode's" nightingale] in a single imaginative act."

The technical preoccupation of *The Hovering Fly* is clearly indicated in these major essays. Realization is the central concern. How does the artist create his "tension" between fact and idea and thus arrive at "knowledge"? The suggested answer is: through the use of symbols which are completely actualized. But it is evident that more than an effort of the will is demanded; an "obscure power" beyond rational definition is invoked, but nowhere expounded. Tate, in this book, seems to be leaning toward a metaphysical source of imaginative power, though he is yet unable to abandon his old rational footholds. In *The Forlorn Demon* (1953) he has made the leap.

There is no public announcement of the author's profession of Catholicism in *The Forlorn Demon*, but a new orientation is obvious in tone, in vocabulary, in authorities quoted, and in the central subject matter. The tone is humble; there are constant disclaimers of knowledge, confessions of inadequacy, and uncertainties in conclusions. The book is described in the preface as a stage in the author's "unfinished education conducted in public over a number of years," and the implication that this stage is not an advanced one immediately disarms the critic.

The new vocabulary substitutes "communion" for the communication which literature essays, and this communion becomes possible ultimately "only through the love of God." The freedom of experiment and inquiry to which the Western world since the Renaissance has been committed becomes now a "demi-religion"; and "Thomists and Scotists" are defended against the charge of excessive conservatism "in refusing to sanction the advances of science as they were made." The basic authorities now cited are Augustine, Pascal, and Maritain.

The most important pieces in *The Forlorn Demon* were all composed as lectures, for Tate has been remarkably active in recent years as visiting poet or lecturer at universities, participant in symposia, and delegate to international conferences. A number of the selections in this book read, even in amplified form, like speeches. Especially is this true of the two opening pieces, "The Man of Letters in the Modern World" and "To Whom Is the Poet Responsible?" and also of the later "Our Cousin, Mr. Poe" and "Is Literary Criticism Possible?" Of these, the first two and the last are of particular interest in setting the new bearings of the critic, and the third in illuminating some bearings of Tate, the poet.

In the Preface, Tate has announced that one of his major themes is the use and abuse of language. The language of literature, he contends in the opening essay, must provide a "communion," an experience of participation, not mere communication. The prime problems which have been concerning Tate, of literature's "knowledge" and its realization, are reworded in the new terms: "Is there in this language genuine knowledge of our human community—or lack of it—that we have not had before?" This theme is further expounded in the following essay, with the larger section a refutation of the old charge that modern writers are irresponsible. The literary man's responsibility is strictly a literary one, Tate contends, "for the mastery of a disciplined language which will not shun the full report of the reality conveyed to him by his awareness."

To this point, Tate has not carried his theoretic discussion substantially beyond the range of *The Hovering Fly*, and the new emphasis has fallen primarily on linguistic discipline. "Is Literary Criticism Possible?" increases this emphasis, stressing grammar and logic as prerequisites to the ultimate mastery of rhetoric—"the use of the figurative language of experience as the discipline by means of which men govern their relations with one another in the light of truth." Certainly this definition is startling in its unexpectedly broad extensions. Not only has Tate extended the influence of literary disciplines to life disciplines, which is surprising enough in a formalist; he has invoked at the trailing edge of the quotation a "truth" which obviously leaps beyond the old "knowledge" to its source. Lest we pull up at a lesser truth, Tate continues by asking:

> Can we believe in the language of human truth without believing in the possibility of a higher unity of truth, which we must posit as *there*, even if it must remain beyond our powers of understanding?

Then:

> Without such a belief are we not committed to the assumption that literature has nothing to do with truth, that it is only illusion, froth on the historical current, the Platonic *gignomenon*?

This strangely Platonic argument, which arrives precisely where the argument on poetry in *The Republic* does not, illuminates Tate's reorientation. Whereas earlier, like Ransom, he had been seeking to justify literature's eminence by granting it an equal footing with religion's revealed truths, in the form of mythic knowledge, he now seeks to justify it simply as a lower human form of higher religious Truth. The language of literature becomes the means, like that of human ritual, to the ultimate vision of unity. Tate's monistic and authoritative system is now secure, but its assumptions are large: that literature is equivalent to human truth, that human truth reflects divine truth, that Truth and hence truth is a unity. This formulation leaves Tate finally a far cry from the dualisms of his fellow Fugitives.

The emphasis on language in this book is now revealed as something quite different from the emphases of Brooks and Empson. Criticism as simple "analysis of literary language, or 'stylistics,' must find its limit . . . in the extreme 'purity' of nominalism or metaphysics," if it be not corrected by a "total rhetoric." Explication of texts is insufficient also unless it be informed by the "historical imagination." In fact, Tate disposes of all critical approaches, and concludes that criticism is "perpetually impossible," but, "Like man's, the intolerable position of criticism has its own glory." After this burst, in "A Note on Critical 'Autotelism,' " which appears later in the volume (though written earlier), Tate soberly accepts R. P. Blackmur's "declaration of critical scepticism," while he agrees with Ransom that the "position is untenable."

"Our Cousin, Mr. Poe" is interesting for its application to the creative Tate. In the author of "The Fall of the House of Usher" the critic discovers a decadent, "a conscious artist of an intensity which lacked moral perspective," and therefore a "cousin." This is not to be construed as a direct confession, for Poe is the cousin of all of us, and the cousin likewise of Tate's own creation, George Posey. But the description, as it applies to the earlier poet and novelist and even the critic, has considerable pertinency.

The core essays of *The Forlorn Demon* are those on Dante and Poe, for they exhibit full-scale applications of Tate's new theses. The reinterpretations of Samuel Johnson and Longinus as critics hold considerable interest, though neither is a crucial study. Johnson, of an age with faults opposite to our own, is described as denying validity to a "poetry of experience," of action or drama, like the metaphysical, because he was immersed in a static culture; while Longinus is reread in the light of the "new criticism," and consciously overread to anticipate many of the emphases of that technique. Both of these essays suggest Tate's reorientations, but "The Symbolic Imagination" and "The Angelic Imagination" fully demonstrate for the first time the possibilities for criticism inherent in the author's new Catholic bearings.

It seems likely that the concept of "angelism," which Tate credits to Maritain, determined the structure of the complementary essays, both of which were originally read as lectures. "When neither intellect nor will is bound to the human scale," says Tate, paraphrasing his source, "their projection becomes god-like, and man becomes an angel." The "angelic fallacy" which Poe illustrates, therefore, is plain abstractionism, the mind and the will working without benefit of "the world's body," and therefore exhibiting a "dissociation of the sensibility." My phrasings here are those of Ransom and Eliot, as well as of the earlier Tate, for I wish to emphasize that these are not essentially new insights. Tate's exegesis of Poe, however, is new and valuable, since French critics for three-quarters of a century have consistently overestimated Poe's literary powers. Tate finds ultimately in Poe a hypertrophy of feeling, which leads to vampirism; a hypertrophy of the will, which projects him constantly above the human moral plane; and a hypertrophy of the intellect, which fails to find proper analogues in the human situation. These analyses, well documented, are more satisfactory than the final explanation of Poe's dilemma done in the new terminology: "He was a religious man whose Christianity . . . had got short-circuited," so that " 'co-ordination,' for a man of his intensity, was difficult if not impossible."

The Dante essay is thoroughly satisfactory as well as thoroughly Catholic. Tate explores here the symbols of light in the "Paradiso" in order to establish the validity of what he calls the "symbolic imagination." This he explains carefully: "To bring together the various meanings at a single moment of action is to exercise what I shall speak of here as the symbolic imagination. . . . The symbolic imagination conducts an action through analogy, of the human to the divine, of the natural to the supernatural, of the low to the high, of time to eternity." He stresses the form of action for the "Poetic Way," as opposed to the static "Illuminative Way" of the theologian and the "Unitive Way" of the mystic. In tracing Dante's development of the theme of light, as a symbol embodied in Beatrice, Tate is at pains to demonstrate that the poet employs it always in active and concrete images. At the crucial point, when Dante reaches the final blinding light of God's presence, which must be by its extra-sensuous nature unvisualizable, Tate exhibits the poet making his daring, but inevitable, leap back to the visual image of the Incarnation at the center of his circles. Tate's conclusion, for which Poe stands as antithesis, might easily have been formulated by Ransom twenty years earlier: "Poetic insight . . . never begins at the top; it carries the bottom along with it, however high it may climb."

Since *The Forlorn Demon,* Tate has printed only one piece of literary criticism, though speeches and sections of a long Dantesque poem have appeared in quarterly magazines. The critical essay, from 1953,[4] extends the thesis of the "angelic imagination" specifically to Hart Crane, almost an obsessive subject with Tate since their days of mutual influence, and generally to the modern poet. Again the "symbolic" referent is Dante, and Crane, though called one of the greatest poets of his generation, is exhibited, like Poe, as failing to submit his individual will to a "Higher Will," and thus as ending in suicidal frustration. Tate invokes his now familiar idiom to speak of Crane as a poet of "sensibility" only, lacking knowledge of a higher "Truth." By way of contrast, Dante is seen as surrendering his will to the "sea" of God's will and thus, paradoxically, keeping his feet solidly on earth.

4. "Self-Made Angel," *New Republic,* CXXIX, 17-18.

In 1956 it appears eminently unlikely that Tate will make new contributions to theoretical criticism. All of the major prepossessions with which he began his critical career have finally found a footing which seems to guarantee their stability. The authority which he has so frequently invoked or assumed has reached home in an ultimate Authority. Traditionalism and its practical handmaid, conservatism, have received the sanction of ecclesiastical, as well as historical, blessing. Literature has been secured in a high place by analogy to ritual, and by reference to Truth, which its truths (or knowledge) reflect.

Theoretically, Tate has no farther to go without reversals which now seem inconceivable. Of practical criticism, however, there is happily no end. It is to be hoped that Tate has not, like Ransom, virtually abandoned the field. For here, as in his readings of Dante, Donne, Dickinson, Hardy, Keats, Flaubert, Poe, and Crane, Tate has made a lasting contribution to modern criticism.

CHAPTER IX

Ransom as Critic

JOHN CROWE RANSOM did not publish his first volume of critical essays until 1938, or until he was fifty years old, and then he termed the book a series of "preparations for criticism," a "sort of apprenticeship." These "preparations," however, are of a sort that few critics ever make; they are an attempt to work out a full-blown aesthetic theory from which practical criticism, of which he includes several examples, can legitimately proceed. It is true that Ransom, the most truly philosophical mind of the Fugitive group, has, like most theoreticians, become so absorbed in theory (and in editorial work) that he has been able to do less practical criticism than his admirers would like. And it is even true that his theoretical positions have forced him into what has seemed a perverse blindness to values inconsistent with them. However, *The World's Body,* at least, has a boldness and excitement about it that has kept it fresh where volumes by younger men have lost their edge. It rips lustily into Shakespeare as well as into Eliot. It can be lightly witty or weightily philosophic, mordantly sharp or graciously disarming; but it is likely to be always at an extremity, in the engaging manner of youth. One can understand readily that Ransom should have formed an early and lasting distaste, if only as a matter of temperament, for that oldest of young men in his generation, T. S. Eliot.

Since that first volume, much of the excitement has faded out of Ransom's writing. He has held firmly to the main lines of his dualistic thesis and he has continued to move, largely into and out of strict formalistic areas; but he has expended much of his critical energy discussing polemically the theories of other critics and rewriting, with minor shifts of emphasis and slight extensions of analysis, his original pronouncements. *The New Criticism* (1941), which has been Ransom's only other critical book to 1956, lent its title inadvertently to the modern movement in criticism which I have called aesthetic formalism. The book does not, however, define either the movement or its practitioners, nor does it aim to. Instead, it examines a rather miscellaneous group of critics and suggests the theoretical bases for an "ontological," or Ransomically realistic, critical approach.

In more recent years, Ransom has begun several major reworkings of his theoretical doctrines, but all of these have been abandoned without reaching full development. Each of these rethinkings has sprung from further examination of familiar theorists, and each examination has tended to reinforce the doctrinal positions from which Ransom, as a philosopher, began his excursions into criticism. In his most recent formulations, he has, in fact, come full round.

In his years of writing for *The Fugitive,* Ransom's fundamental critical orientation was established. Later, in *God without Thunder,* he had elaborated the basically humanistic, but Judaistically weighted, philosophy which underlay his aesthetics. Indeed, if we recall that Ransom's first critical piece was a rational, typically eighteenth-century formulation, involving the dualism of form and content, that his "ironic" philosophy was predicated on the dialectical opposition between man's rational, moral pretensions and nature's—or God's—nonrational, extra-moral prerogatives, we are adequately prepared for the variations of form or of philosophical alliance which might seem to belie a consistent theoretical position.

Ransom has redivided and subdivided his original oppositions. He has allied his theories to those of a string of major English poets, to those of a number of philosophers, chief of them Kant, and even to those of Sigmund Freud. In his latest formulation (1954-55) he has returned to Kant, with an emphasis on the dualism of man's moral universals and "the purposive concrete of Nature." If, in this discussion, his aesthetic analysis arrives at a trinity, "the head, the heart, the feet," it is not that he has foregone his dichotomies, but only that he recut his cloth, with the "head" retaining its full half measure, and the remainder split.

For Ransom, whatever his occasional vagaries, remains an unreconstructed rationalist, determined to account for the virtues of his long-beloved literature in terms of her real—or ontological—characteristics. He was the first to go overboard for her, to claim for her graces the accolade of "knowledge" and the sisterhood to revered religion or "myth." He was also the first of his group to insist on divorcing her appeals from any practical or useful consideration. Both anti-Platonic and anti-Aristotelian, opposing both the practical moralist and the scientist, he has enshrined literature, along with religion, as mediator between the world's fact and man's ideals. He has strongly opposed all theories which tend to reduce her status, whatever their origin, but he has never admitted metaphysical criteria to support her position.

More and more since the date of his second book, however, Ransom has tended to shift the site of literature's prime dwelling closer into the orbits of common life experience. The thinner altitudes were never congenial to him, and he has increasingly found the pure air of aesthetic criticism too rare for his humanistic lungs. In earlier years, he had complained that "art for art's sake" doctrines tended to pale into "life for art's sake" bloodlessness. Now he has begun again to speak of "substantive values" and "moral Universals" in contradistinction to aesthetic values per se. He has even talked the heresy of a separable content which may be discussed on its own merits without damaging the work of art to which it belongs, and which may "enter into the conduct of life."[1] In his reasserted humanism, Ransom has been left stranded while the fresher

1. "The Shores of Criticism," *Partisan Review,* XX, 111.

currents of suprarational and prerational criticism break around him. The suspicion remains, however, that his solid principles may endure longer than those of the swimmers with the flood.

The World's Body (1938) sets out what the Preface calls "various versions of what approaches, I think, a fairly single and coherent poetic doctrine." In sum, the doctrine holds that true poetry is "the act of an adult mind," wanting "only to realize the world," which is to say the full "body and solid substance of the world" which our practical and scientific abstractions have kept from us; it is "a kind of knowledge." This is the major of Ransom's theses; the other appears on page 4, where he speaks of the "strain of contraries, the not quite resolvable dualism, that is art," a dualism between "the poet and the man, the technique and the personal interest." Later, this dualism extends to one between the "logical object or universal" and a "tissue of irrelevance" in the art work, those elements later to be distinguished in Ransom's most useful terms, "structure" and "texture."

The "knowledge" theory proposed here by Ransom should be distinguished from that later formulated by Tate, though the acknowledgment to this volume speaks of "obligations to Allen Tate . . . whose views of poetry I share . . . with fewest and slightest reservations." At the heart of Ransom's conception is his original view that art is a form of man's revulsion against too much abstraction or practical science. This is not to denigrate science, which Ransom never really does. It is to insist that art is one with religion and manners as a mode of ritual, but "its field is wider than that of manners, or than that of religion." The purpose of the artist is not, like that of the scientist, to bring the object under a "system of control," but to "know it for its own sake." And, Ransom adds,

> . . . this is the knowledge, or it ought to be, which Schopenhauer praised as 'knowledge without desire.' . . . a knowledge so radical that the scientist as scientist can scarcely understand it, and puzzles to see

it rendered, richly and wastefully, in the poem, or the painting. The knowledge attained there, and recorded, is a new kind of knowledge, the world in which it is set is a new kind of world.

Here, as often elsewhere in this volume, Ransom limits his description of aesthetic "knowledge" to the perceptual, with the artist's imaginative contribution completely omitted. In "Poetry: A Note in Ontology," he states that art "means to reconstitute the world of perceptions"; and the essay on "The Mimetic Principle" insists that the reconstitution is accomplished by literal imitation, which should exhibit "an infinite degree of particularity." Plato, the moral abstractionist, he remarks, "could see no sense in the artist's imitation of natural objects, as if that were something to do. . . . I suggest that the artist is not necessarily doing anything else." The "necessarily" would seem to save the theory here, but Ransom unfortunately, like Plato, uses painting for his illustration and allows only for a painstaking naturalism, where "the pains measure the love."

But the critic does not remain on this level. In several of the essays he insists on the form which the artist imposes between himself and his object. Then, in successive discussions—"Poetry: A Note in Ontology" and "A Psychologist Looks at Poetry"—he broadens the base of his theory to include three types of poetry and to admit cognition and the imagination. The types are: pure or "Physical Poetry," that simplest type, which "is the basic constituent of any poetry"; "Platonic," or poetry of abstract ideas; and "Metaphysical Poetry." Ransom finds that "Platonic Poetry is too idealistic, but Physical Poetry is too realistic, and realism is tedious and does not maintain interest." Metaphysical Poetry, which is "the extension of a rhetorical device" (metaphor), adds a "miraculism or supernaturalism. . . the same miraculism which supplies to religions their substantive content."

The effect of this essay is to relegate the still basic perceptual knowledge of other essays to a contributory status, to refurbish and admit science's conceptual knowledge, and to discover in their fusion through the device of metaphor the higher aesthetic knowledge. The agent of this fusion, we find in the essay on I. A. Richards, is the imagination:

> The imagination supplies the form of knowledge for poetry. . . . I should say that imagination is an organ of knowledge whose technique is images. . . . The poet . . . animates nature . . . abstract qualities, abstract collective or quantitative terms . . . gives them body, life, and mind. . . . I prefer to think that these images or assertions which exceed observation are the form that certain cognitions take with us because of our natural propensities as knowers.

The enlarged conception which Ransom arrives at in this formulation brings his theory close to that of his subject, Richards, and to that of Tate, to whom he acknowledges obligations, though Tate's full-blown theory did not appear until some years later. But both Richards and Tate, later, describe their "mythic knowledge" as an interaction between a mind and the external world. For Ransom, this is insufficient, since scientific knowledge is describable in the same terms:

> It is philosophical to say that all knowledge is an impure product, or compound, of two factors, a subjective constitution and an external object, but in having said that we have not settled any aesthetic problems. We have laid down a proposition which governs all our knowledges, and governs them equally whether they appear in poems or in sciences.

Ransom's solution to this dilemma is nowhere propounded, but his preferring to think of poetic "images" and "assertions" as the forms of cognitions taken "because of our natural propensities as knowers" suggests that Kant is in the background. The imagination would appear to be a Kantian category, which determines the forms of our aesthetic responses.

However we may assess Ransom's "knowledge" theory in its several forms, and it shares with Tate's the failure to provide verification outside itself, we recognize the strength of the compulsion behind it. Ransom needs to assert poetry's right to equal consideration with both religion and science. Even more important, he is calling for a new emphasis on an *appreciative* approach to life, despite life's tragic character. "Love not use" is the key to Ransom's attitude toward the world he lives in, and therefore toward art.

In this volume, Ransom's dualistic prepossessions lead him to elaborate a number of distinctions. He even breaks down his "aesthetic knowledge" into "alternate forms": the sentimental and the formal. These forms, corresponding roughly to the romantic and the classic, are by no means of equal value for Ransom. He obviously prizes the formal discipline in poetry as in manners, for, while it removes the artist into a virtual "anonymity," it enables him to transfer his experience from an instinctive level to an aesthetic one. The essay on "Lycidas," which opens *The World's Body,* applies this thesis brilliantly.

A less fortunate distinction is that between "Pure and Impure Poetry," described as the alternate forms into which "modernist" poets have been forced in their efforts to purge their verse of the nineteenth-century "moral effect." The "pure" style is illustrated from Wallace Stevens in a poem which, Ransom says, "has no moral, political, religious, or sociological values"; in fact, the "subject matter is trifling." Tate's "Death of Little Boys" illustrates the "obscure," where the poet, "as if conscious that he is close to moralizing sententiousness, builds up deliberately, I imagine, an effect of obscurity." He introduces "bright features . . . to his total image without permitting them to reveal any precise meaning, either for himself or his reader." One cannot avoid sympathy with Yvor Winters who was driven into a quiet rage by this essay. If the analysis is correct—which I think it is not in either case, despite Ransom's intimacy with Tate—it clearly gives warrant for much of the grosser criticism of modern poetry.

Ransom's most impressive dualistic venture in this volume occurs only as a brief postscript to "Criticism, Inc.," the final essay. The critic, he suggests, however he express himself, must recognize that "two terms are in his mind, the prose core to which he can violently reduce the total object, and the differentia, residue, or tissue, which keeps the object poetical or entire." Ransom does insist, in formalist fashion, that the poem is a "living integrity," to be separated into its component elements only for the purpose of analysis, and he insists that "the character of the poem resides . . . in its way of exhibiting the residuary quality." However, in the earlier essay on Millay, he had proposed as a "staple consideration" that "the poetry on whatever level must make as consistent sense as prose." The way is fully prepared here for Ransom's most important and useful dualism, that of "structure" and "texture."

In the large, "Criticism, Inc." is a plea for an objective and philosophical critical procedure, which should exclude impressionism and minimize extra-critical studies. Ransom wants a "professional" criticism, thoroughly organized and "scientific," one that disregards the emotional component of poetry as non-objective and undiscussible, and concentrates on properly aesthetic considerations. This is good formalism, though perhaps more rigid in its controls than other formalists would allow. There is, however, one qualification—one on which the essay on "The Cathartic Principle" also had insisted:

> The good critic cannot stop with studying poetry, he must also study poetics. . . . I think the taboo may have originated with Mr. Eliot . . . or in some narrow trades-unionism that the guild had adopted, perhaps by treaty with the professional aestheticians who resent poaching on their trade.

"Criticism, Inc." must for Ransom be buttressed by a not yet incorporated theory. His abiding interest, like that of most pure rationalists, has been philosophical speculation, so that the aesthetician in him poaches even on the scientific, or empirical, critic called for in this final essay.

The most stimulating and most capricious of the essays in *The World's Body* are, surprisingly enough in view of "Criticism, Inc.," those of practical criticism. In particular, that on Eliot displays rather flagrantly the old animus against the author of *Murder in the Cathedral*. Ransom finds this play, as he had once found *The Waste Land*, a series of "brilliant discords," which "must come out of personal disintegration and unfaith"—an inference hardly deducible from "properly aesthetic" considerations alone. "Shakespeare at Sonnets" comes off little better. Here the critic's increasingly exclusive attraction to Metaphysical Poetry betrays him into unorthodox and unjustifiably harsh verdicts. His application of Donne's standards to Shakespeare, who "had no university discipline," leads him to conclude that the poet wrote naturally a romantic "associationist poetry," and that his attempts to employ the Metaphysical manner were largely failures for lack of intellectual control. The discussion of Macbeth's "Tomorrow and tomorrow" soliloquy in terms of Donne and out of dramatic context is again a flagrant violation of the critic's own prescriptions.

Even with all its unsatisfactory aspects, *The World's Body* remains a highly readable and stimulating book. Its immediate effect was to provoke discussion of aesthetic problems in critical magazines on an unprecedented scale. In conjunction with the neo-Aristotelian "critical revolution" at the University of Chicago, it was a major factor in swinging large sections of the academic world away from historical and linguistic studies and toward formalist critical doctrines and procedures. With Brooks and Warren's *Understanding Poetry* of the same year to serve as practical handbook, and Tate's earlier volume to buttress it, Ransom's book invaded university classrooms to pave the way for a decade of ontologically minded "new critics."

Another important result of *The World's Body* was the establishment of *The Kenyon Review*, worthy successor to *The*

Southern Review, which was to survive only until 1941. Ransom left Vanderbilt in 1939 to accept a Carnegie Chair of Literature at Kenyon College and to found there the quarterly which he has edited since. The move which took Ransom out of the South for the first time since his student days signaled his abandonment of Agrarian doctrines and of creative work in poetry. From this time on, his writing is exclusively critical, and his preoccupation with theory becomes more and more pronounced.

At Kenyon he set to work immediately on a series of critiques in which he reviewed in detail the theoretical positions and predispositions of his contemporary critics. His resulting volume, *The New Criticism*, appeared in 1941, when aesthetic formalism was entering its period of widest influence. Almost at once, the critical world adopted his title to describe the loosely related body of critical innovation represented in the book. But the designation of "new critic" was quickly extended to include the author and his Fugitive colleagues, then to such critics as Burke and Blackmur. If the term finally has come to have a limited reference, it applies to that body of critical writing which I have referred to as aesthetic formalism.

Ransom begins with I. A. Richards once again, but Richards appears now in a new role, his earlier "scientism" forgiven. Ransom's objections to Richards' new emphasis centers on the "affective fallacy." For Ransom, the emotions have never been legitimate subjects for critical discussion, for they are intractable and far too imprecise for logical, objective analysis. "The specific quality of any emotion," he says now, "is all but indefinable in pure emotive terms, and that seems to be because the distinctness that we think of as attaching to an emotion belongs really to the object." He feels, therefore, that the "critic is faking his discovery of emotion when he cannot make out its object." The "emotions are correlatives of the cognitive object." As Yvor Winters has noted, Ransom's doctrine here exactly reverses Eliot's celebrated account of the "objective correlative." The reversal, however, is simply a matter of point of view, Eliot writing from the poet's standpoint, Ransom from the reader's. Still, Ransom as poet too would insist that he begins with the object.

The logic of Ransom's position is that of Symbolist or Imagist poetry (or his own "Physical"), rather than that of the Metaphysical which he chiefly defends; and it would effectively exclude Shelleyan romantic poetry for its failure to provide concrete correlatives to which the emotions should attach. But Ransom's primary interest is to clear the ground under his own "knowledge" theory. In a summarizing passage he remarks that, to Richards, "poetry is a very good thing, but it has no rating as a way of knowing the world. Its service is not cognitive, but psychological." Though he admits that Richards and his follower, Empson, are at times engaged by the "cognitive content," he insists that "Richards always holds . . . that the heart of the aesthetic experience is the affective activity." In a drastic simplification, Ransom proposes his own version in the form of a definition: "A beautiful poem is an objective discourse which we approve, containing objective detail which we like." It is this sort of statement that has led Winters to speak of Ransom as a "hedonist," but this is to ignore his fuller statements, such as that in his Santayana critique (*The World's Body*): all the arts, "even music must symbolize life." The definition here merely wants to underline objectivity.

Between the discussion of Richards and the concluding plea for an "ontological criticism," Ransom analyzes Eliot as a "historical critic" and Winters as a "logical critic." Eliot is "historical" in that he approaches literature with a "characteristically comparative" method; he tests by reference to the poetic tradition, though he also exercises "independent critical judgment." "It is likely," Ransom concedes, "that we have no better critic than Eliot." But: "A historic critic in this sense is a man with touchstones, and a man who quotes."

On the theoretic level, he is weak; in fact, his aesthetics produces "one of the most unmanageable theories that a critic could profess." Eliot's accent on emotions and feelings is subject to the same criticism as that of Richards. Ransom is able to translate Eliot's "big emotions" and "little feelings" into his own "structure" and "texture" as their points of attachment, and thus avoid "vagueness"; but "fused" or "transmuted" emotions remain meaningless concepts for him. The famous "depersonalizing process," with the poet as catalyst, Ransom will not allow, since it reduces the creative act to a kind of "poetic automatism."

When Ransom discusses Eliot's use of tradition and religion (and elsewhere in this volume as well), he reverts to many of his pre-Agrarian positions. His new independence of his Fugitive colleagues appeared in the Richards essay, where he disagreed with Brooks on the centrality of irony; now he disagrees with Tate as well. He categorizes Tate with Eliot among those who "do not propose to have commerce with the world," because they are "very distrustful of naturalists and positivists." Eliot, in particular, he objects, holds that "poetry is in some manner exempted from having to furnish a real factuality for its . . . objects, since it only wants to offer emotional experiences, and these can feed on fictions and fancies." This places it, even by Eliot's standards, in the same position as religion. But Eliot prescribes a "suspension of disbelief" for poetry, a dogmatic belief for religion; he "believes in believing the religious dogmas, not the affirmations of poetry." Even science can admit that its "truest" hypothesis is speculation, despite its "brilliant precision." "But religion is reluctant to concede that its 'revealed truth' is speculation."

It is evident in this essay that Ransom has gone back at least as far as *God without Thunder*. Only his new terms, "structure" and "texture," provide the novelty, and these terms must bear the full burden of the expanded "knowledge" theory. The texture now supplies the "world's body," the full particularity of physical knowledge. Texture can provide a "factuality" for poetry equivalent to that which the "myths" of religion provide for it. But Ransom now wants an equivalence with scientific knowledge as well. He finds it in his old "logical sequence," now reintroduced as "structure." Science is a formulation of experience with its "truth," comparable to the "truths" of religion or poetry; but, unlike theirs, its "truth" is one of an abstract and logical character. Now poetry, in its abstract and logical aspect, as "structure," acquires science's order of knowledge, as well as religion's. Ransom's theory gains a new balance and completeness, though the term "knowledge" retains its dubious character as a description of the poem's communication. Furthermore, Ransom is able to restore that rational, logical element to which his essentially Cartesian mind had always inclined him. "If Shelley's argument is foolish, it makes his poetry foolish," he can now say, with evident satisfaction.

If Eliot neglects structure in his poetic theory, Yvor Winters, the "logical critic," Ransom says, is our "best at pouncing upon the structure of a poem." And Winters is, by no means, "blind to texture; but his conscious theory does not know how to take hold of texture." Ransom's basic objection to Winters' theory is that it "subordinates the poetic interest to the moral, or . . . denies the poetic interest," for "Winters believes that ethical interest is the only poetic interest." It is true, certainly, as Winters objected, that Ransom interprets "moral" and "ethical" here in a narrower sense than Winters himself does. But, in his turn, Winters interprets Ransom to mean didacticism, a narrower concept than Ransom's. Winters wants to say, with Arnold, that all poetry, even "pure" descriptive poetry, is a comment on, or an interpretation of, experience. Ransom is only anxious that such evaluation be not overt in the poem. Therefore, Ransom would concentrate on the objective aspects, where the evaluation appears in solution, while Winters would crystallize out this "moral" aspect and treat it separately, performing his own evaluation upon it.

Ransom is particularly happy with Winters' analysis of the structural types developed by the "Experimental Generation of poets." "What Winters impeaches [in these modern poets] is their structural confusion," and, with Eliot the chief offender, Ransom endorses the judgment. He is enthusiastic also about Winters' attention to metrics, which he feels have been much neglected, not only by critics, but by the poets of our time, who "have been insensitive to metrical niceties as the poets of no earlier period have been." Ransom's dualisms are being multiplied at this point, so that a strong metrical texture is now required to act as a "conventional" opposition to balance the "meaning."

The final chapter of *The New Criticism*, entitled "Wanted: An Ontological Critic," is an elaborate elucidation of the theses which Ransom has been developing through the earlier chapters. First, poetry "is a kind of knowledge" that "treats an order of existence, a grade of objectivity, which cannot be treated in scientific discourse." The argument for this premise is substantially that offered in *The World's Body*, though it is couched now in the more technical terms employed by Charles Morris. The structure-texture theory, on the other hand, undergoes a process of redevelopment. The process begins with a complete reversion to the earliest of Ransom's formulations, to "suggest that the meter-and-meaning process is the organic act of poetry, and involves all its important characters." He even repeats his old phrase that the poet is "metering his argument." But a new element must be introduced to account for the intractable textural qualities. Ransom provides for it in a concept of "indeterminacy."

"An argument," he says, "which admits of alteration in order that it may receive a meter must be partly indeterminate. Conversely, a metrical form must be partly indeterminate if it proposes to embody an argument." What Ransom does, therefore, is to split up his logical element into "determinate meaning" and "indeterminate meaning," and his metrics into determinate and indeterminate meters. "I cannot but think," he adds, "that the distinction of these [four] elements, and especially of the D M and I M, is the vocation *par excellence* of criticism."

The process of creation sounds singularly rational and uninspired in Ransom's description, the poet working preformed arguments into preformed meters, until:

> . . . in the experiment of composition, . . the imagination of the poet, and not only his verbal mechanics, is engaged. . . . The meter seems only to harm the discourse, till presently it works a radical innovation; it induces the provision of icons among the symbols. This launches poetry on its career.

The unexpected importation into this pedestrian account of the "imagination" and of forces which work radical innovations, provide icons, and actually produce the poetry, leaves the reader wondering why the fuss about D M, I M, and the rest. Had not the critic done better to have begun with these crucial subjective forces? The dilemma is a typical Fugitive one: the rational, objective argument leads only up to the crucial point. Ransom will soon be toying with Freud's irrational elements.

The New Criticism ends with a brief look at the condition of modern poetry. Despite their stated respect for poetic tradition, modern poets "make wide and deliberate departures from it for the sake of their own poetry." In their anxiety for a "more direct and less formal knowledge," they "irregularize and de-systematize the 'old practice.' " Ransom finds them "committed on principle to an unprecedented degree of indeterminateness in the meaning," yet at the same time seeking indeterminateness in the meters. "The effect is an ontological density which proves itself by logical obscurity." The balance of opposing forces which Ransom always requires is hopelessly upset.

The occasion of so sudden a flight may be simple nostalgia, looking backward. But also it may be a reluctant testimony to real ontological efficacy, very much as it has been arrived at in the past experience of the race with its language.

This final statement is Ransom's valedictory to his fellow Fugitive theorists, whose insistent dedication to the strange gods of modernism has tried his traditionalist patience too far. His ideas are no longer "close together" with those of Tate and Brooks. Effectively separated in his own Northern bailiwick, buttressed by his own magazine, Ransom can afford to woo old loves and cleanse his hands of the modernist taint, which had never penetrated subcutaneously.

By the end of 1956, Ransom has published no further volume of criticism. However, during his long period of editorship of *The Kenyon Review*, he has pursued his investigations into aesthetic theory and printed a number of reviews and topical articles. At the same time, in lectures and public discussions, he has continued to emphasize the basic doctrines which he had first formulated in *The Fugitive* years.

Quietly, but none the less certainly, Ransom has retreated from the advanced and involved dialectical positions in which "Wanted: An Ontological Critic" had embogged him. He has given up his D M's and I M's, and his iconological phraseology, derived from Morris. Substantially, too, he has abandoned his "literature as knowledge" theory. In 1943 he still finds that poetry "seems to reflect a kind of ontological principle, or 'reality principle,' " and even that "Poetry would seem to exercise our proclivity for a dangerous kind of knowledge."[2] Even here, the accent, with its "seems," is soft; in following years the theory never reoccurs in its original force.

Perhaps the most important development in Ransom's critical writing during the last decade and a half has been its isolationist character. He had already cut away from formalist and modernist trends in Brooks and Tate in the last chapters of

2. "Positive and Near-Positive Aesthetics," *Kenyon Review*, V, 443-47.

The New Criticism. Shortly afterwards, in a backward glance at the Agrarian movement,[3] he removes himself from the settled convictions of two other former colleagues, Davidson and Lytle, who have remained unreconstructed Agrarians. Ransom's position is that the contemplated recommitment to farm life, never actually practiced by its advocates, would have amounted to a lifelong penance for intellectuals in the modern world. He does not make explicit the sin for which the "mode of repentence not itself to be repented" could be considered an expiation, but there is no question that Ransom no longer shares his associates' continued enthusiasm for the program.

The new critical isolationism exhibits itself most clearly in a suspicious and almost truculent attitude towards critics who represent positions relatively close to his own. At one point, he draws a rather scornful distinction between his own sort of "professional" critic and the "academic variety," a "subtle version of the old town and gown controversy," as he calls it.[4] This comes somewhat strangely from a career professor. For him, the Chicago Neo-Aristotelians are, of course, too prosaically logical, despite their professed regard for the "poemness" of the poem. But the "new criticism," in the hands of a Brooks or an Empson, has also become academic and disappointing to the "professional." Brooks is castigated for his scorn of the logic which the Chicagoans emphasize, and for his attempts to limit poetry to the play of paradox. "I think," Ransom says, "that mystification, at the level of literary criticism, is no longer a good strategy."[5] The revival of Coleridge as a critic—by Richards primarily, one supposes, but by Brooks, Tate, and especially Warren later—is "obfuscating and dull." But Warren, Ransom testifies to feeling, was for a time at least "on the way to arguing that poetry is science, and even to being a Positivist"[6]—still the final heresy. Having thus sharply cut

3. "Art and the Human Economy," *Kenyon Review*, VII, 683-88.
4. "The Bases of Criticism," *Sewanee Review*, LII, 570-71.
5. "Poetry," *Kenyon Review*, IX, 439.
6. "Positive and Near-Positive Aesthetics," *op. cit.*, p. 444.

off both the right and the left of his own position, Ransom speaks of the "messy present state of poetic theory."[7]

In the area of literary modernism, Ransom similarly burns many of his old bridges. In an unreprinted essay from 1939,[8] Ransom had attacked Joyce's *Finnegans Wake* in terms reminiscent of his early attack on *The Waste Land.* Joyce was seen as "on the side of the angels" in his obvious "reaction against the processes of science," but Ransom would have none of his "prime devices for obfuscating discourse." Later in this essay he threw up Joyce to Richards as an instance of Richards' dictum that anything belonging to the "psychological situation" is relevant to the "total meaning," and he accused Empson of reading by "homophones" in the way Joyce writes. Four years later, Ransom is back again at Eliot, with the same type of objections reflecting the old antipathy.[9] "Eliot's structures are as far short of those of traditional poets on the semantic and logical side as they are on the phonetic or metrical side." In this essay, also, Warren is criticized for not giving a place to "texture" in his theoretical statements.

If the impression begins to form that Ransom has grown old, set and crotchety in his ways, it is belied by his more recent attempts to rework his theoretical position in terms of other men's premises and conclusions. In 1947 he looks again at the "messy state of poetic theory" and decides to begin again, this time on a basis on Freudian psychology and, to an extent, on logical positivism.[10] Ransom's formulation here is not so new as its apparent sponsors would seem to make it look. The old structure-texture dualism has a new framework in ego-id psychology, with the (paraphrasable) "thought-work" as ego and the "play on substance" as id. The critical function, once regarded as distinguishing D M and I M, becomes largely a matter of rationalizing the "id motive."

7. "Poetry," *op cit.*, p. 447.
8. "The Aesthetic of *Finnegans Wake*," *Kenyon Review*, I, 424-28.
9. "Inorganic Muses," *Kenyon Review*, V, 278-300.
10. "Poetry," *op. cit.*, 436-56, 640-58.

In this formulation, what is new is Ransom's admission of the emotive element, which he had hitherto rigidly excluded as inaccessible to rational discourse. "Poetry," he now says, "is language in the pathetic mode, which is the mode not of logic but of feeling," or in the "substantive mode," which emphasizes the emotional referents. There is also a "logical, functional mode," and Ransom continues to insist on the objective "precious objects" of aesthetic regard, which are to be distinguished from objects "for use in the desire process." But only the simplest poetry, he now finds, evokes the precious objects; "good poets . . . can manage without . . . or with very few."

Ransom's attempt here to reconcile his old and "precious" theories of "the world's body" with new concepts out of psychology and logic is by no means complete in his two essays. He once announced a third part of the study, but the continuation was abandoned without explanation. When he finally returned to basic theoretical problems, the reversion was to another old favorite, Immanuel Kant.

Before reaching Kant, Ransom introduces one more variation into his system. Again discussing Brooks and the Neo-Aristotelians,[11] he proposes, not a dual nor a quadripartite, but a "trinitarian existence" for the poem. In the discussion of Brooks, he recalls, "I had the idea of a poem as a great 'paradox,' a construct looking two ways, with logic trying to dominate the metaphors, and metaphors trying to dominate the logic. . . . But now I suggest that we must reckon with the meters too." He repeats the suggestion in his criticism of "Humanism at Chicago." Clearly no change of heart has taken place; Ransom has simply, in the interests of economy, given up his distinction between determinate and indeterminate meters.

The tripartite division continues to dominate the first part

11. "Why Critics Don't Go Mad," *Kenyon Review*, XIV, 331-39; and "Humanism at Chicago," *ibid.*, pp. 647-59.

of Ransom's 1954-55 reworking of his theory, entitled "The Concrete Universal: Observations on the Understanding of Poetry."[12] After recording his reservations to W. K. Wimsatt's treatment of the "concrete universal" in his volume, *The Verbal Icon*, Ransom offers his trinity in organic form, as "the head, the heart, the feet." Most of this essay is spent in the head area, and the critic is defending the logical "universals" which appear, imperfectly embodied, in poems. He insists that paraphrases are not damaging, are, in fact, useful, and are not importations, as Brooks and others would have it. "There is nowhere in the world for the logical paraphrase to have come from except the poem, where it is implicit." Ransom illustrates current neglect of this "head" aspect by citing what he calls the hitherto overlooked intellectual content of Wallace Stevens' poetry, which he construes "as a set of Notes Toward the Definition of a Secular Culture."

In this essay and its sequel,[13] Ransom clarifies his own secular humanistic code and reaffirms his commitment to "the dreadful facts of life and the pusillanimous dialectic by which poetry deals with them," in preference to "the security of dogma." His return to Kant is to the apostle of "aesthetic humanism," who reconciled "the free moral world which is wholly inner" and purposive, to the natural world outside us, which "likewise seems free and purposive." He offers as Kant's a definition of poetry very like his early ones: "Poetry is the representation of natural beauty," with the "spectacular faculty of imagination [as] its agent." On the other hand, his own structure-texture formulation—he says he was never satisfied with the term "texture"—is translated into Kantian terms: the "moral Universal" and "the purposive Concrete of nature." The play of these two elements is both "unpredictable and inexhaustible." Illustrating the process with excerpts from 300 years of poetry, Ransom demonstrates two strategies, in

12. *Kenyon Review*, XVI, 554-64.
13. *Ibid.*, XVII, 383-407.

which one or the other element dominates. The processes correspond closely to Tate's account of beginning at the "extensive" or "intensive" end of the scale. But for Ransom there is no poetry of the "middle," no pure "tension."

Ransom's dualisms remain inviolate, free from any taint of a Hegelian, or even a Tatean, synthesis. Temperamentally and philosophically, Ransom cannot forsake his oppositions, for the human condition is to him an ironical opposition between man's desires and his potentialities, between his moral propensities and the world's indifference. No science and no religion can, in Ransom's book, resolve these oppositions. Where other critics have found their reconciling principles in some form of positivism or in dogma, Ransom has held to his rational humanism, stubbornly and alone seeking a solid grounding for his clear-headed view of the poem as an objectively analyzable phenomenon of "precious" value.

Chapter X

Tate's Fiction

Allen Tate's short career in fiction began in 1933 and ended abruptly in 1938, considerably before he had displayed a critical interest in the art of fiction. His attraction to the medium as a means of creative expression coincided with the Agrarian excitement and followed his incursions into the field of biography. His theory, as he was developing it in relation to poetry, insisted upon the primary reality of imaginative works over those whose ontological status depends on literal fact. The turn to fiction thus represented an attempt to reach a higher level of historical truth, for the fiction, as we should have predicted, dealt exclusively with the historical background of his own heritage. Tate's short stories, "The Immortal Woman" and "The Migration," were printed in 1933 and 1934. Though the first of these forecasts the novel *The Fathers,* that book was not published until 1938 and no further stories came in the interval.

"The Migration," printed in *The Yale Review,*[1] purports to relate, from the point of view of a son, the life of one Rhodam Elwin, a late immigrant to tidewater Virginia (in 1794), and the related lives of his family and neighbors. What Tate is evidently at in this dryly told narrative is a further attempt to define the "Old West" culture from which his own has sprung. Here he traces, not the aristocratic F.F.V. tradition, which is shown already, as his protagonist defines it, effete and degenerate, but the later Scotch-Irish artisan element which moved, via North Carolina, over the mountains into Kentucky and Tennessee. Tate does not argue a case; he pre-

1. Vol. XXIV, 83-111.

sents simply a life that he regards as typical, not minimizing its faults and weaknesses, but offering its solid virtues in contrast to the ostentatious "nouveau riche" of Nashville, to the elegant and still feudal aristocracy of Virginia, and to the "poor white" of the back country. He emphasizes the family's moral and social code and its ability, therefore, to absorb pain and evil. Further, he highlights the agrarian practicality of the elder Elwin, who repudiates the Europe-oriented tobacco economy of the Eastern seaboard for a sounder corn and wheat economy in his adopted Tennessee homeland. The story ends, in fact, with a repudiation of the now migrating Tidewater element, who drive in politely to ruin the country with tobacco planting and to lure poor white followers behind them. Father Elwin at his death frees his first-bought slave, gives him $50 and his Revolutionary captain's uniform coat, and suggests that he buy a hack and an old horse: "you will get all the tobacco-makers riding behind you," he says.

As fiction, "The Migration" is not impressive. The form is pure narrative—all "pictorial," in Henry James's terms, nothing "scenic." There results no presented drama, and no reader commitment. Since the style is a sparse antipoetic re-creation of mid-nineteenth-century agrarian prose, no special interest accrues from a diction without metaphor and without intimacy.

Tate's other short story, which appeared in *Hound and Horn*[2] and was selected for O'Brien's *Best Stories of 1934*, develops more fictional interest. "The Immortal Woman" is much more complex than "The Migration," though it attempts something of the same sort of historical re-creation. The point of view in this story provides an immediate challenge, for the narrator, a Civil War veteran invalided, comes from the North, of an impoverished Pennsylvania family now located in Georgetown. Tate thus boldly offers a "foreigner's" perspective (a "foreigner" become sensitive through his invalidism, and thus

2. Vol. VI, 592-609.

perhaps equivalent to the modern Southern poet) on a significant aspect of the Tidewater heritage. The view is further complicated, and perhaps made more modern, by the fact that it appears through a decadent post-Civil War present, so that the culture it means to present can come to life only secondhand, by the expedients of overheard conversations and belated, severely limited, observation. The old lady who is the focus of the story is the Jane Posey of *The Fathers*, here long married to a Westerner, hopelessly lost to the traditional life, but yearning back to it in the form of the decaying mansion in which she had once lived.

The point-of-view character, who "can know things only in action," as he admits, is quite inadequate to interpret the old lady's behavior or the motivations behind it. He can see her floating walk, symbol of the gliding progress through life of the oriented culture of the old South, and he can sense that the old house is "not innocent enough" for his own abstract training to compass. In his own predicament he can feel, too, the lady's harassment, her "perfection of untested desire," "as perfect as a cyclone, as terrible, with the same suffocation vortex inside." This description, prefiguring as it does the description of George Posey in *The Fathers*—the George Posey of this story is described as "in a rage all his life"—indicates the true bearing of the story in its relation to Tate's agrarian-traditionist position in the thirties. The "immortal woman" of the narrative represents, like the house, a city-decadent phase of a border Southern culture; the stronger stock, like the Elwins, had moved West. The inner fury which for Tate characterizes this phase results from the abandonment of an organized, land-based way of life and the substitution for it of a commitment to pure contingency. Now the lost lady is seeking a place in which to die, a means of fulfillment in terms of the earlier cultural pattern which has been denied her.

The story's ending turns what has been ostensibly an indirect chronicle of a life, and a disturbed way of life, into naked allegory. A young man, strong and well dressed, suddenly appears, kisses the old lady, looks at the house, and leads her away, she in tears but leaning on him. There is no speech, but he smiles as he guides her off confidently. The youth has not appeared before nor been mentioned nor suggested. He enters evidently only for the purpose of completing the author's ideational pattern. As a representative of modern man, he is bestowing on her a benevolent kiss of a death, and leading her, as the remnant of the ante bellum tradition of the Tidewater, to effectual oblivion, ironic immortality.

"The Immortal Woman" received due acclaim when it was selected by O'Brien and in 1937 when it was reprinted in *A Southern Harvest.* Complexly organized, reflectively and sensitively presented, honest in its evocation of a society compounded of graces and corruptions, it promised much of its author. Only its ending, forced in the interest of completing an ideological pattern, imposed rather than organic, betrays a weakness. Its highly distanced point of view obviated the necessity for presenting a full texture of life being lived. Though the distance device does not militate against the conviction here, it will no longer serve when the author gives himself the scope of the novel. There is little indication of Tate's power to create the immediate illusion of life in either of his short stories.

The novel for which "The Immortal Woman" had served as a preliminary exercise was published as *The Fathers* in 1938 and was chosen as a Literary Guild selection. It proved not only a well-written, historically convincing, and soundly plotted novel, but a continuously absorbing and exciting one. For the critic-historian, it provides much more: an early example of the archetypally planned or myth-conscious novel, a fascinating illustration of some of the author's poetic theories, an excellent index to the strengths and weaknesses of Tate as a creative artist, and a useful introduction to the symbolism of his later poetry.

Setting the story in the home country of his family tradition, Fairfax County, Virginia, Tate offers in concrete and active terms an extended critique of the tradition itself and of the "modern" forces which destroyed it under the specific pressures of the Civil War. The protagonist and "hero" of the story is the destroyer—modern man personified in the form of George Posey, the charming, rootless, and therefore ruthless, city product to whom the narrator, as still more modern man, ironically and somewhat implausibly, remains dedicated. The book begins with a long, carefully detailed and animated description of ritualized death under the code-protected ante-bellum dispensation, and proceeds through the unnecessary and violent deaths of the early crisis period, to end in more and more desperate tragedies as the War violence and displacement affects the principals. Yet *The Fathers* is by no means a morbid book. It is a tense and finally a feverish one, but, at the same time and more centrally, it is reflective and even philosophical. And its major weakness is a function of these virtues: the intellectualism that assures its effectivenss in terms of theme and structure at the same time tends to defeat its convincingness as human chronicle.

The Fathers is a further testimony to Tate's clear-sighted, historically honest treatment of the heritage to which he has devoted much of his creative and critical life. The evocation of manners, codes, and prejudices, the reactions to change and violence are managed in the large with skill and conviction. He glozes no individual faults in the traditionally oriented circle—the father's harshness and even injustice in his adherence to his code, Semmes's weakness, John Langdon's pure natural depravity—and he omits none of the positive evils developed in a slave-holding society. If the picture of town life is less sucessful than that of the country, the case is that Tate shows us Alexandria and Georgetown only in times of extraordinary stress and upheaval, when his thesis of the city as a breeder of aimless motion, rather than of purposive life, is most apt. Only in the small island of the Buchan home, transferred from the country, does life continue its patterned round, and even here Tate demonstrates that the insulation is precarious. High-society life and political life are caricatured but not directly glimpsed, and the life of business is portrayed only in George Posey's doubly shady midnight dealings between lines.

The planning of the novel is careful in the large and in detail. The central action—movement from regulated country life to more and more hectic town life as the divisive war threat intrudes, and finally to the country again in war itself and in war-bred destruction—manages to compress into fourteen months the whole social history of the region as Tate interprets it. Paralleling this larger movement, the progress of George's character downward is from the chivalric gentleman of the opening pages, through dark dealings, to the chameleon of the last section, shifting rapidly from tradesman to householder, to soldier, and finally to a simply pragmatic disguise as itinerant apothecary, man of science. In contrast, old Major Buchan stands unyielding in his stiff integrity, oblivious to all the hurricanes of family and social pressures until his inevitable fall with the fall of the ancestral home.

The minutiae of the novel are consistently selected with a Flaubertian attention to visual, aural, and olfactory naturalism, and, at the same time, to their symbolic significance or their relevance to the thematic structure. George's original gift, which assures young Lacy Buchan's lifelong devotion, is prophetically and symbolically a gun, which knocks him down at the first test. George's personal servant is Blind Joe, a " "rabbit-eyed" Negro, whose "blindness" is symbolic of his master's lack of inward vision, and whose rabbit eyes project George's basic fear. Only one minor detail seems unduly emphasized by the author, a bit of leather strap which Lacy absently picks up and which he must return to during the long day of his mother's funeral. The strap clearly represents the past which he must hold on to against the loss he has suffered, and the idea is psychologically sound. But the insistence on the detail in context makes it appear a kind of author rigging to ensure a Ransomic "tissue of irrelevance."

The long succession of absent or vacant looks, looks "off into space," and "unfocused eyes" is another matter. Once it becomes clear that these abstracted expressions are symbolic of modern abstraction itself—Major Buchan is always attentive to his company—the device becomes an irritating repetition, like a Dickens character tag.

Most of the symbols and themes which recur in Tate's poetry are exploited in this novel, so that it could serve as a sort of exegetical text reference for the poems. Perhaps the most important of the symbols, beside the "motion" image for purposeless activity—George is "like a tornado. His one purpose is to whirl"—is that of darkness or night, a symbol which is similarly prominent in the poetry of these years. Practically all of the violence in the novel happens at night, as do George's business activities. But night has a double significance in Tate's usage. Lacy phrases it in Ransomic terms when he says:

> Nobody today, fifty years after these incidents, can hear the night; nobody wishes to hear it. To hear the night, and to crave its coming, one must have deep inside one's secret being a vast metaphor, controlling all the rest: a belief in the innate evil of man's nature, and the need to face that evil, of which the symbol is the darkness, of which again the living image is man alone. Now that men cannot be alone, they cannot bear the dark, and they see themselves as innately good but betrayed by circumstances that render them pathetic.[3]

Violence, which Tate uses similarly in his poetry, is conceived as ultimately and always self-violence. Violence results from a lack of positive will, not from negation. George never

3. *The Fathers*, pp. 218-19.

has "the intention to do evil but he does evil because he has not the will to do good." Lacking organized values by which he can recognize good, he must act suddenly, on impulse, if he is to act at all, and he must be constantly doing. Impulse is violent, and since man is essentially depraved, his violence is essentially evil. So George drives his wife mad; kills his faithful brother-in-law, Semmes; destroys his chance of redeeming himself in war by suddenly shooting his superior in the face; causes his father-in-law's death and the destruction of the family place—all acts against his will and self-destructive.

George stands at the crux of the argument of the story and at the heart of the human story; Tate therefore expends his major effort on making him convincing. He must embody a concrete universal in his person, and the burden is heavy. George, it must be admitted, does not stand up under it. An ultimate irony of the Fugitive war against abstraction is that they too often create abstractions which are therefore unequipped to sustain the argument. This is particularly true of George Posey and of the novel as a whole.

George is introduced to the reader as the brave, strong, brilliantly adroit, irresistible suitor for the hand of narrator Lacy's sister. But shortly we see the bold George: 1) unable to attend a funeral from fear of the presence of death; 2) unable to face the fact of sex, in the form of a young bull mounting cows; 3) unable to place a wreath on his fiancée's head after a chivalric victory in her name. Lacy never for a moment wavers in his devotion to his hero: George has only to say, " 'You're my friend, Lacy,' " and he is. Susan announces her engagement to him shortly after the public slight—he merely tosses the wreath into her lap and laughs.

For the author, George must possess all the easy attraction and victorious way of pragmatic scientism; at the same time, he must sum up in himself all the destructiveness, the disjunction and narcissism which Tate attributes to modern pragmatic man. The character, overweighted by all this, breaks down fictionally before the story is far advanced. With a lifeless abstraction at its center—"I believed that he was imponderable, that I could have put my finger through him,"[4] Lacy truly remarks at one stage—the novel inevitably lacks that sense of "felt life" which was Henry James's prime requisite in fiction. Inevitably, too, the disease spreads to George's young sister, Jane, who asks Lacy to "tell me about dead people" and who responds to Lacy's and Semmes's love like a cardboard marionette, but who can be frightened almost to death by a Negro's look at her. And to his baby daughter, who repeats much too patly, "Papa make money, Papa make money," and to the other minor and wholly symbolic members of the family.

The authority of the narrator himself is impaired by the exigencies of the symbolic extension. Lacy, necessarily perceptive both as child and as old man narrator, must analyze George's weaknesses and fix responsibility on him for the destruction of his entire family, but still must "love him more than I love any man," to quote the final line of the book. The fact is that the old, wisely perplexed physician, who is Lacy grown old, completely disappears as narrator in the later stages of the story. He is so far forgotten, in fact, that, as we see and hear through the suddenly matured young Lacy, the novel ends with a first person present point of view: "I'll go back and finish it. . . . It won't make any difference if I am killed." Near the end also, the point-of-view failure requires the importation of a ghost grandfather to point the dilemma and relate it to the Jason-Medea myth, of which it is the avatar.

The more we examine this novel, the more it appears that Tate's fundamental weakness as a creative artist is a function of some failure of sympathy or, perhaps better, of empathy with his human subjects. It is not only that George and those connected with him particularly lack the humanity which would render them "real" to the reader; it is the consistent failure of the novelist to describe an emotional crisis in convincing terms. The critical moment of the entire novel occurs when

4. *Ibid.*, p. 256.

Lacy is waked by the screams of Jane, who presumably has been violated by a half-breed Negro whom she had offended by her unreasonable fear of him. Tate projects the experience for Lacy, who has been dozing, in terms of "the panther whose scream now came with the rhythm of breath, low on the intake but rising to a high wail with the heave of the expulsion."[5] This is essentially the image which appears at the heart of "Ode to the Confederate Dead," where it is similarly associated with night. In both instances, the "panther" and the "jaguar," self-victimizing violence seems suggested. But the novelist is presumably in Lacy's mind, and Lacy is presumably in love with Jane. The image has an abstract logical rightness, but humanly it rings false.

Then when Lacy enters the room, Jane, the apparent victim, is lying unconscious on the floor. "The light suffused Jane's face. The mouth was open. Her skin was tight and chalky, like pressed muslin. I thought it a shame that any girl should be lying there humiliated, so young."[6] The crucial sentence here is a clear echo of Webster's "Cover her face; mine eyes dazzle; she died young," a line which Tate has cited as a touchstone of tension in poetry and Warren has used in a short story to prompt the intellectual awakening of a youthful protagonist. Lacy's reaction is a literary importation here, not a human emotional response.

Tate has not again ventured into creative fiction, though he has extended his critical theories and methods into the area of the novel. The evidence of this one provocative, but ultimately unsatisfactory, book confirms the wisdom of Tate's decision to concentrate his energies on poetry and criticism. Certainly his large talents are less suited to fiction, unless it be pure allegory, than to any other literary medium. His mind finds its most congenial occupation in analysis and abstract formulations. Fiction requires an intuitive feel for the living, an ability to project into other and essentially foreign lives. In these senses, Tate is inherently weak.

5. *Ibid.*, p. 223. 6. *Ibid.*, p. 226.

CHAPTER XI

Tate as Poet

ALLEN TATE reached the peak of his reputation as a poet in the early 1930's. At that period only Hart Crane among American poets was receiving greater critical acclaim. If, in the years since, his achievements have come to seem somewhat less spectacular, it is not that Tate has failed to fulfill his earlier promise, but that the critics had overlooked his basic limitations as a poet and these have become more apparent on rereading.

Tate's poetry of the thirties and forties continually gains in tonal control and in technical handling of verse forms. The tension which characterized his earlier poems does not relax, and the themes do not change fundamentally but are extended in several directions. As the pose of his apprentice verse is altogether abandoned, a naked, hard-pressed sincerity is exposed behind the dense curtain of his language. The note of desperation is heard only occasionally now; for the most part it is subdued in the irony of taut understatement or intricately involved in a play of bitter wit.

During the earlier years of this period Tate, returning from travel in Europe, is back home and involved with Ransom, Warren, Davidson, and others in the Agrarian controversy. The renewed contact with Fugitive colleagues is evident in a temporary waning of the influence of Eliot and Crane and a re-emphasis on Ransomic ideas and Ransomic formalism. Echoes of *God without Thunder* are heard through much of Tate's poetry in the thirties, though the ring is always personal, in the pitch of Tate's peculiar anguish. With the arrival of the forties, the obsessing themes of death, animation of the past, and modern mechanistic violence and abstraction are lent new immediacy by their application to a world at war. A spate of satire is the first reaction to the war situation, which seems an overt expression of his dark theses. But the more lasting effect is one which leads him back toward Eliot and into Dante's *Inferno*. *The Winter Sea* (1944) is full of Hell, concentrated especially at the seventh circle, where the violent are punished.

By 1947 Tate has completed the third phase of his poetic development, and he pauses here to revise and select, then to issue a collected volume, *Poems: 1922-1947* (1948). When he writes poetry again, he has followed Dante and Eliot into Catholicism.

The body of Tate's mature poetry, as it has been culled and reworked for the 1948 volume, leaves a uniform impression, despite unevennesses and varying degrees of complexity. The poems, whether they originate in an abstract idea or in a concrete situation, create in the process of development a kind of dramatic tension which Tate himself has been at pains to define in terms of symbolist and metaphysical poetry. Typically, Tate's abstractions are constantly driven toward their concretions in images, while the images or situations are driven toward their abstract significances. In discussing Emily Dickinson's poetry, Tate has noted that she "perceives abstraction and thinks sensation."[1] This describes Tate's process more exactly than it describes Dickinson's. It is "a kind of intellectual eyesight," to use Delmore Schwartz's phrase, "which dominates the poet's sensibility."[2] In the texture of the poems it operates continuously—"We are the eyelids of defeated caves"—and in the structure, it works from either extreme toward the other. "The Mediterranean," for example, opens with "Where we went in the boat was a long bay"—an immediate situation; after three stanzas, however, we are led to an abstract consideration of our heritage, though all the final section is com-

1. *Reactionary Essays*, p. 17.
2. "The Poetry of Allen Tate," *Southern Review*, V, 431.

pact with concrete images as it develops its intellectual core. On the other hand, "Ode to Fear" begins with an abstract invocation to "memory" and ends with the concrete image of "a dry storm" bursting "on a child's long day."

The peculiar tension of the poems is determined, therefore, largely by a kind of vision and a habit of language. But the effect is constantly heightened to drama by the internal conflict which is thus presented. Poem after poem derives its dramatic quality from the opposition of two antithetical forces coexistent in the poet. Tate treats himself consistently, not as a "romantic traditionalist," but as a modern man inevitably conditioned by the despised scientistic world into which he was born. At the same time, as what might be termed a classical traditionalist, he feels within him the urge of his heritage striving to give him a direction which neither he nor his ancestors, reanimated, can define. Thus, typically, death for the ancestors had a meaning, but a meaning that depends on the future's constantly redefining and fulfilling their purposes. Modern Tate cannot redefine or fulfill, so that the dead are thwarted, their deaths vain. The poet becomes at times a sort of improvident ghoul, plundering the graves of his forebears without gaining thereby himself (except in the resolution that is the poem), without even providing a meaning for his own death to come.

It is this conflict, with its schizophrenic overtones, which provides the base matter of the poems and which gives them their special pitch. The conflict is not, however, the overt theme of many poems. As I have indicated, Tate has, in these poems, extended his earlier themes without altering them. Perhaps as a result of his European travel, the problem of the tradition has been extended beyond that of the immediate Southern heritage to that of its origin in Europe. In the first two poems of the 1948 *Poems* the line is traced back to Aeneas, at once the traditionalist bearing the older civilization into the Western world and its betrayer, "unmanned" by his conquests, founder of predatory Rome.

In another direction, with the theme of the modern dilemma, the extension leads down into Hell: the Inferno of Dante, a Sartrean "No Exit" hell, and a burning Platonic cave. On a more personal level, represented chiefly in the Christmas sonnets, the problem of religious belief is added. An earlier poem, "The Twelve" (1931), presents directly and effectively the thesis of a "God without Thunder," while others—"The Eagle," "The Cross," "Last Days of Alice," "Fragment of a Meditation"—incorporate it. But the two groups of Christmas sonnets relate the theme to the poet's childhood guilt and his present struggle with the religious problem. The temporary solution appears in I of "More Sonnets" with:

> Ten years are time enough to be dismayed
> By mummy Christ, head crammed between his knees.

A further ironic extension occurs in sonnet III, where the war provides the setting. Here it is in the name of Christ, as modern god of Love, that Western man goes about his destruction of enemies "unstalked by Christ."

Tate continues in these later poems to exploit and develop the images and symbols which the early poems had introduced. The most notable additions, both of them from the forties, are those of the cave and those deriving from the *Inferno*. The patterns which dominate this poetry are the contrasts of darkness and light, night-day, blackness-sun, and, closely related, winter-summer. Many of the poems are set at twilight and several others at night; and even in the day-poems a blanketing (once a "fiery") shade is common. Darkness, always used with symbolical force, carries a special ambiguity which can best be glossed, as I have noted, from Tate's novel, *The Fathers*. At the crisis of the book he speaks of "a belief in the innate evil of man's nature, . . . of which the symbol is the darkness." For modern man, lacking this belief, night is evil itself—his fear, or inner darkness, made manifest. For the more realistic ancestors, night was welcome as a reminder of man's natural depravity and of his mortality, a challenge against which he could assert his human dignity.

In contrast, day is the constant symbol of the modern "light" of science, of an innocent ignorance of evil and of original sin. At its point of highest illumination it becomes the "great Day pure and dazed" of "Jubilo," symbol of the innocent belief in the triumph of innocence, when evil itself will be canceled out. At the weak extreme, there is the thin light of Plato's cave of abstraction, which finally produces "Albino man bleached from the mortal clay." Between the extremes, a daylight world of boyhood innocence is allowed, but this is a precarious, short-lived day.

Twilight becomes Tate's particular time, since it offers a symbol for our dying "day" life and an entrance into the "night" world. This is the period, too, of reflection, when the day life can be assessed, when the shades of the past come with their importunate questions. Tate constantly envisions himself as a "twilight" man, product of the day world, racked by the oncoming night.

Intimately attached to the dark-light symbolism is that of blindness. The blind have been blinded by the dazzling light of science, by the "pure" religion of love or of good without evil. Tate's exploitation of this symbol closely parallels that of Sophocles in *Oedipus Rex*. In Sophocles only the blind (Tiresias) see beyond logic and the accidents of vision; Oedipus, the daylight man, is essentially blind until he symbolically blinds himself. With Tate the "eyeless with eyesight only," "we, a blind race," are those who see with sight and mind, but lack vision or focus, a sense of direction, ultimately a code of values. Our blindness in particular obscures for us the meaning of the past, the forms of the dead and the significance of their deaths.

Winds hot and cold, tempests, and hurricanes blow through these poems with a uniformly desiccating breath. Like modern man, and especially like George Posey of *The Fathers*, the winds are "By motion sired, not born; by rest dismayed." Knowing no direction, "will-less" as well as restless, the winds symbolize unbodied abstraction. Their humanized body-born opposite is the "breath." In contrast to air, the full-bodied sea has many positive connotations for Tate. "How absolute the sea!" the poet exclaims in "Message from Abroad." In "Winter Mask" he finds at length "The sea worth living for." The symbol receives its fullest development in Tate's most ambitious poem of the forties, "Seasons of the Soul." Following the "Summer" (or air) section and "Autumn" (or earth), "Winter" employs the sea, explicitly the winter sea, as its ruling metaphor. The "sea-gods are dead" as is "the drying God above/ Hanged in his windy steeple," but there is still "shade for lovers" beneath the "shuddering foam" of the sea. For the sea, with all its richness in good and evil, promise and menace of the "swift shark," is Tate's essential reality, the only medium in which love can exist. The "pacing animal" of lust is caged beyond the sea cove, and beyond too are the self-violent lovers (*Inferno* XIII) who, encased in tree-like coral, resist the sea. Finally in "Spring" (or fire), "thin Jack-and-Jilling seas/ Without the human will" appear, the tepid juice of spring in the blood, essentially a meaningless mockery of reality and love.

"The Seasons" is not only ambitious in theme and symbolism (Tate's *Four Quartets,* perhaps); it is also the prime example of Tate's final control of his medium. The sections are developed in parallel, each dealing not only with a season and an element, but with a time of life. A major symbolic cluster controls each unit, and the Hell images, varied from section to section, provide a common symbolic core. (The epigraph to the poem from *Inferno* XIII—"Then I stretched forth my hand a little forward, and plucked a branchlet from a great thorn; and the trunk of it cried, 'Why dost thou rend me?' "—refers to the first of the self-violent sinners in the second ring of the seventh circle of Hell, Pier delli Vigne, who, after being blinded and imprisoned, committed suicide.) Epithets and textural images, as well as the symbols, continually recall Dante. As Tate comes nearer again to Eliot in the later forties, his approach is through Eliot's ultimate master. At this point, however, Tate is fixed in the fire and ice of the *Inferno*, while Eliot has moved into the refining fire of the *Purgatorio* with reaches, at the end of the *Quartets*, into the *Paradiso*. But for Tate, as for Eliot, Dante supplies the example and the means for a strict poetic organization of longer units, for integrating current experience with history and the personal past, and for clothing the abstractions of mental and spiritual life in concrete images. The central Dantean pattern of the circle and dome first appears as an epithet in "Summer":

> The hot wind dries and draws
> With circular delay
> The flesh, ash from the ember,
> Into summer's jaws.

The epithet quickly becomes an image and a symbol, the "blue, empty, and tall" sky dome of fall,

> Where burn the equal laws
> For Balaam and his ass.

Quickly then it takes on added spiritual connotations in the "winding hell" with its "vast concluding shell" where the first section ends. In "Autumn," where the theme is the personal past, the image appears immediately: "I was down a well," connecting with the Inferno passage just cited. At the end of the stanza, the image widens:

> And when I raised my hand
> I stood in the empty hall.

The hand-raising recalls the epigraph, while the hall, with its "round ceiling" containing the dead, continues further to extend the symbol. "Winter" takes up the dome and inverts it again as the "hollow rind" of the sea, while it picks up the aspect of circular movement in "Bodies that wheel and drop" and "the circular miles." "Spring" first suggests the cycle of life-death-rebirth in the "ancient pun" on dying (the Elizabethan euphemism for orgasm) and in the conception of a "new star" rising from the holocaust of war. It ends in a final variation of the Inferno symbol:

> This earth—Platonic cave
> Of vertiginous chance!

In addition to this sort of image control, Tate has mastered new and effective metric forms. "The Seasons," as well as the "Winter Mask," illustrates his mastery of a verse form which Yeats developed in his later poems, the trimeter stanza with a refrain line. In both of these poems Tate varies his refrains. The result is both more flexible and less artificial than Yeats's standard. In "Summer" of "The Seasons" only the final word, "paws," remains constant; in "Autumn" only the final "hall." "Winter" shifts from "living wound of love" to "livid wound of love" and back significantly to "living"; while only "Spring" is consistent in its retention of "mother of silences." However, it is this last section which demonstrates most effectively Tate's skill in handling the form. The recurrence of the refrain causes no strain in the larger movement of the poem as it progresses from an impersonal "the cooler day/ Of the mother of silences" to an apostrophic "Mother of silences!" and finally to a beautifully modulated combination of the two in the last lines:

> Whether your kindness, mother,
> Is mother of silences.

A new intimacy is developed here, both from the shortened form of the apostrophe and from its suppressed position at the end of the line. This suppression in turn gives additional emphasis to the initial "Is" of the final line, and the question which it generates becomes the crucial issue of the section and of the poem, as it alters the hitherto accepted significance of the refrain. *Is* death truly and irrevocably the propagator of silence alone? (Alternatively, *is* the Virgin propagator only of a dead religion?) Is spring, as it has appeared, "just a mime/That rises in the blood," or is the "ancient pun" still viable? Is, finally, the succession of the seasons—and the succession of man's stages of life—meaningless?

Tate employs a variety of verse forms in the thirties and forties, none of them so free as his earlier "Prufrock" and "Gerontion" type forms. Three highly traditional patterns occur with the greatest regularity: the sonnet, the pentameter quatrain, and blank verse. For his own effects he borrows and adapts freely, but not only from Yeats and Eliot. In "Pastoral" and "False Nightmare" he employs a shortened trimeter version of Dante's *terza rima*. "The Traveller," dedicated to Archibald MacLeish, uses the run-on quatrains of that poet's "You, Andrew Marvell," and succeeds in putting Tate's own sort of hard body into the skin of that soft original. "The Eagle," in verse form as well as in ostensible subject, parallels Elinor Wylie's "The Eagle and the Mole." Tate experiments with something like a Negro spiritual stanza in "Jubilo," with an "Eclogue" form *à la* Landor, and with other stanzas traceable perhaps to Ransom.

In all of these forms Tate exhibits technical skill and ingenuity. At the same time he noticeably lacks the suppleness and ease of the natural poet, of a Yeats or an Eliot or an Auden. There is always a sense of effort, of forcing his effects in any sustained passage. His individual lines are too often cramped into the metrical exigencies of his patterns. When he remarks, in "To the Romantic Traditionists," "We speak the crabbed line," he too well describes his own practice. In his theory it is, of course, impossible for our age to sing—and Donald Davidson's natural singing voice went hoarse in imprecations against his unsympathetic world. But Tate's crabbedness must be seen less as a historical symptom than as an index of his poetic personality. For what Delmore Schwartz calls a "certain unique harshness of diction and meter" is joined to "an equally curious violence of imagery and sentiment."[3] The poet's view of the world is itself harsh and crabbed, governed by an intensely critical attitude.

Though Tate, as we have seen, includes himself as one of the damned in his indictment of his age, the inclusion does nothing to humanize the hot and cold passion of his strictures. With few exceptions, the poems are keyed up into a hard intensity of thought, diction, and meter. The concentration is such that the reader does not, cannot, participate in the emotional life of the verse. Instead, he, in his own hard concentration, reads it with a sort of fascination. He stares at it and into it, but Tate's world impinges so narrowly on the fuller, common world of emotional and intellectual life that it affects him at best only peripherally.

This is not to say that the poems' problems are singular and unsympathetic per se. It is simply that the emotional tone, the manner, the means, all make up a complex that is finally repellent to the reader's sympathies. In the first place, the thematic and emotional areas with which Tate deals are held to so exclusively that they leave no space in which the whole man can feel at home. The poet himself, "burning with a single flame," is never given an enclosing body. When, for example, young love is treated in "Shadow and Shade" and "Pastoral," it is described in terms of a "barbarous" "stalking tide" or a "black surge," "this lust," "their agonies," and "mental ire." The poet seems to have been exposed too early to Eliot's typist. Secondly, the passion that gives intensity to the expression is at once fiery and cold, a sort of congealed and congealing fury that allows itself and the reader no moment of relaxation, admits no palliatives. Finally, one can only feel

3. *Ibid.*, p. 419.

that the excitement is generated exclusively from the mind and nerves. Tate makes large use of "blood" and "heart" in these poems, but they come to seem an overemphasis, covering a paucity of real warmth. There is no joy, no humor (for the satire is invariably acid), and only a mask of humility. The spirit remains strictly critical, with only a rare trace of charity, no acceptance, and therefore no ease. The surface resemblance to Donne's poetry has been often noted; but noted less often is the absence of the pulsing blood that warms Donne's wit-play into moving expression.

Ultimately Tate's poetry exhibits the limitation that has been noted in his fiction. In the latter case, the substitution of abstractions for full human beings, what Kenneth Burke early diagnosed as a lack of "*physicality*,"[4] vitiates the authenticity of the critical insights. In the poetry, this is far less true. Only as we see the body of his best poetry as a whole (which Tate himself has bid us do) is the limitation apparent. Individual poems retain an effectiveness that is a product of sharp perceptions and brilliantly developed imagery, brought to life by a realized emotion—the first of the "Sonnets at Christmas" and "The Oath," for example. Others, more abstractly conceived, are yet personally related and under the control of an integrated sensibility. "The Mediterranean," "The Eagle," "The Wolves," "The Twelve," "The Traveller," "The Cross," and, with reservations, "The Seasons of the Soul" and the revised "Ode to the Confederate Dead" are certainly among the best of these. Many of the other poems are distinguished by insights, by sharp and illuminating imagery, and by complex ordering and manipulation of symbols. Only a few of the lyric pieces are strained beyond patience: the first of "More Sonnets," "The Last Days of Alice," "The Paradigm," and "False Nightmare." The satires are generally less successful, though Cleanth Brooks finds that each of them ends "with a serious

4. "Tentative Proposal," *Poetry*, L, 98.

ironic view of our plight."[5] Their topicality too often betrays the poet into venomous criticism of men and groups, on whose immediate activities he has looked with something less than a proper aesthetic distance. Often the lack of charity and humility manage only to turn the satire back on the poet himself—see especially the harsh "Ode to Our Young Pro-Consuls of the Air," "Causerie," and "Retroduction to American History."

Tate's more recent poetry, all of it dating in printed form from 1952 and 1953, is a direct product of his conversion. He has printed the first, third, and sixth parts of what is termed a "long poem," evidently confessional in tone, and evidently modeled to a considerable extent on Dante's masterpiece. It is, of course, too early to assess the full enterprise, but it is not too early to indicate the general bearing of the poem and to discover in its abstract and often esoteric symbolism some interesting developments. The poem is clearly allegorical as well as personal, two of its printed parts taking the form of dream visions, and all three of them are couched in the English equivalents of Dante's *terza rima.*

The announced purpose, as stated in Part I, "The Maimed Man,"[6] is "to rehearse pastoral terrors of the youth still in the man," as an aid in teaching the poet "to fast/ And pray." At the opening of this poem, the poet, in Miltonic fashion, invokes his Muse while rejecting the counter-Muse. The Apollonian laurel of enlightened reason provides the inspiration, and the myrtle of Aphroditean sense the antithetic temptation. The poem proper describes a dream in which the poet, young, meets a headless man who has only bluegrass in the "slot" between his legs. Later this figure is identified as a distorted image of the poet himself; but, "How could I know this friend without reproach?" Further, he discovers of the "maimed man" that, "My secret was his father, I his tomb," and recalls that "I," as poet, wrote "iambics willed and neat," and, out of a "love disordered," "clutched shades forbearing in a family well."

5. "Allen Tate," *Poetry,* LXVI, 326. 6. *Partisan Review,* XIX, 265-67.

There is candor and some overzealous exaggeration in this confession, as we recall Tate's strictures against "poetry of the will" and his accent on the "historic myth," among other things. However we may take these apparent disavowals—and I have sufficiently indicated my critical judgments of the earlier poetry—there must still be remarked in the allusive invocation and in the highly allegorical method of presentation here of the narrative element a renewed accent on the rationalist, now Thomist, as opposed to the mystical, or neo-Platonist, in Tate's religious emphasis.

"The Swimmers"[7] is marked as Part III of the still-to-be completed poem. Unlike the other two sections, this one is presented as a direct boyhood recollection of an objective experience. The narrative is remarkably uneven, at times clear and swiftly moving, at times turgid and willfully ambiguous in syntax. Five named boys, including "Tate with the water on his brain" (a multiple and self-deprecatory pun), on their way to swim witness a twelve-man posse going out under a worn-faced leader, then returning without the leader but with a lynched Negro's body. Tate calls them

> Jesus Christers unmembered and unmade,
> Whose Corpse had died again in dirty shame.

Since the body is referred to again in capitals later as "It," the association of the Negro's lynching with the Crucifixion is inevitable. The "Jesus Christers," with their leader disappearing as Judas did from the Last Supper, seem to refer to the Disciples, though the qualifying participles are difficult to justify in these terms. A stranger (Joseph of Arimathea?) with the sheriff's help (Nicodemus?) tie the body to the saddle, and the boy, stricken, watches it being dragged, with a soon "faceless head" jouncing behind, to the town.

The invocation to this section indicates that this experience was "the spring of love and fear" in the boy,

7. *Hudson Review*, V, 471-73.

When a thrush idling in the tulip tree
Unwound the cold dream of the copperhead.

Presumably, then, for the poet, the witnessed incident becomes the prefiguration of his understanding of the Passion, his awakening to knowledge of man's corrupt nature and, at the same time, to redemption through love. The incident itself seems fully adequate to support the fear aspect of the symbolism —Tate has always been most effective in his nightmarish evocations—but neither the Negro-as-Christ symbol nor the actions of posse and stranger as disciples seem significant or portentous enough to bear their apparent symbolic extensions. Nor does Tate's dry style of narration carry their burden for them, as a Faulkner's conceivably might. Finally, in this section, the Dantesque form appears to impose an unusual strain on the poet, forcing at times both diction and image.

In "The Buried Lake,"[8] labeled Part VI of the full poem, the invocation is to Santa Lucia, "Lady of Light," who evidently serves, as she does for Dante, as guide to Divine Wisdom, or Catholic revelation. The concern of this section, with its highly involved allegorical dream sequence, is again exploration of the poet's past, but now chiefly in terms of sexual love and art, with the denouement in a mutual discovery of religious "light." The poet traces the Eliotic "way and way back," "Where Myrtle twines Laurel"; and symbolically details his failures with a "stately woman," and with the violin he "had come to play." Finally, he can "bend knees" and find the "day," as she has. (It is impossible here to refrain from referring the reader to Caroline Gordon's—Mrs. Tate's—recent novel, *The Malefactors*, for they seem to project imaginatively, and at a small remove from fact, a joint experience which involved Dorothy Day.)

What seems most certain in the sections of the projected poem thus far printed is that Tate has set his poetic future in

8. *Sewanee Review*, LXI, 175-80.

close resemblance to his recent analysis of Dante's "symbolic imagination." Keeping his feet firmly on the ground of his personal experience, real and visionary, while he describes a progress toward salvation, he will doubtless carry the reader through at least a kind of *Inferno*. There are already obscure individuals introduced by name and reference, like those from Dante's past, and there are difficult references to private happenings. Furthermore, the whole would seem to be couched in dream-allegory terms for the most part, replete with hellish images.

This will be, evidently, a highly intellectual, and even abstruse, work. Judging perhaps prematurely from the three printed sections, one may hazard the opinion that the sincerity of the emotional commitment which it embodies will hardly redeem it from the chilly passionateness that has characterized Tate's poetry almost from the first. Though the poet has seen the light of a Catholic "day," his imagination is still gripped by the fascination of an infernal night world. Pagan, Judaistic, or Christian, this essentially surrealistic creation is exhibited under the constant control of a rationally ordered, critical intellect.

CHAPTER XII

Warren as Poet

ROBERT PENN WARREN's first volume of poetry, *Thirty-six Poems,* did not appear until 1935, following not only his graduate work in the United States and at Oxford and his early teaching career, but also his reassociation with the Fugitive-Agrarian group and his editorship with Cleanth Brooks of *The Southern Review* at Louisiana State University. The book represents a selection of his poetry from *Fugitive* days through 1935, with the major accent on his production of the late twenties and early thirties. This volume was followed in 1942 by *Eleven Poems on the Same Theme,* a publication in the Yale Younger Poets series. From this corpus, with the addition of two longer poems, "The Ballad of Willie Potts" and "Mexico Is a Foreign Country," Warren chose his *Selected Poems, 1923-1943* (1944). After a dozen years, this book fully represents his achievements as a lyric poet, since his only subsequent poetic publication has been the long narrative, *Brother to Dragons* (1953).

The *Selected Poems* establishes a rather arbitrary division between "Late" and "Early" poems, since it includes in both categories work first printed serially in 1934. Furthermore, the distinction cannot be justified in terms of maturity of concept or mastery of medium, for the later sections of "Kentucky Mountain Farm" are among the finest lyrics Warren has written, and "The Return: an Elegy" is as advanced conceptually and structurally, at least, as the author's 1943 essay on "Pure and Impure Poetry." To ignore the late-early distinction, however, is to ignore a clear development, from the probing of experience—particularly experience of the natural world and of personal dilemmas—to definitions of attitude and testing of attitudes in a broader setting.

Warren's analysis of the human condition has always leaned heavily on Ransom's dualism, but the disposition of his more mature poetry, as well as of his fiction, has been to reach beyond analysis in order to seek out meaningful patterns of living in the community of the world. Where Ransom remains content with his role of ironic observer, Warren has continued his restless testing, for it is not only the conditions of the mind which he would satisfy, but the conditions of an active world that demands practical adaptations. In the early poems generally Warren explores the conditions and suggests tentative attitudes; in the later ones, he subjects his results to continuous test in quasi-narrative patterns.

The "Kentucky Mountain Farm" sequence, which dates from 1928 to 1932, projects a series of attitudes, all deriving from sharply focused observations of nature. The opening sections, which I have discussed earlier, first propose the mountain rocks as stoic preceptors, then discover their vulnerability, as "the frost has torn/ Away their ridged fundaments at last" and carried them back to the "absolute deeps" of the primal creative-destructive matrix of nature. The third section, insisting further on man's vulnerability, suggests the ideals of the past, only to find them incomprehensible to modern man.

The three following sections of this poem, all products of the first years of the thirties, exhibit Warren at the peak of his lyrical power. "The Cardinal," "The Jay," and "Watershed" are beautifully realized nature lyrics, each projecting its attitude wholly in terms of its imagery. "The Cardinal" carries its major theme in the flashing bird itself and the evergreen cedar; the "vision of scarlet devised in the slumberous shade" suggests a Marvellian retreat into "the mind's undated shade." The counter-images of rock and lizard, presented in religious terms, "devout as an ikon," suggest fixed creeds which may "southward fail" without affecting the evergreen inner calm.

"The Jay," with bird and tree images again dominating, carries forward to autumn and winter, where "blatant and blue" the "outrageous sergeant of the summer's rout" troubles the recluse with memories of active life, the old lure of adventure. "Watershed" centers again on a bird, the gold-eyed hawk at sunset, and the rock, now raised into the mountain divide. At this altitude, with man's impermanent habitations seen from the hawk's eyes, both the meditative shade of "The Cardinal" and the call of "The Jay" are dwindled. The perspective of the hawk now prompts the recognition that

> Not love, happiness past, constrains,
> But certitude. Enough, and it remains, . . .

The concluding poem, "The Return," adds no new attitude beyond the hawk's purview. Instead, it removes the "Watershed" attitude from its bleak heights and sets it down in the world of personal relations, amid Warren's most persistent and characteristic imagery: the autumn tree shedding its leaves and the moving stream. (It is not, as Southard has it, "night all day long"[1] in Warren's early poetry, but autumn all year long, where, beyond desire, ripeness waits.) Specifically, "The Return" suggests the Heraclitan flux, where memories and images, "all/ Familiar faithless things," are "lost/ In the water's riffle, the wind's flaw." Here the motif of "History among the Rocks," the past as possible mentor, is reduced to the personal plane and finally rejected. Retreat to the past, like the cardinal's retreat, is a luxury which man in a changing world cannot afford. The sycamore, "burly and clean," enduring the changing seasons, remains, an image, like that of the hawk, adapted to the harsh facts of its world and strong above its flux.

Two other fine poems of the period add notes to this attitude, while they echo the late autumn imagery. "So Frost

1. W. P. Southard, "The Religious Poetry of Robert Penn Warren," *Kenyon Review*, VII, 656.

Astounds" discovers in a frail older woman's willed calm, "forever beyond the accident of flesh and bone," a proof against the frost—"I have thought: this will I find." In "The Last Metaphor," a typical Warren "old fellow," meditating that "no leaf clings mortally," finds a further suggestive metaphor:

> . . . when the leaves no more abide
> The stiff trees rear not up in strength and pride
> But lift unto the gradual dark in prayer.

This Ransomic conclusion to an essentially Ransomic poem—there are numerous recalls of Ransom even in the poem's diction—rounds out the attitudinal foundation on which the later poems begin to build.

Warren's most ambitious poem of this middle period in his poetic development is "The Return: an Elegy," first printed in 1934 and classified as "Early." Though its theme is more immediately personal and the emotional commitment more direct and intense than anything in the later poetry, its strategies and rhetorical complexities connect it with *Eleven Poems*, rather than with earlier work. The "Elegy" is a completely "impure" poem in the sense of Warren's definition. It mixes present reflection and memories of the past, natural image and abstraction, tender emotion and callow flippancy, Latinic diction and homely colloquialism in order to "earn" its final image of loss. The poem proceeds in a series of shocking tone shifts, as moods, recollections, and passing glimpses from a train window present images and feelings clustering about the death of the poet's mother. But Warren's control is everywhere evident. The "roaring cubicle" of the Pullman car, plunging through darkness and rain amid "the stiff pine," develops metaphorically into the coffin in which the mother will be confided to "earth's absolute chemistry," and into an image of the poet's own sealed anguish. Contributory details are flashed out of the mind or the scene, to be picked up and transformed in the final synthesis. The closing "earned" symbol—"the dark and swollen orchid of this sorrow"—emerges out of the early image of death's chemistry, which burns the bones "like faggots in—of damp and dark—the monstrous bulging flame," and out of the face of grief itself.

Despite its artistry and despite the intensity of emotion which surcharges it, the "Elegy" is not a complete success. Like a Borromini sculpture, it is baroquely overwrought, leaping from hollow to height in an almost feverish attempt to prove itself capable of balancing the heavy affective freight it carries. The final image is masterful, but it cannot fully redeem the over-violent insistences and tone clashes of the poem's body.

Warren never repeats the personal emphasis of this poem, but its stylistic devices, the taut elisions, the juxtaposition of philosophic abstraction and homely detail, the alternation of mood and movement, and the structural principle of building through fragmentary images to a concentrated metaphor, all remain typical strategies of Warren's later poetry. The late style, however, does not arrive immediately. A group of five poems printed in *The American Review*, one in *The New Republic*, in 1934, and "Ransom" of 1935 seem to reflect a kind of nostalgia. Previously assimilated influences reappear again in undiluted form. "Toward Rationality," for example, echoes both Tate and Ransom, and Eliotic notes are sounded throughout "Ransom." The one new element here is the increasing use of historical, and especially historico-religious, referents: Christ in "Ransom"; Christ, Pilate, and Orpheus in "Aged Man Surveys Past Time"; The Persians and Ptolemy in "Toward Rationality"; and a generalized journey which is a version of the Exodus in "To a Friend Parting." Like Tate at this same period, Warren is widening his horizon, finding, as "Ransom" puts it: "Our courage needs, perhaps, new definition." No new definition is suggested, but the exploration continues now with history as both a subject and a referent.

The year 1935, when Warren joined Brooks in founding *The Southern Review,* marks one of the important turning points in Warren's career. Not only did he commit himself to editorial work and criticism, but he prepared his *Thirty-six Poems* for publication. Included in this volume were five distinguished poems first printed during the year serially: "Letter from a Coward to a Hero," "History," "Resolution," "Man Coming of Age," and "The Garden." The level of these poems is considerably above those of the previous year, the first two and the last ranking among Warren's finest works. The most perfect of these, "The Garden," continues the "Kentucky Mountain Farm" series in mood and in imagery—autumn, the sycamore, the jay and cardinal—and it projects a serene acceptance of life's conditions. But whereas "Resolution" and "Man Coming of Age" are content with the Shakespearean dictum that "ripeness is all," "The Garden" goes farther to define the ripeness as a new sacramental innocence that may be won beyond knowledge and beyond "appetite." Using as his model, both for tone and for verse form, Andrew Marvell's poem of the same title, Warren has "bemused" by frosts the "green shade" and ripened the "green thought." Marvell's Edenic innocence, discovered in nature and the mind's retreat (as in Warren's "The Cardinal"), is replaced by a postfall innocence found in the bare ruined choirs of stately trees and in a knowledge beyond desire.

The sustained and unforced eloquence of "The Garden," its thematic maturity carried in sharply evoked and symbolically rich imagery, make it his finest single nature lyric. Later, only in the first part of "Bearded Oaks" does he reach this height, but the besetting abstractionism of the "Late" poems intrudes somewhat too heavily in the later stanzas of this otherwise fine poem.

"Letter from a Coward to a Hero" and "History" introduce a free, intermittently rhymed verse form deriving from Eliot and Pound. Terse descriptive fragments are blent here with terse abstract formulations under the domination of a controlling imagery. The violent alternations which characterized the "Elegy" have been subdued into an over-all tonal harmony, and the emotion has been objectified. In form, the "Letter" is a controlled modification of the "Elegy" and, like it, earns its final metaphor from an accumulation of memories, moods, and images. "History," on the other hand, presents directly a quasi-historical sequence—as it were out of Exodus—in the manner of Eliot's "Journey of the Magi" and in a diction sometimes directly Eliotic:

> We came bad ways,
> The water courses
> Dry,
> No herb for horses. . . .
> Sleet came some days,
> At night no fuel.

Both these poems in effect extend the conclusion of "The Garden." After knowledge and a kind of religious acceptance, there remains the problem of action. How to behave, how to adapt attitude both to the necessities of one's own nature and to the compulsions of social living? The "Letter" examines the "heroic" response, dedication to an abstract conception. A further examination of the theme of "History among the Rocks," the poem elucidates the natural unearned evil against which the man-made heroic concept is blindly pitted:

> Admired of children, gathered for their games,
> Disaster, like the dandelion, blooms,
> And the delicate film is fanned
> To seed the shaved lawn.

This fine image, drawn out of the earlier childhood reminiscences, objectifies the "coward" poet's rejection of heroism: "But I/ Am gunshy," unlike the brave trained dog. The hero is seen finally in an image of pristine innocence, again from childhood:

> Clutching between the forefinger and thumb
> Honor, for death shy valentine.

If the abstract ideal, then, is equivalent to uninstructed innocence, what has full knowledge and acceptance of the condition to offer as guide to action? "History" is a post-fall poem in which we, the chosen race, are poised at the moment before action, after the rough journey, "pain past," surveying below the comfortable fields waiting to be won by our assault. Foreseeing the empty prosperity which lies ahead in the traditionless future of the "promised land," we are tempted to delay in the "myth's languor," musing on the past. But we are doomed to act, and "The act/ Alone is pure," beyond desire. "We shall essay/ The rugged ritual, but not of anger." Commitment is the price of life, though it involve us in rapine, acceptance of unsought luxuries and ease, and loss of old values.

This commitment, which is clearly related to the *engagement* of the French existentialist philosophers, whose analyses also resemble Warren's, provides the thematic basis, not only for Warren's later poems, but for his novels as well. Ransom's ironic detachment, proceeding from the same premise, has no further validity. How does one live? succeeds: What does one make of the absurdity of man's situation? as the question to which Warren sets himself.

Eleven Poems on the Same Theme contains two groups, the earlier one consisting of four poems directly related in mood and theme to "The Garden." All of these—"Bearded Oaks," "Monologue at Midnight," "Picnic Remembered," and "Love's Parable"—are recollections of love-innocence, contrasted with its sequal of knowledge-disillusion. A new image dominates the first three and particularly the best of them, "Bearded Oaks": a submarine setting of sun filtered through summer trees. This innocence symbol, with its womb-safety connotations—used extensively later in *All the King's Men*—is opposed to the "vault of dark," "the positive night," the "coldness of no dawn," which subsequent knowledge discovers as the symbol for the human condition. The tentatively religious attitude of "The Garden" finds expression in "Monologue":

> Our mathematic yet has use
> For the integers of blessedness,

and in the final question of "Picnic Remembered": is the soul a hawk, reflecting "Uncharted Truth's high heliograph?" But the only positive response comes from "Bearded Oaks": "If hope is hopeless, then fearless fear."

All these are tighter poems, both metrically and structurally, and denser than those of any earlier group. The influence of John Donne has become paramount, and the result is a loss as well as a gain. The image no longer seems to develop its own symbolic overtones as it interacts with the intellectual processes. Logic often creates its own symbolic imagery, or forces extensions of meaning, in the manner of Tate. And abstractions begin to figure more prominently. "Bearded Oaks" is much the most successful of these poems, developing its taut submarine imagery under fine tonal control; but the later stanzas move off even here through abstractions to an abstract conclusion not wholly warranted by the occasion.

The later group in *Eleven Poems*, all dating from the early forties, includes the strongest and most provocative poetry that Warren has written to this point, though the old lyric grace and clarity has been sacrificed in the achievement. The trend toward abstractionism increases, as it is doing in the work of the other Fugitives, but these poems come more sharply to grips with the immediate problem of adult living in a Ransomic universe than anything earlier. In concentrated language and imagery, they forecast all the issues which his novels will examine in broader, more leisurely terms. These are difficult poems, in that they compress themes and images under a highly intellectual discipline, and their resolutions are uniformly in terms of a symbolic image. Elipsis becomes the typical mode of expression, and the abstractly conceived metaphor, an additive factor, the typical conclusion. But all of the poems are charged with vital images out of the modern age of anxiety, and all of them develop with a relentless poetic logic.

In "Revelation," a boy making his first break out of "the submarine glimmer" of the mother-love cocoon, earns, through separation, the grace of love, transcending idea and romantic abstraction. "End of Season" displays a slightly different version of innocence, "the annual sacrament of sea and sun," the vacation recapturing of the voiceless "glaucous glimmer" which lived briefly under the "Bearded Oaks." Now the contrast is not the dark, but the pressing reality which waits: "the mail lurks in the box at the house where you live." And "you must think/ On the true nature of Hope, whose eye is round and does not wink." This final symbol is derived from the sun image which has dominated the beaches, but becomes now a pitiless eye, insistent on the reality, the Truth, the hopeless Hope which must be faced.

"Question and Answer" has been set by Warren in the *Selected Poems* directly following "History," which was first printed some six years earlier. The later poem repeats the short-line, irregularly rhyming form of the earlier one, and it follows fittingly in that it suggests alternative solutions to the problem of commitment raised in "History." "Question and Answer" re-examines "What has availed/ Or failed?/ *Or will avail?*" The poet discovers no suitable answer now in "Hawk's poise," nor in "looking back." Neither nature nor love supplies a permanent answer, for man must constantly redefine and redetermine his values. Finally, the poet suggests that we, like Moses, must strike out of the hard rock of fact "the living stream's delight," or shoot directly at a Judaistic "God's black, orbèd, target eye." However interesting to Warren, as to Ransom, may be the God *with* thunder projected alternatively here, we can only feel that the poet's own commitments at this point leave him striking the not always fluent rock.

The other poems in this sequence—"Terror," "Pursuit," "Crime," and "Original Sin"—are conceived very much as short stories or novels in brief; in fact, "Original Sin" is subtitled "A Short Story." From this point on, Warren's imaginative thinking begins to assume a narrative form, and in each of these poems he is sharply condensing a story pattern in which the problem of continuous living in a real world is explored and commented upon.

The theme of all these poems, in one form or another, is that of guilt, and the address is now always direct—to "you." While God's "monstrous guilt" (as "Mexico" has it), the guilt, that is, of setting man and his ideals against the natural order with which he must live, remains, the emphasis is generally shifted to the personal knowledge of guilt in each of us. In "Original Sin" the "nightmare" is our individual sense of guilt, which we escaped only at the cost of our divorce from the human community; in "Crime" our memories add the guilty responsibility for our conscious transgressions. These two complementary poems define the individual burden; "Terror" and "Pursuit" exhibit modern man's attempts to put off the burden, which he is inadequately equipped to shoulder. In all of these poems, the imagery is violent, the texture dense, the irony harsh, and the diction more "impure" in its mixture of the colloquial and the high rhetorical than in anything earlier of Warren's, with the possible exception of the "Elegy," and perhaps than in anything by other modern poets.

These poems are nominally conventional in their metrics, but within their stanza patterns Warren allows considerable freedom in rhyme and more in rhythms. The constant substitution of anapests and spondees for iambs, together with the continually shifting caesura and the frequently lengthened final line of stanzas, deprive the verse of any felt norm. The result in sound is a sort of dense free verse with occasional rhyme, a style which reflects the author's shift from a lyrical to a narrative-reflective form.

"Original Sin: A Short Story" reads like a tightly condensed and highly figurative version of a Warren novel. The poet follows the life-pattern of one of his typical protagonists: the discovery of evil or guilt in the family heritage; the escape to college where, after the first homesick acceptance, the guilt sense is lost in the "quantum glare" of abstraction, of "classic prudence or fondled axiom." But the attempt to capture "a new innocence" in science or in nature or in travel later is doomed. The nightmare returns in the final three images, domesticated, mourning back toward childhood, useless and mindless, but still precious in its reminder of the common human situation.

"Crime," with ruthless irony and vivid cancerous imagery, tells its brief story of mindless murder, bidding us "envy the mad killer" who cannot "remember what it was he buried under the leaves." Though now he "lies in the ditch and grieves," he was seeking, like us, happiness and peace. He went for them directly out of his own secret need, but he is to be envied for, unlike us, he has no memories of his guilt to drip like "a pipe in the cellar-dark." For responsible man, who must remember his guilt, happiness is a toadstone charm "you have no use for now," and "the peace in God's eye" which we innocently desire is an immoderate hope.

"Terror" is the harshest and most topical of these poems, its ostensible theme a favorite one of Tate's especially, that modern man is "born to no adequate definition of terror," or evil, and therefore his attempts to act become gestures of meaningless violence. Out of "passionate emptiness and tidal/ Lust," the "unsatisfied and sick" are lured to other people's wars in Spain and Finland, seeking in abstract causes a fulfillment that their lack of faith and code makes impossible. The others, the "you" of the poem, "guiltless, sink/ To rest in lobbies, or pace gardens/ Where the slow god crumbles." Ignoring the world threats, not even asking what has become of faith, "you" cannot have an adequate image of evil—"you see an empty chair."

The subject of "Pursuit" is pain, or the pursuit of its opposite, happiness or pleasure. The parable here leads "you" to science, the doctor, who prescribes a "change of scene," a "change of love." These failing, you escape into yourself, "alone—which is the beginning of error—"; for "Solution, perhaps, is public, despair personal." And you come back to the pain you tried to escape (as you did the "nightmare") and discover that only out of the acceptance of suffering does hope for happiness spring. The final image is that of a bereaved, blinking old lady's "crutch, which may put forth a small bloom, perhaps white."

All of these poems exhibit a vivid, and varied, succession of concrete images through which the narrative and meaning development is carried. Their progression is always basically logical, rather than associational or "qualitative," to use Kenneth Burke's term for describing Eliot's characteristic moodal or affective method. Their difficulty for the reader lies in the weight of the load which the images are required to carry. For through them alone, often, we must comprehend the narrative line and the developing pattern of moral or philosophical meaning beneath it, as well as the emotional or attitudinal movement. Most often the images succeed with a startling brilliance, for Warren's eye is sure, his conceptions and attitudes firmly held, and his attention unflagging. But at times the images pile too thickly, their referents become too involved, or their associations bristle out in too many directions. The last stanza of "Terror," for example, projects the "you" in lobbies unheeding the Hitleresque figure of present danger:

> Nor give the alarm, nor ask tonight where sleeps

That head which hooped the jewel Fidelity,
But like an old melon now, in the dank ditch, seeps;
But you crack nuts, while the conscience-stricken stare
Kisses the terror; for you see an empty chair.

The third line here is a perfect Warren signature for the later poems, in its graphic, somewhat horrific, concrete image, in its broken rhythm, and in its concluding, isolated, let-down verb. But the total configuration of image is over-dense, riding too many horses at once. The head, once haloed, but also enclosing in its sanctified round a jewel of fidelity, is now severed, cast off into a ditch to seep, a rotting melon. The crucial jewel—this doubtless Conrad's "idea of Fidelity" on which his world rested—is lost like the halo in the complications, and the abstract head was never given a body to be parted from. (The severance itself is an inference I take from the parallel of Ransom's "Painted Head," as a symbol of modern dissociation, but it is hardly a fact of the poem.) Finally, the "empty chair" symbol, which, Warren has stated, derives from *Macbeth*—Banquo's ghost seen by Macbeth only—adds a still further complication of images, to which the clue is obscure, at least until the final words.

The difficulty with "The Ballad of Billie Potts," the first, as well as the latest written, of the poems in the *Selected Poems*, is of a different order. This poem is of particular interest in that it stands as the transitional piece between the semi-narrative group just discussed and the full-length novel-poem of 1953, *Brother to Dragons*. More and more in the forties, Warren's interest turns toward the larger patterns of experience and their interpretation in terms of his extensions of the essentially Ransomic analysis of the human situation. Here, as in the novels, the fable has a fact basis in history, and an idea structure emphasized by an included commentary. The story pattern is simple: the evil parents, the son blundering in imitation of them, his departure West and return, rich and unrecognized, and his final murder by the parents in ignorance of his identity. In the commentary, however, Warren makes this unpromising story line carry a tremendous burden of symbolic meaning. It must bear the theme of history and its meaning for us; the problems of innocence and knowledge; the pattern of flight from self and false redemption; the themes of self-definition and of the acceptance of heritage.

These are, of course, all the major concepts which are given full treatment in the novels, where the narrative complexes are sufficiently rich and varied to carry them. In the "Ballad," however, many of them are introduced as gratuitous extensions of the story recorded, rather than interpretations of it or emotional configurations discovered within it. The narrative itself, as given in history, does not cover all that Warren wants to tell, or to comment upon. One result is that the commentary sections bulk too large, and the ballad proper shrinks in proportion. Another is that the form of the total poem is weakened. The commentative sections, after the first, tend to become discrete, separately developed poems, in the free-verse patterns of poems like "History," or in the tighter modes of "Original Sin" or "Terror." Meanwhile, the ballad itself undergoes an expansion of form, from the original seven-line stanza with an internal refrain and with Warren's characteristic flat unrhymed last line, to the long couplet paragraphs of the final sections. Despite, therefore, a great deal of true poetry—the whole of the next-to-last commentary poem, for example—and often excellently handled vernacular narrative, the "Ballad" is not a completely successful venture. It suffers, like many Fugitive creative works, from the vice of overintellectual formulation and stretching of material on a Procrustean bed of pattern.

Not until he had completed his first four novels, in 1953, did Warren publish another poem; and the poem when it appeared was evidently a combination of the novel and poetic genres. *Brother to Dragons* is called in the subtitle, "A Tale in Verse and Voices." It represents an extension of the narrative and commentary form of "The Ballad of Billie Potts" both in scope and in complexity. Its major technical improvement, a crucial one, appears in the dramatization of the commentative voices. The narrative is no longer broken to admit evaluations and speculations; all the voices narrate and contribute to the intellectual-emotional development at the same time.

One can best approach this poem through the symbolic meaning patterns which are imbedded in the narrative. Jefferson's first long speech establishes the chief thematic poles and much of the major symbolism which clusters about them. The dream that Jefferson had cherished and lived for was that of man at length become perfect, his potentialities for good realized, an image

> angelic, arrogant, abstract,
> Greaved in glory, thewed with light, the bright
> Brow tall as dawn.

In a further image, he speaks of

> Green germ and joy and the summer shade, and I have said:
> Beneath that shade we'll shelter,
> Green grandeur and unmurmuring instancy of leaf.

Here, connotations of innocence and rapport with nature are added to the God-man, abstraction and rational aspects of the first image; and the green shade symbol amplifies the glory-light-dawn cluster. These groups establish the pre-poem Jefferson, and they carry over in varying combinations and extensions to the members of his family who are principals in the narrative.

A disillusioned Jefferson establishes the other pole in a group of Minotaur-labyrinth images:

There at the blind
Blank labyrinthine turn of my personal time,
I met the beast.

Then,

No thread, and beyond some groped-at corner, hulked
In the blind dark, hock-deep in ordure, its beard
And shag foul-scabbed. . . .

The beast waits. He is the infamy of Crete.
He is the midnight's enormity. He is
Our brother, our darling brother.

The beast-man, natural malignancy, the dark and blindness, and ordure cluster at this pole, and are identified by Jefferson in the final line with Lilburn Lewis, the murderer and Isham's "darling brother."

Both symbolic groups are strongly reinforced as R. P. W. describes his visit to the ruins of the Lewis house in Kentucky. It is summer, bright, but hardly the light-and-shade summer of the pre-poem Jefferson:

the sun insanely screamed out all it knew,
Its one wild word:
Light, light, light!
And all identity tottered to that remorseless
vibration.

The land which Charles Lewis would have redeemed from savagery is rock and thorn and ruin; the shade he would have established is "The tall hot gloom of oak and ironwood,/ Canted and crazed," the cultivation a huge grapevine, "hung in its jungle horror,/ Swayed in its shagged and visceral delight." But chiefly there are the heat and light, which prefigure the central tragedy. For at the climax, the insanity, the scream, the wildness, the tottering, the vibration from the "*light*" quotation are all concomitant elements of the murder scene. And the obsession with one word, one idea, traceable to the "light" delusion, is the indicated motivation of the murder.

Once at the ruin itself, Warren offers an alternate beast image in the blacksnake which flows out of the dark pile, "as though those stones/ Bled forth earth's inner darkness to the day." The brilliant description of this encounter forms one of the two reference frames between which the main narrative is swung; the other, following the action, is a return visit to the ruin in winter. The beast element, like the harmless snake, is itself innocent; only as it combines with the specifically human —the Minotaur symbol—does it become knowing and therefore, in the Jefferson view, responsibly evil, with the "immitigable ferocity of self." Throughout the poem metaphors of coiling and "humping" in the dark accent this element, and the earth itself humps up or "heaves" in earthquake tremors at the climax. At the climax, too, the "jungle" image from the scene at the ruins reappears in the extended metaphor of a parasitical flower which "swells/ From the blind nutriment of Lilburn's heart" as he approaches the murder.

All of these symbols of evil have further projections in the characters, but they are primarily emanations from the disillusioned bitterness of Jefferson. The innocent ones, personified chiefly in Meriwether Lewis, whom Jefferson sent West in the thought that "Man must redeem Nature," emanate from the pre-poem Jefferson. The mind of Jefferson, therefore, stands at the center of the poem; Lilburn's crime destroys his Rousseauism and the aspirations which accompanied the philosophy, and Meriwether's suicide confirms the destruction. The image of flames dances around the funeral pyre of Jefferson's hopes: first, the parasite which unfolds "foliage convolute like flame" within Lilburn, then the lurid fires which light up the meathouse scene and consume the victim's flesh. Lilburn's only appearance as a voice in the poem prefigures this destruction as he draws an image out of childhood: lying in the dark with "just one light, one candle flame"; then a cold gust, "and the flame snapped," and "put out the light." Jefferson finally clinches the symbol by his late discovery that man must provoke "in the midst of our coiling darkness/ The incandescence of the heart's great flare" to illuminate his creative hope.

Lucy Lewis, then Jefferson and R. P. W., finally project beyond Jefferson's despair a new innocence born of knowledge, that which Warren first offered in "The Garden." Lucy tells Jefferson:

> my love and your aspiration
> Could not help but carry some burden of ourselves,
> And to be innocent of that burden, at last,
> You must take his hand, and recognize, at last,
> That his face is only a mirror of your possibilities, . . .

Then Jefferson sees that

> we must
> Create the possibility
> Of reason, and we can create it only
> From the circumstances of our most evil despair. . . .
> In creating yourself, you will create
> The whole wide world and gleaming West anew.

R. P. W. on his return to the ruins projects the same vision, and endows it with a new set of images drawn out of the major clusters, modifying them. Under a pale "lemon light" in winter, when "all things draw in," a snow "thin and pure"—of the new innocence—covers the earth. (An earlier icy and stormy night image of "lethal purity" and "desperate innocence" has prepared the symbolic extension here.) Then, there is the reflective moon, like a "mirror to the human heart's steadfast and central illumination." And R. P. W. says:

> If there be glory, the burden, then, is ours,
> If there is virtue, the burden, then, is ours . . .

The recognition of complicity is the beginning of
innocence,
The recognition of necessity is the beginning of
freedom.

In this new illumination, the grapevine, once "big as boas" in a jungle setting, is now "scraggly-thin and hanging like it's tired/ From trees gone leafless now, and not so tall." The snake has withdrawn to sleep "in earth's dark inwardness," and the river below bears away the "Ordure of Louisville," becoming the image of "our history" and also of "some faith past our consistent failure, and the filth we strew."

As a more personal *exemplum* and image of the final stage of reconciliation in responsibility, Warren introduces briefly another winter scene, this time of a modern man and woman and their first cold kiss:

We kissed in the cold
Logic of hope and need. It was not joy.
Later, the joy. . . .
Since then I have made new acquaintance with the nature
of joy.

It was "joy" that Jefferson first sought, and that others of the characters had desperately looked to find. The word is a constant reference point through the poem, and a balance for the terror of the central incidents. Now it becomes possible, and the ideological and symbolic patterns have moved in unity throughout until they reach their earned resolution.

Brother to Dragons is almost certainly, as several distinguished reviewers have found it, the most successful long narrative poem of our era; it is in many ways also the most completely successful of all Warren's works. Its form seems better suited to his manifold talents than those of the lyric, the drama, or the novel, all of whose specific effects he is able to use without strain or violation of the form. The narrative constantly moves and holds the interest; the telling is varied by the voices which pick it up and add the dramatic conflict of differing points of view to the flow of the action. At the same time, the heightened pitch which the poetic medium requires affords a free release for lyrical flights and for the imagery which wells up spontaneously when Warren sits to write. Finally, the Eliot-like philosophic commentaries, which sometimes strike us as intrusive and overpitched in the novels, have dramatic place and a proper key in this form. There are occasional pieces of overwriting in this poem, and at least two breaks out of character in the voices, but the work as a whole is remarkably textured, as well as remarkably readable.

Much of the texture is gained by the variation of speech styles. Though the poem is written basically in a free blank verse, there are many tones of it. R. P. W.'s is naturally the freest voice. In its lower range, it moves from a short matter-of-factness:

> The sheriff came too late. He found it done.
> But that account's not true. Too bad, it's tidy . . .

to a homely slang, and to the raciness of a Kenneth Fearing:

> for virtue is
> More dogged than Pinkerton, more scientific than the F.B.I., . .
> More remorseless than the mortgage or glitter of banker's *pince-nez*, . .
> And that is why you wake up sweating before dawn
> And finger the cold spot in your side with no fancy now for the matitudinal erection.

In the high range, it has a number of lyric and dramatic tones, topped by the Warren "high rhetoric":

> Let now the night descend,
> With all its graduated terrors,

And in its yearning toward absoluteness now amend
The impudent daylight's velleities, and errors,
And let the dark's most absolute shame
Amend the day's finicking shamelessnesses
And in that dark let the absoluteness of hate's dark flame
Consume, like pitch-pine, the heart that had longed for
love's timid and tentative caresses.

Jefferson is both quieter and more smoothly lyrical than R. P. W. in his innocence mood of reminiscence, and more violent—even nightmarish, as Tate can be—in disillusion. All the rhetorical excesses in the poem are Jefferson in his over-violent reaction to the discovery of basic evil in "angelic" man. Against these two sustained extra-cast voices, major contrasts are sounded in Isham's early frontier dialect, fumbling for understanding—this reinforced by the Brother's querulous bumptiousness—and in the cadenced and cultured dignity of his mother Lucy's intelligence. Somewhere between these two we hear Laetitia's homespun, gently baffled speech, while at the dialectal extreme sounds Aunt Cat's innocent-cunning Negro talk.

The characters built in these voices are not so fully blocked in as the characters in Warren's novels, but, in so far as the quasi-dramatic form allows, they are individual and often movingly realized. Of the principals—R. P. W. and Jefferson, outside the action proper, are disembodied reactive agents in the main—only Meriwether Lewis, whose narrative is an addendum, fails to come alive. Lilburn certainly is so darkly controlled, his historic actions so unspeakably sadistic, that he shakes our credibility, as does the Gran Boz of *World Enough and Time*, but we cannot fail to recognize his potential life in ourselves. The all but ineradicable weakness in Lilburn's portrayal, however, makes for the strength in Laetitia's. Her reactions to the incredible Lilburn's acts and moods establish a vital and affecting portrait. As Robert Lowell has noted,[2] Laetitia and

2. "Prose Genius in Verse," *Kenyon Review*, XV, 622.

Lucy are Warren's "triumphs" in this poem; where Lucy charms, Laetitia overwhelms. Isham, too, is a success, a dog-like, brother-worshipping ally in evil, whimpering for Lilburn's love and respect, stupidly baffled by the kicks and curses he inevitably receives.

Warren has dealt with history in this poem as he has dealt with it in all of his novels, accepting its facts and exposing them to the action of the imagination. Here, as always, he is concerned to probe out the meaning pattern and project it in terms of the symbolic patterns of imagery which the facts themselves suggest. The hazard in this method is in its liability to author imposition, and the one real weakness in *Brother to Dragons*—the major weakness of the novels also—is a narrowness of construction which the author's philosophical commitments forces upon the action. Both Lilburn's and Meriwether's stories are strained in the interpretation, though not in the presentation, so that they may be accommodated to the exposition of Jefferson's errors. Both of these characters must become embodiments of the Rousseauistic fallacy and illustrate, therefore, the deceptive principle which Jefferson advocated and America adopted to precipitate, finally, our modern cultural dilemma.

But Warren proves in *Brother to Dragons* that he remains a major American poet of our time. The lyric quality, which seemed threatened in the later poetry of *Selected Poems,* is still much in evidence, and he has added to it dramatic power and narrative movement. He has not lost touch either with the natural world of tree and rock and bird or with the human community to which he as man and as philosophic mind has been committed. His poetry has gained in depth and density, and it has lost only in the constriction which set patterns of thought have impressed upon it. It would appear certain that Warren's career as a poet is not complete in the mid-fifties.

Chapter XIII

Warren's Fiction

"The philosophic novelist," Robert Penn Warren has written, ". . . is one for whom the documentation of the world is constantly striving to rise to the level of generalization about values, for whom the image strives constantly to rise to symbol, for whom images always fall into a dialectic configuration, for whom the urgency of experience, no matter how vividly and strongly experience may enchant, is the urgency to know the meaning of experience. . . . For him the very act of composition [is] a way of knowing, a way of exploration."[1]

We require, I think, no better definition of Warren's own practice as a novelist than this, from his introduction to Conrad's *Nostromo*. To a considerable extent this definition will apply to the body of the more significant fiction of our time, the particular heritage of Flaubert, and especially to the more significant fiction of the Southern literary renaissance. In Warren, however, we have our purest exemplar of the type, for the vivid naturalism which characterizes the surface of his stories is never without its reflection into the depths where its meaning patterns are formed, and configurations are never allowed to distort, in the fashion of allegory, the literal rendering of observed experience. Warren's apparent superfluities, therefore, even his "rhetoric," must be seen always as relevant to the meaning patterns which his novels develop. His books are conceived like poems of at once lyric intensity and reflective brooding, so that they must be read like poems, with full concentration on image and tone and the "dialectic configurations" which these ultimately produce.

1. "Nostromo," *Sewanee Review*, LIX, 391.

Warren served his apprenticeship in fiction largely during the era of *The Southern Review,* though his first published story, "Prime Leaf," was written in 1930 and printed the next year. These early stories have been collected, along with two later ones, in *Circus in the Attic and Other Stories.* "Prime Leaf" is not only Warren's first considerable short story, but the first of several re-creations of the historic background of his region. Furthermore, it is interesting as a preliminary handling of the subject which his first novel, *Night Rider,* will treat more complexly and more "philosophically." In this case, Warren goes directly at his subject, without tactical maneuvers and without the addition of any special stylistic increment such as will distinguish the novels. The theme is already, in simplified form, one of Warren's particular themes, the conflict between the ideal and the practical, the problem of ends and means. The point-of-view character, old Mr. Hardin, who is the prototype of Captain Todd of *Night Rider* and represents the unyielding integrity of the gentleman-farmer traditions, is pitted against his stubbornly practical son and finally against the whole organization of night-riding tobacco growers, whose zeal in their clearly just cause has led them into violent tactics. Since the point of view, and therefore most of the sympathy, is carried by a character who remains solidly fixed in his position, the conflict lacks the complexity lent it in *Night Rider,* where protagonist Percy Munn must face the outer struggle and the reflection of it in his inner conflicts at every step.

This story, further, lacks the symbolic richness of Warren's later work. For the most part, he is content with his "documentation of the world." "Prime Leaf" develops a final tragic irony as the son, now following to the letter the uncompromising code of old Mr. Hardin, is shot down by those whom he had previously defended. Though the meaning pattern is thus completed, it is not reinforced by a contained pattern of imagery. Warren's documentation of his characters and the setting is careful and convincing, as his action is firm and compelling, but the images do not "rise to symbol," so that the story does not reach to the status of, let us say, poem-myth, to which his later work constantly strives.

In the other early stories, it is largely the realistic texture that absorbs the author. They are a series of explorations into the life of his region, the inflections of its voices, the rounds of its habits, its secret guilts and satisfactions, the moods of its rocks and fields and streams. Sometimes these stories recall the vignettes of *Winesburg, Ohio,* without the pointed preoccupation with psychic frustration and with a more inclusive, more evenly modulated, if often ironic, sympathy. Often, too, they bring to mind Chekhov's simple pathetic chronicles and his significant glimpses of small experience. Only occasionally does a story, like "The Patented Gate and the Mean Hamburger," extrude its point—in this case Agrarian—or not quite convincingly enforce its irony, like the stories about college professors, "The Life and Work of Professor Roy Millen" and "The Unvexed Isles."

The life in these stories is varied and often richly textured in the telling. The embittered animalish life of a shiftless sharecropper family is pictured in "Christmas Gift" against a finely etched foreground of winter snow, rocks, and mud, and presented in the light of a prematurely tough young boy's responses. In "Her Own People," the pathetic story of an uprooted and stubborn Negro servant is exposed through the comico-serious give-and-take of the master-mistress intimacies. The desperation that forces itself into the placid life of an average town girl ("The Love of Elsie Barton") is chronicled in a level Chekhovian style that suggests the level of town comment. And the hidden sin which occasions "The Confession of Brother Grimes" is revealed by means of a salted ironic commentary which forecasts the style of *All the King's Men.*

There are several boy stories, compounds of pathos and irony, and a fine old-man–boy story, "When the Light Gets Green," a delicately handled boy's view of a grandfather's ultimate capitulation to the basic indifferences of nature and man. In most cases, the life chronicle or the notation of an incident is offered without commentary, but with a sidelong glance down the direction of the pattern's significance. When the point of view is limited by a first-person presentation, it is a boy's view or a removed view, so that a comprehensive understanding is automatically ruled out. In the removed view of "Goodwood Comes Back," for example, the important crises are simply reported to the narrator, and only in Goodwood's own inadequate reminiscence and in the severely limited speculation of the reason for Goodwood's murder are there hints at the total ironic configuration.

In the third-person stories, Warren's practice is to limit the comprehension either by the point-of-view character's inherent limitations, as in the professor stories, or by the implication of point of view carried in the style. In the latter case, the style is flavored generally to a sort of man-about-country-town level, an amalgam of amused gossip and mildly ironic comment, but limited by an implied narrow range of understanding and by similarly implied observational restrictions. "The Patented Gate" illustrates the type. Though an "I" is casually inserted early, the narrator soon becomes completely absorbed in the communal view. Here, there are a number of independent comments on various stages of the family transfer from country to city life, but a complete absence of total evaluation, save as the bold symbols of farm gate and hamburger stand supply it. "The Love of Elsie Barton" projects its major incidents in a dramatically presented sequence, and the style level is keyed down to the "average" level which Elsie represents. No comment is offered until the final, "they drove off into the enormous world which she would never understand." The statement comes out not as an author conclusion but as a kind of communal head-shaking over the noticeable lack in Elsie, which is unexplainable by the common lights.

All of these stories illustrate Warren's acute ear for the

various vernaculars of the region, as well as his eye for the illuminating detail and his command of the striking phrase. Furthermore, almost all of them exhibit a wide range of human sympathy and understanding. The rather pervasive ironic view has much of Ransom's aloof observer incorporated in it, but it seems always more immediately concerned than Ransom ever allows himself to appear. There are stories in which the harsh irony of many early Ransom poems obtains: "A Christian Education," "The Confession of Brother Grimes," and "The Life and Work of Professor Roy Millen"; and it is noteworthy that these concern the professional preacher and the professional educator, both abstracted in the event from large contact with "the world's body." But Elsie Barton, the town girl; "Milt's little bastard," the sharecropper son; the uprooted servant Viola; Jeff York and his city-yearning wife; ballplayer Goodwood; and the dying grandfather are all treated with notable, if often gently ironic, sympathy.

Few of these stories carry a symbolic extension to any considerable degree of complexity or depth. It is different, however, with the other two stories included in *Circus in the Attic,* both of them written after the first novels had appeared. "Blackberry Winter," which was originally published in a limited special edition in 1945, is, I think, one of the finest short stories that American writers have produced. It had its origin, Warren has told us, in a group of recollections of farm boyhood: a boy's outrage at incongruously cold unbarefoot weather in June, an outseason flood, the equally incongruous appearance of a city-bred tramp coming from the wrong direction and wanting farm work. All these "blackberry winter" elements were originally set down in their compelling naturalistic detail before the congruity of the incongruous images began to find its ultimate extension. Warren nowhere in the story sacrifices the original sharply registered surface: the drowned chicks with their feebly curled feet and "the fluff plastered" to the limp bodies, the necks "long and loose like a little string of rag," the eyes "with that bluish membrane over them which makes you think of a very old man who is sick and about to die"; the sharecropper boy who, in his patched overalls and "mud-stiff brogans," surprises himself by saying out loud, " 'Reckin anybody ever et drownt cow?' " as he watches the flooded stream and its cargo; the train play with the little colored boy playmate set against the colored mother's "woman-mizry"; the indecent fastidiousness of the tramp and his flick knife.

But all of the details are finally relevant, and poignantly so, as the tramp's parting words, cursing the boy who cannot help trail after him as he leaves, echo back: " 'You don't stop following me and I cut your throat, you little son-of-a-bitch.' " And the boy-narrator adds, "But I did follow him, all the years." All the incongruities and the contrasting stabilities, both with their own meaningful ambiguities, come suddenly into focus: the deadness of the chickens and their finicky handling, the train playing and the "mizry," the cow and the hungry boy, the firmness and gentleness of the father, the tricks of the boy to stay illegally barefooted, the oak-bodied everlasting Negro hand who finds that "the yearth is tahrd," plain "tahrd of sinful folks."

"The Circus in the Attic," which dates from 1946, has less immediate surface interest and develops at a slower pace. A late example of the life chronicle which Warren first had tested in stories like "Elsie Barton," and which he had developed in the "bump" stories included in the novels, "The Circus" reverts to the communal viewpoint, supplemented here by direct native comments through the course of the narrative. In addition, analyses of motive and states of mind are introduced, but these are always partial and held within the limits of the character's own insight. Direct scenic presentation is necessarily confined to brief climactic moments, but the vigorous and often poetic narrative style is constantly enlivened by the colorful voices of the town.

"Circus in the Attic" is the chronicle of a man, Bolton Lovehart; of a town, the Bardsville of *Night Rider;* and of Southern town aristocracy in general. A mature example of Warren's typical, several-leveled complexity, it exhibits amply his "philosophical" transformation of image into symbol and of human experience into patterns of meaning. The first section of the narrative gives us the town, sharply described in its modern dress of factory, Negro slum, business center, and residential heights; and its early ambiguous history, which is symbolized in the now neglected heroes' monument to the Civil War town "saviors," one a "likker killer" only, the other a stubborn defender of his rights. The second section introduces the protagonist, descendant of pioneer long-rifle stock, exhibited first as a child in the image of an effete aristocracy, a velveted Lord Fauntleroy. Soon the image becomes that of a puppet, manipulated carefully and sheltered against the touch of the "common" by his mother, who embodies both the emasculating social snobbery and its supporting unrealistic religious heritage. (The ironic development has the church supply Bolton with an eminently realistic Snopesish wife, who actually descends from Bolton's own stock.)

From the beginning of the story, metaphors of the "circus performer" and "celluloid film" have been introduced; in the second section there are further images of this artificial life: the puppet, "spangles," a skirt flaring "like a dancer," "a photograph in an album," prepare the major symbol. When the circus actually appears, it is "barbarous" to Bolton, and his love-smothered need for animalism, for sin, drives him to it. Later, it is this same need, "like a blind fish from a cave, hurled into light," which drives Sara Darter to seduce Bolton under the portraits of her grandfathers. Trapped again by his mother, his first refuge is the new movie theatre, where, as ticket-taker, he acts the part of an "impressario." Finally, the secretly carved circus succeeds as the substitute for the real life that has been continually thwarted. An artificial life, an art for life's sake life, has replaced the attempt to live. Bolton learns now that "you can only love perfectly in terms of a great betrayal." His mother has pointedly identified herself with Christ and become absolutely necessary to the Judas role which enables him to live in a semblance of the good-evil world of reality.

When his mother's heart proves in its turn a Judas to her, Bolton's circus loses its *raison d'être* and becomes a sacrifice on the altar of his new commitment to life, in marriage and in vicarious war participation. Only when he is betrayed, first by his stepson's death in the Italian campaign, then by his wife, who is killed in the process of an adulterous affair, does Bolton revert permanently to the circus, which has now become coterminal with death, with the now artificial tradition of "aristocratic" Southern town life, with the "heroes," early and late, and with Bardsville itself. And it is the final pattern of Bolton's life.

"The Circus" is less poignant, less immediate in its appeal than "Blackberry Winter." Its drama and its color thin out during the war era sequences where too much must be presented in summary, but it has brilliant moments: the opening section of description; and the old-timer's version of the historic raid, particularly the scene of her heart's final betrayal of "pretty little, nice little Louise Bolton" Lovehart (the ironic significance of the name is apparent). Chiefly, however, "The Circus" provides a useful introduction into Warren's novelistic methods.

All of Warren's novels are pegged to the realism of historic events, to recognizable localities and people; and they are concerned with man's usually tragic attempt to impose pattern and meaning upon the raw stuff of his world. This structural opposition of real and ideal is reflected on the textural surface in a sharply observed and colloquially recorded realism contending with a rich and sometimes high-flown rhetoric. The profuse life is always corralled into meaningful patterns, the profuse imagery is directed by the patterns of its symbolic extensions.

The most fruitful approach to the novels is that of poetry, for Warren has organized them like metaphysical poems, as well as like the later Elizabethan drama—as that drama has been interpreted, at least, by modern "expanded metaphor" analysis. Each of the novels is dominated by a strong set of images, which assume more and more significance as they undergo variations and expansions until they culminate in symbolic action. A more specialized imagery often attaches to individual characters, thus lending their particularity a symbolic force. Finally, an independent localized imagery wells up in a spontaneous flow, as if to give body to Ransom's theory of textural irresponsibility.

But the novels are drama also, poetic drama of the Shakespeare, Webster, Tourneur sort, with "romantic" heights and earthy depths. This type of metaphysical poetic drama, as a form, offers many advantages for the novelist. It permits, even demands, a plot of action, and therefore a romantic or melodramatic appeal on the primary level. Like Shakespeare and the others, Warren derives his plots largely from historic events of a violent nature. Again, on the level of the pit, Warren is enabled to indulge an earthy humor and salty wit issuing naturally from "low comedy" characters. Balancing this element, boldly poetic rhetoric can be introduced in soliloquies and scenes of high emotional stress. Yoking such opposites together becomes the primary function of the controlled symbols, as well as the developed patterns of meaning which inform all levels of the action. Warren is, furthermore, enabled to embody in prose form the major theses of all the Fugitive critics: Ransom's dualism of "physical" and "Platonic" poetry, with its ideal resolution in metaphysical poetry; Tate's "tension" between extensive and intensive factors; Brooks's doctrine of irony and paradox; and Warren's own concept of "impure" poetry.

Warren's first published novel, *Night Rider*, establishes its basic image patterns in the opening scenes. The crowd and the crowd pressure to which Percy Munn is subjected on the opening page as he prepares to leave his train at the Bardsville station fix one symbolic pole—the political one—for the novel's action:

> The gathering force which surged up the long aisle behind him like a wave took and plunged him hard against the back of the next man. . . . Mr. Munn again resented that pressure that was human because it was made by human beings, but was inhuman, too, because you could not isolate and blame any one of those human beings who made it.

After the crowd on the streets and the subsequent group pressure which forces his commitment to the mass action of the growers' Association, and after his own too successful speech, Munn recalls "how incredibly brilliant and empty had been the sky from which the light poured over the landscape and the innumerable faces." This emptiness, which is the "tremendous emptiness of the crowd" itself, and is attached to the light of naked idea, gradually takes form, or at least outline, in the figure of Senator Tolliver, who is seen almost at once staring, "cold and abstract," at a "blankly sunlit wall." Tolliver is a moral hollowness surrounded by political man, and it is finally with Tolliver that Munn is forced to identify. Equivocal, like all of Warren's symbols, the crowd represents the real world of men and action to which Munn secretly yearns, and at the same time it presents to him the image of his own inner lonely emptiness.

More obvious, as well as more complex, is the pervasive symbolism of light and darkness, and its extension in terms of warmth and coldness. The opening page's "glare of the morning sun . . . half-blinding him after the dim interior of the coach," marks Munn's emergence from the cocoon of his marriage into a world of fact and activity. But the full light of responsible public action for Percy Munn hardly survives his maiden speech. From the moment of his complete involvement in the Association's business, he becomes a creature of the night. The first evening in the hotel he cannot sleep and rises to watch and listen to the crowd below, with "disgust not only for them but for himself." The revulsion he feels for them and for his own act, committing himself to them, is balanced by a new wave of exultation, an orator's gesture in the night—he would "tell them what he knew to be the truth." The accompaniment of this commitment to the "Word" is the singing in the streets below to the tune of "John Brown's Body," a significant reference, since Warren's early biography of Brown pictures him as an archetypal image of man given over to the abstract idea. Munn's gesture thus becomes his renunciation of his own essential humanity and of his proper self-realization.

After the inauguration of night-riding activities, every important event in Munn's life occurs under the aegis of night, with the coldness of stealth, lust, and violence gradually mastering every phase of his activity, until he lives in a cave—a reversal of the opening brilliant empty sky image—and dares not appear in daylight. Only occasional flickers of light and warmth penetrate to him through the body of the novel until the climax of night-riding brings the great burst of flame from dynamited warehouses. But the moment of apparent fulfillment which this artificially enkindled light and heat of destructive violence provide for Munn is soon itself a cold blackened ruin. On a grander scale, it is the oratorical gesture in the hotel room, and its apotheosis.

The false heat and light of fires provides the accompaniment for the love affair of Munn and Lucille Christian. Their desperate search for fulfillment in each other, since they have not the means to find it in themselves, is a clandestine action like that of the night-riding which parallels it, setting off their flame of passion with the flames of burning barns. The affair ends with the destruction of two once-potent centers of real warmth, Lucille's father and Munn's home. And the double catastrophe by night and fire discovers to the lovers their essential coldness, isolation, and emptiness.

The image pattern is completed and its elements merged with the "blunt, frayed flame" of Munn's pistol punctuating the night, the pistol with which he has been unable to kill his hollow father-surrogate and alter-ego, Tolliver. For the trapped and dying Munn, this final scene becomes a reversion to the lost innocence of childhood, with the voices of his assassins—the now deadly crowd—sounding to him "like the voices of boys at a game in the dark." Thus the symbolism which began with the dimness of innocence from which Munn was emerging has come full circle, back through night abstraction with its false lights to the dark womb of innocence and death.

Warren's second novel, *At Heaven's Gate*, is ideologically a study of modern "freedom," liberation from the decadence of the past and its moral restraints into the rare air of unsupported pragmatic creeds; hence the ironic title, applying primarily to Sue Murdock—"my lady sweet, arise." This is Warren's only city-bound novel, and its central imagery reflects an adverse agrarian verdict against a form of life dominated by finance capitalism and cut off from its roots in the soil.

The novel develops two large symbolic clusters: those relating to decay, disease, deformation, and the like; and those which may be termed unreality images. The focus of the first group is Lemuel Murdock, whose murder of a rival politician in defense of his honor, as he and his code understood honor, has left him "mountainously decayed, sagging from the big maned head, the gray streaked yellowly as by old rust stains, the whole mass sagging, as by long slip and erosion." Symbolically, he is the tradition itself, the South, a monstrous ruin in the new order of finance which his son represents. Similarly, the backgrounds of the younger characters all abound in images of decay, deformation, and filth. In Jerry Calhoun's agrarian home there are cripples, foulness, and rot; in Dorothy

Murdock's peeling family house rotting Revolutionary War boots; in Duckfoot Blake's slum bungalow a "distorted parody of an old man"; in Sweetwater's decaying family home "dust-smelling horsehair furniture" and "gray-faced old ladies," whose breaths smell "like stale cooked turnips."

But images like these are by no means one-directional, for they are exploited just as insistently in the city life of the younger generation. While the repulsive heritage represented by Lemuel Murdock may be taken as sufficient cause for the unprincipled, artfully smooth and attractive surface which his son creates, the moral emptiness and human coldness of that life is sufficient to drive his daughter, Sue, into a restless career which reflects distortedly, invertedly, the images projected directly by the figures of decayed tradition. Sue's city world is dominated by the overt images of the cripple, Rosemary, of Sarrett's ambiguous sex, of Sweetwater's scars, Blake's splayed feet and "farts." But it is the inverted reflection of these images that gives them symbolic weight, for they represent the moral perversion and distortion of values implicit in their lives. So Sue must compel Jerry to take her first in the family library, repository of the tradition, then on the cripple's bed, where he must feel "as though he clasped that other body, small, bony, twisted." She must wear Rosemary's dress and sleep on her patch of warmth in her bed, and call Jerry an "emotional cripple." The characters pick their psychological "scabs," "boil out" their mental "pus," exhibit their ambitions "like boils"; they need to squeeze their emotional "pimples," they slobber or vomit or feel like it, spit or "dribble saliva." Art in Sarrett's circle becomes a growth out of "dung and offal," poetry "the glitter of pus," criticism "at its worst . . . an attempt to disintegrate the rose into the dung which fertilized the root," and discovery of a sympathetic role in the theatre "like first menstruation."

Art, and particularly theatre art, along with sport, supplies a major division of the unreality images, which symbolize a contrasting but intimately related aspect of the traditionless lives. The specific unreality images revolve generally about two centers: Bogan Murdock, who is a "solar myth" or "just a dream Bogan Murdock had"—"When Bogan Murdock looks in the mirror, he doesn't see a thing"—; and Slim Sarrett, persuasive exponent of the reality principle, but himself a whole-cloth creation. Bogan personifies the chimera of finance capitalism, a "wonderful idea" without tangible reality. It is Bogan's moral nonexistence (reflected also in the sport-for-appearance images surrounding him) which gradually steals from his wife her sense of reality, and which, by the specious glitter which surrounds it, attracts Jerry Calhoun, only to leave him finally with the memory of "events and persons . . . as shadowy as frosted breath on the air." And it is this blank heritage which Sue, as the modern experimental spirit, attempts to fill with a series of desperate liaisons: first, with the American dream hero, up from poverty through football to banking (Jerry); then with the irresponsible aesthete (Sarrett); finally with the ideology hero (Sweetwater).

Sarrett personifies the artistic-intellectualist denial of the world of fact. His attributes, the strict athlete's discipline, the hard surface and penetrating insight, the androgynous character, the alienation from and by society, and the retaliatory attack on society, are those of modern art itself. Sue, attached to Sarrett's as well as to Murdock's unreality center, experiences her most significant moments in non-self-identifications: on the stage, particularly as the innocent victim, Cordelia; in the utterly detached artificiality of her participation in Sarrett's parties, where she acts merely as a bright reflecting surface; in the self-forgetfulness of drink and sex; in her times of pure emptiness, when her overpowering urge to be loved and to be identified through love has left her and she is the nothingness which Bogan has passed down to her. The numerous images of gold and glitter link her with her father's world; those of freedom, power, and powerlessness, with her attempt to find a self in the world of abstractions bounded by

Jerry, Sarrett, and Sweetwater. To the end, her cry, that of the "freed" generation, is "'Oh, what am I?'"—but she remains a mirror only, reflecting her own inner emptiness.

All the King's Men is a novel of redemption and the only one of Warren's, therefore, which permits the protagonist, who is again a personification of modern man in quest of self-identification, to emerge from his ordeal to the hope of a new and oriented life. The symbolic fable of this book embodies the world of fact in Willie Stark ("stark" fact) and the world of idea or abstraction in Adam (innocence of the world of fact) Stanton, while the Eves of the piece, Anne Stanton and Sadie Burke, are the agents by which knowledge of evil is transmitted to Jack Burden (who must finally bear the full burden of knowledge, as he is regenerated).

The pervasive imagery of this novel enforces the redemption-rebirth theme, as Norton Girault has noted,[2] and the related Eden-fall-knowledge motif to which the title obliquely refers. The early episodes dealing with the childhood idyll of Adam, Jack, and Anne are saturated with water imagery. The womb-innocence connotations are underscored by the numerous childlike features and attitudes which Jack notes in Anne. But the major image of Anne, that of lying back gazing up or with closed eyes, whether she is floating on water or reclining on the seat of a roadster or waiting naked on the bed for Jack, is one of expectancy and receptivity to real experience. Jack's preservation of this image, which he understands only in its aspect of innocence, and his inability to violate it are the indices of his subconscious urge to hold on to a kind of innocence or to return to it. So Jack is thinking in terms of an "aqueous green" forest coolness with himself as a bird diving into it—as Anne had once dived—while Anne is destroying his memory picture by accepting Stark as a lover, embracing the realities which

2. "The Narrator's Mind as Symbol: An Analysis of *All the King's Men*," *Accent*, VII, 220-34.

Jack shuns. When he discovers the violation, for which the receptive aspect of the image should have prepared him, the water symbol becomes "green scum on the shrunk pool around which the exposed earth cracks and scales like a gray scab." (Jack is still unprepared in a final sequence when Anne opens her door to him with, " 'Of course I'd let you in.' ")

The rebirth symbols appear on several levels and in various tones throughout the novel. The episode of Willie Stark's enlightenment, when he changes from a "country sap" into an astute practical politician, is dominated by images of conversion, ritual killing, and revival. Stark had heard the call to politics "as for a saint," had been "the little white lamb of God." In the crucial scene, he becomes "the sacrificial goat . . . the ram in the bushes." He passes out cold to be referred to as "the remains" with a "face pale and pure." Jack's morning midwifery produces "a high and pure and transparent look like a martyr's face," and Jack can soon comment that "he's been on the road to Damascus and he saw a great light." The scene ends with Willie's eyes shining "and over him God's bright, brassy, incandescent sky." All this forms an ironic prelude to the final enlightenment and rebirth of Jack Burden. Willie is reborn into "realism," and it is under the aegis of Willie and realism in its various forms that Jack is to live. On one level, this novel is a testing of philosophic realism, as *World Enough and Time* will be a testing of romantic idealism.

As early as page 11, Jack's resistance to the rebirth which comes from knowledge of self and world has been presented in a graphic image:

> But the clammy, sad little foetus which is you way down in the dark which is you too lifts up its sad little face and its eyes are blind. . . . It wants to lie in the dark and not know and be warm in its not-knowing.

(The contrasting image for Willie in his pre-Damascus phase is: "inside himself . . . something was swelling and growing painfully and dully and imperceptibly like a great potato in a dark, damp cellar.") Jack's progress toward enlightenment is a reverse movement, marked by running-away images and by the womb returns called "Great Sleeps." The climax of this process occurs in Jack's mechanistic phase—the Sleeps separate his adoption of various realistic philosophies. He watches Adam perform a prefrontal lobotomy, designed to provide the patient with a new personality by purely mechanical means, an operation, Jack thinks, "more radical even than what happened to Saul on the road to Damascus." Like Willie's, this ironic rebirth-conversion previews Jack's, but now more explicitly, for the image cluster includes the "white nightshirts" of a revivalist baptism, and Jack insists that the patient "is born again and not of woman. I baptize thee in the name of the Great Twitch, the Little Twitch, and the Holy Ghost. Who, no doubt, is a Twitch too."

One further false rebirth symbol is associated with Jack's "father," the Scholarly Attorney. Here the religious aura, the "hanged man" symbol (George, the more or less adopted son of the Scholarly Attorney, was "the man who got hanged" in the circus), the bed wetting, the "maternal little noises," the metaphor of the "saint" to describe George's masticatory bliss—all support a downward-to-false-innocence redemption and regeneration. And since George has become the stand-in for Jack in a doubly false or unreal situation, the ironic application of the scene is clear.

After this preparation, the true redemption of Jack Burden occurs, but only when he has accepted responsibility for the deaths of both his father-imago and his real father. The ritualistic shedding of the father's blood has prepared him and purchased knowledge, for all knowledge that "is worth anything . . . has cost some blood, and knowledge is redemption"; "the truth always kills the father."

Jack's rebirth is heralded by his mother's scream, "which snatched [him] from sleep" with its "bright, beautiful, silver purity of feeling," by her moaning and drugged behavior. The scream is a revelation of her capacity to love, and it gives Jack a new mother, a new, if dead, father, and "a new picture of the world." At the same time, Willie Stark's "greatness," which "perhaps he spilled . . . on the ground," as Onan his seed, has a dubious reincarnation in the illegitimate perhaps-grandchild whom his widow adopts and names "Willie Stark." The contrast and irony are complete with the parallel established between this offspring of spilled seed and Jack, with his hard birth into responsibility.

World Enough and Time, a novel in which Warren tests various versions of philosophic idealism, offers a symbolic pattern oriented about primitivistic ritual—centered in the sacrificial shedding of blood—and the ritual's idealization in romantic tragedy. The key image for the first cluster is developed from the Indian conception of Kentucky, defined by Warren as the "Dark and Bloody Ground . . . a holy land . . . a land of mystery . . . for the gods lived here." The principal dramatic images reflect Jeremiah Beaumont's view of himself "mounting the high stage" to perform a "noble" tragic action.

Blood imagery dominates the early wilderness scenes in which Jeremiah's character is formed, the climactic episodes involving the sacrificial killing of Colonel Fort, Jeremiah's father-surrogate, and the final retributive section. The development of these blood images culminates in the symbolic hacking off of Jerry's head—the Platonic idealist severance of mind and body which Ransom had brilliantly exploited in his metaphysical poem, "Painted Head." However, the blood pattern is initiated quietly in a description of the acres of wild strawberries on the father's home site, so thick that "his boots were red and bright with juice as with blood." Jeremiah adds: "But I remember from my own time how they were sweet to the tongue." This association of sweetness with the blood image is indicative of Jeremiah's—and romantic idealism's—distortion of natural violence, and it sets the referents for the following religious conversion scene. The revivalist's sermon, visualizing God as a great bear whose "fangs drip wrath" and the victim-to-be-saved as a lamb offering its throat so that its blood will spurt under the Divine jaws, is prefaced by words touching "for their sweetness," and followed by the exhortation: "let there be sweetness in your terror." At this point there recurs to Jeremiah an ambiguous sacrificial and sadistic image from early childhood of a young woman martyr at the stake in flames. Thus the total major symbolic complex of blood-sacrifice, sweetness, and "high stage" is complete.

As Jeremiah approaches his sacrificial murder of Fort, the revivalist imagery controls his thinking, for in his own mind he is avenging martyred innocence and therefore purifying himself. "The blood of Fort would clear him. . . . He would bathe in it and be clean." He goes off on his "errand of blood" like a knight of romance, with a red ribbon "the color of blood" to fly "as a pennon for victory." When the deed is done, the thought of his own blood to be shed in retribution starts a sudden feeling of "great lightness and cleansing, as though he . . . *was* innocent and could trust his innocence."

The final sequence begins with Jeremiah's flight to the West—a constant false-innocence motif in Warren. Here the God-bear image recurs, but now ironically twisted, as Jeremiah seeks an animal-innocence in the body alone. His guide, "smeared and stained" with juice of the wild grape, seems "savagely painted for ritual, or as though [he] had fed on dripping flesh and the waste blood had caked about the muzzle." In the retreat of the Gran Boz, where it is now Rachel who wears a red ribbon in her hair as she goes sacrificially to visit the monster, the religious ritual is perverted to drunken fornication at the side of a man bleeding to death; and Jeremiah contracts a venereal disease from the "corrupt blood" of the woman. After the severance of head from body and the burial of the "ideal" head alone, a final note of irony is appended when Wilkie Barron, who personifies the realist way of the world, shoots himself so "tidily" through the heart "that he leaves not a single spatter of blood on the floor."

The symbolism of the drama, representing Jeremiah's idealistic version of his own action and later Rachel's forced version of hers, plays a constant accompaniment to the blood motif. For Jeremiah in his first retreat with Rachel, the world of affairs is a "mock-show" but soon it becomes a retreat "from another more dire mock-show" of his own mind's creation. From this perception, Jeremiah rises to imagine and then to enact his "secret drama," in which Fort is villain, he hero. But it must all be played in the dark, out of the light of realism, and he must draw Rachel onto the shadow stage with him. The high tragedy has its ironic climax when poison fails to produce more than a retching sickness:

> So after the fine speeches and the tragic stance, the grand exit was muffed. The actors trip on their ceremonial robes, even at the threshold of greatness, and come tumbling down in a smashing pratt-fall, amid hoots and howls from the house.

The world of reality has the last laugh. The primitive ritual of hunting and bloodshed—the pure earth-born violence apostrophized by Faulkner and Hemingway—as well as the ideal drama have been perverted by man's inability to coordinate the two aspects of his nature, until the error-strewn course comes to its end in animal reversion and corruption and in comic "pratt-falls." In contrast, unalloyed realism bows off triumphantly, and in the wings manages its own bloodless self-defeat.

The structure of Warren's novels, which is reflected in the symbolism, and furthermore in the style, is based on the dualistic ideology which he inherits from Ransom. It is a structure of primary oppositions, expressed variously as: ideal and real, or idea and fact; man and external nature; innocence and guilt; ends and means; science and religion or art; heritage and revolt, or father and son; history and the individual life. The attempt to resolve or to balance these antinomies in terms of the integration of personality and in terms of moral adjustment to an active life in the world is the burden of the fables. In each novel, the protagonist—or protagonists in one case—is in quest of his own identity and of his role in social life, a quest successfully concluded only in the case of Jack Burden. But always the protagonist's search is set off against others which embody a variety of opposing and related approaches to the problems set.

All of the novels begin with historic fact, the actual historic set of events. The facts are ordered, altered, and probed until they yield up meaningful patterns in terms of Warren's ideological predispositions (since history itself, as Jack Burden discovers, and Tate especially has reiterated, is a meaningless compilation until it is reinterpreted by and for the living). *Night Rider* exploits the facts of the 1909 "tobacco war" in Southern Kentucky between growers and buyers' agents, the subject of Warren's first long story, "Prime Leaf." Its thematic pattern is discovered in the career of Percy Munn and his quest for self-identification and for direction. Opposed dead-end solutions for his ends-means dilemma are embodied primarily in Dr. MacDonald's behaviorist scientism, in Professor Ball's pragmatic idealism, in Lucy Burnham's blank retreat into the past, and in Ianthe Sprague's equally blank commitment to an unexamined present. Meanwhile, Willie Proudfit's agrarian realism-plus-religion and Captain Todd's traditionalist code offer successful examples of integrated and purposeful adaptations to life.

At Heaven's Gate offers the same practice in more complex form. Here Warren draws on the modern history of Nashville: the famous Carmack shooting of 1902, the career of the World War I hero, Sergeant York, and the financial manipulations of Colonel Luke Lea during the 1920's. The thematic pattern in this case develops out of the interacting quests of several characters, all of them in revolt against their heritages, seeking desperately in a series of pragmatic experiments in living to discover a *modus vivendi.* Opposed to them chiefly are Bogan Murdock, who has successfully sloughed off all moral concern and with it his whole humanity, and Ashby Windham, the religious fanatic who alone accepts guilt and responsibility and provides the example of a meaningful life.

In *All the King's Men,* the rise and fall of Huey Long supplies historical base material for the long education of Jack Burden. Willie Stark's pragmatic realism and Adam Stanton's idealist-scientific innocence are the major foils here, but it is Cass Mastern's acceptance of guilt and responsibility which forecasts Jack's illumination.

The political battle between advocates of the Old Court and New Court of the 1820's (a reflection of the Old and New Deal conflicts of the 1930's) becomes the background for *World Enough and Time,* while the famous Beauchamp murder case in Frankfort of that era supplies the foreground drama. Jeremiah Beaumont's tragic search for a way of life which will embody his romantic ideals is played off against the worldly opportunism of Wilkie Barron, the sheer animalism of the Gran Boz, and Percival Skrogg's fanaticism of the idea. Again it is a peripheral story, that of his religious conversion told by Munn Short, which prefigures Jeremiah's final recognition of his errors.

Since, for Warren, history as record has no importance, his presented life patterns never become, as they do for Faulkner, patterns of collective experience. Warren's are philosophically probed moral lives and deaths of everyman. He does not, therefore, tell his stories, as Faulkner does, in the portentous direct style of myth or legend. Instead, he must probe from several points of view, turning each event over and about like a piece of a jigsaw puzzle until its color and configuration reveal its position in the developing design. This tentative, trial-and-error method, while it lacks the immediate impact of Faulkner's revelatory manner, draws the reader into more immediate participation, so that illumination and discovery are developments in which he shares. For the organization of his books, however, Warren's method presents difficulties.

The fullest reader participation requires absorption in a single point of view, but the fullest interpretation and evaluation require more than one limited perspective. Hence, Warren consistently resorts to the device of the commentary. All of the novels include peripheral stories which serve the commentative function. These stories are never so discrete and unattached as the "Old Man" story in Faulkner's *Wild Palms,* but they are, from a structural point of view, excrescences.[3] In *At Heaven's Gate,* the frequent shifts in point of view among the central characters provide sufficient commentary on one another. However, an additional form of commentation is employed extensively in the third and fourth novels. The narrative technique here is that of the re-creative confession or journal. Warren uses the device, as André Gide does, to gain multiple perspective without sacrificing intimate reader participation. In *All the King's Men,* Jack Burden tells his confessional story from a double point of view: that of the moment when the action occurs, dramatically; and that of the period of his enlightenment, reflectively. *World Enough and Time* adds further perspectives: there is Jeremiah's journal, like the double view of Burden's story, but there are further speculations by the historian-author looking back from a century and a quarter later, with the further aid of trial records and other documentary material. The author tells us on the second page that "We do not know that we have the Truth." We do have additional commentative and speculative opportunities, at all events; so many, indeed, that in this book the commentation threatens at times to overwhelm the narrative.

The "philosophical novel," particularly when it is based on history, is necessarily interpretive, and Warren, like the other Fugitives more and more absorbed with meanings, has

3. Warren's term for these stories is "narrative bumps," but he is certainly facetious in implying that they are introduced to "bump" up a flagging narrative interest. They serve rather as interruptions to the narrative interest.

increasingly squeezed his incidents for motives and patterns. On the other hand, he has consistently balanced the slow-paced reflective element with violent action in the manner of Elizabethan tragedy. It is Shakespeare, in fact, who is cited in *At Heaven's Gate* as authority for what has been Warren's major theme, and as a prototype for what is Warren's basic narrative pattern. The key word in all the novels is "knowledge." "The end of man is to know," says Jack Burden; and Jeremiah later echoes, "If we can only know!" To know is, first of all, an introspective process, and all of Warren's major characters are engaged by the necessity for learning to know, or to "identify" themselves. Slim Sarrett's attribution of this classic theme to Shakespeare is as follows:

> The theme underlying Shakespearean tragedy—Elizabethan tragedy, in fact—is usually misstated. . . . The tragic flaw in the Shakespearean hero is a defect in self-knowledge. . . . Bacon wrote: Knowledge is power. Bacon was thinking of knowledge of mechanisms of the external world. Shakespeare wrote: Self-knowledge is power. Shakespeare was thinking of the mechanisms of the spirit, to which the mechanism of the external world, including other persons, are instruments. In other words, Shakespeare was interested in success. By success, he meant: Self-fulfillment. But his tragedy is concerned with failure. Naturally the successful man . . . has no story. He is pure. But poetry is concerned only with failure, distortion, imbalance—with impurity. And poetry itself is impurity.[4]

In this paragraph the heart of Warren's ideological and aesthetic insistences are clearly expressed. Self-knowledge—and, following upon that, knowledge of the world outside the self—is the one sure approach to directional, and hence successful, living. In the absence of a compelling religious belief, which he constantly interprets as a means to self-knowledge, Warren is propounding a Renaissance view of man's self-sufficiency in an alien world. But self-knowledge implies for him a knowledge of one's own essential depravity, or in religious

4. *At Heaven's Gate*, p. 64.

terms his fallen state. Himself corrupted in a corrupt world, whose challenges he must face if he would be counted man, he must steer a resolute, but by no means uncompromising, course. Like Gilbert Mastern, he must try "to do a little justice in terms of the great injustice." Necessarily he requires ideals of conduct and reason as guides, as he requires the guidance of his tradition, but the pitfalls of an uncompromising idealism or rationalism are as dangerous as those of pure pragmatism. Jeremiah sums them up at the end of *World Enough and Time:*

> He had thought that the idea in and of itself might redeem the world, and in that thought had scorned the world. But that thought . . . had led to a second error, which must always follow from the first when we find that the idea has not redeemed the world: the world must redeem the idea . . . 'man will use the means of the natural world, and its dark ways, to gain that end he names holy by the idea. . . .' But there is a third error . . . that follows from the second: to deny the idea and its loneliness and embrace the world as all.

Pure idealism smashes itself up against a recalcitrant reality; pragmatic idealism corrupts the end by employing the corrupt means of its enemies; and pragmatic realism is a surrender of the essential humanity of man. All of these types of failures occur in all of Warren's novels. Jeremiah's answering hope is merely "knowledge," but there are many ingredients in this knowledge in addition to knowledge of self per se. There is first acceptance of primary guilt, then of total responsibility for one's every act. Further, there is the directional bearing that can be found only in the acceptance of one's own heritage, however corrupted—hence Warren's very liberal use in the novels of the father-surrogate, rejected and rediscovered father motifs. "Direction is all," Jack Burden can say, and insist that there is no future without a past accepted; and conversely Percy Munn must find that "because the future was dead . . . the past too . . . began to fall apart."

Warren offers no panaceas and no rules of thumb; he is generally "concerned only with failure," since he is writing tragedy. And it must be emphasized, to correct certain critical misconceptions, that he does not advocate reactionism (Kazin), acquiesce in *"real politik"* (D. Trilling), or write historical romance with an eye on Hollywood (several generally reputable critics). Warren is a "religious" writer, in the sense that he emphasizes Ransom's "god of thunder," "original sin," free-will and its responsibilities, and a kind of redemption. However, his equal emphasis on man's ultimate self-sufficiency to his tragic role in life and on the equation of religion and art puts him, again with Ransom, on the side of classical humanism —and therefore of democracy. In embracing the twin heritages of the Western world, his doctrinal position is at once rational and secularly metaphysical, ultimately morally oriented—the typical Fugitive position.

The "rhetoric" of Warren's novels, particularly that of *All the King's Men*, has been harshly treated by several competent critics without reference to its functional relation to the themes and structures of the novels. "Rhetoric" is the proper term for Warren's style if it be understood in its Elizabethan and baroque-metaphysical sense as the art of effective speech. In literary temperament, as we have noted, Warren is closer to these models than to modern simplicity cults which have attached pejorative connotations to the term.

Warren's normal prose style derives from the Ransomic dualism which underlies his themes and his own theory of impure poetry. To do justice to the "complexities and contradictions of experience," language must reflect in a constant counterpoint both the ideal-romantic and the crude fact-animalism of man's dual nature. To disallow either of these aspects of Warren's writing in their contexts (critics have referred to them as "fancy writing" and "vulgarity," thereby revealing much of their own limited monistic tendencies) is to rule out Warren's philosophic and literary premise. These stylistic extremes are not what these critics imply, lapses of taste or self-indulgences, but technique, and technique that has been fully integrated to theme and structure.

Each of the novels is, in fact, a different stylistic, as well as symbolic, compound. *Night Rider*, the least complex, told from a single author-over-shoulder point of view, proceeds largely in graphic and forceful, but always decorous, style, slightly elevated to the tone of the idealistic Southern landholder, who is not primarily farmer. (The constant use of titles for the characters, especially the author's consistent reference to his protagonist as "Mr. Munn," is largely a tonal device suiting the natural aloofness of the type.) Counterpoint to this normal style, which is often poetically heightened in Munn's thought monologues, is supplied chiefly by dialogue: the colorful, earthy comments and explosions of Bill Christian, the only less vivid realism of Dr. MacDonald, the harsh dialects of farmers and softer ones of the Negroes. Finally it is broken by the long, finely sustained dialect passage of Willie Proudfit's tale.

At Heaven's Gate, with its shifting multiple viewpoints, employs a variety of counterplayed styles, from the densely metaphoric mountain-evangelist dialect of Ashby Windham to the brittle, nervous city language of the Slim Sarrett episodes or the tough-gentle humor of organizer Sweetwater. Through such ground styles as these run variations like Blake's gamey naturalism and Uncle Lew's rural crudities, the hysterical ritualistic dialect of Negroes in torture-sport and in fear, Murdock's pretentious self-salesmanship, and Sue's bright schoolgirl disillusionment. In this Babel of speeches, reflecting the city setting with its confusion of purposes and creeds, there is no center. There is, instead, the gradual intrusion of an impersonal, yet cynical, news reporter style which ends by dominating the closing sections. The abstract belief-less voice of the city as a whole finally prevails.

The "smart-aleck" commentary, as well as the high-flown rhetoric, of *All the King's Men* has been unduly censured by puristic critics. Once the role of Jack Burden, the narrator, is seen in its true centrality, with his dual nature objectified on the one side in Willie Stark's factualism, on the other in Adam's abstract and romantic idealism, the necessity for the stylistic alternation becomes evident. The cynical smart-aleck pose—the "fancy writer," the smothered and hence romantic-ironic ideal of himself—is Jack's defense against a world that has alienated him. These two continually warring stylistic elements are further overlaid by the retrospective reflections of the mature, philosophic Jack Burden of the book's end. Most characteristic of the base style is the appended tag which snatches a sharp insight, a lush description, or an indulged emotion from its flight and realistically grounds it in the manner of *The Waste Land;* the late style often retrieves it to middle space. Then there are the brilliantly mixed descriptions of scenes and people, such as the one that opens the book, recklessly paced kaleidoscopic successions of imagery and metaphor, quick observation and comment, humor, earthiness and beauty. This is Jack (and perhaps Warren) letting himself go as man of fact, man of idea, and ironic mature philosopher at the pace of the modern world he is depicting.

Extended philosophic passages, in this book always metaphorical and somewhat racy, and the formally paced speculative style of the Cass Mastern story reveal new stylistic veins which come to dominate *World Enough and Time.* This fourth novel, despite its several perspectives, offers an evener tonal surface than any of the earlier books. Jeremiah's formal vocabulary and often stiltedly romantic phrasing is modified in the historian's controlled language, but there is no sharp contrast and both are predominately speculative. As in *Night Rider,* the "world of fact" contrast is supplied in the dialogue and in the peripheral story. The ready spittle-punctuated realism of the common speech and its dialectal color comes through unpurged in Jeremiah's report, where it stands as the groundling commentary on the "high stage" performance of Jeremiah and his peers. Munn Short's story, like the earlier story of Willie Proudfit, adds the sustained note of earth-bred realism.

In all these voices, there is little repetition from book to book. No other writer of our time, with the possible exception of W. H. Auden, has exhibited such fluency and narrative ability in so many styles. Only Faulkner has approached his mastery of vernacular speech, and even Faulkner, whose highly personal flavor so permeates everything he writes, does not achieve the individualized authenticity or the wide variety of Warren's dialects.

Warren's ear is uncommonly acute, but his most valuable faculty is a shrewd and at the same time sympathetic ability to penetrate into the inner life of his characters. In the most caustic vignette offered through Jack Burden's squinted eyes, the pity of human wastage is never lost. Warren's sense of "irreducible evil" and of inborn human frailty permits an extremely wide range to a natural fund of sympathy which is completely devoid of sentimentality—ironic therefore in the I. A. Richards sense that it provides its own immunity to irony. The sympathy does have limits, marked at one end by a Bogan Murdock and at the other by a Carlos Bumps, the upper and lower cases of the dollar sign. But the humanism that can embrace the Senator Tollivers, the Lew Calhouns, the Sugar Boys, the Sadie Burkes, and the Percival Skroggs gives to the ideological and symbolic dialectic of the novels a compassionately moving concretion.

Warren's fifth novel, *Band of Angels* (1955), reflects the new thematic emphases which appeared first in *Brother to Dragons* and have dominated his work since, in particular the series of poems to his young daughter[5] and the cogent booklet on the segregation problem.[6] Both themes are evidently involved with important personal experience: freedom, which has

5. "To a Little Girl, one year old, in a ruined fortress," *Partisan Review*, XXII, 171-78.

6. "Divided South Searches its Soul," *Life*, XLI, July 9, 1956, pp. 98-99, 101-2, 105-6, 108, 111-12, 114.

seemed to Warren to require new definition in view of the recent Southern outbreaks over integration rulings; and joy, which his marriage to Eleanor Clark and the birth of a daughter has brought into new relief.

At the end of *Brother to Dragons*, Warren's self-image, "R. P. W.," made the crucial discovery: "The recognition of necessity is the beginning of freedom." But the actual achievement of freedom, *Band of Angels* demonstrates, is a complex process, involving recognition and acceptance of responsibility, of personal guilt, and of the true character and human limitations of the self. These are familiar concepts with Warren, both in his poetry and in his novels. What is new here are the form, the setting, and the protagonist.

The problem of freedom in *Band of Angels* is boldly embodied in the first-person life story of the beautiful half-breed daughter of a slave-holding Kentucky farmer. Lending depth and the dimensions of history to the personal story, the Civil War turmoils involving freeman-slave issues in and about New Orleans are re-created from multiple viewpoints as the susceptible Amantha is shifted about among contending parties and cultures. Since Amantha is largely a discontented product of events, history here not only supplies a counterpoint to the main action, as it does in Warren's other novels, but becomes a central actor. It is necessity, and it is the antithesis of the personal, the antagonist of freedom until Manty learns the true nature of emancipation.

As others of Warren's novels have explored the consequences of materialism, relativism, and other modern philosophies, this book explores determinism. Everything happens to an essentially irresponsible and reactive Amantha, and she remains essentially incapable of becoming more than events make her. To herself, she is only "poor little Manty" in her frequent moments of self-pity, and she feels an illusory "joy" whenever fortune treats her kindly. Like the doll which figures largely in the early childhood episodes, she is an object to be protected and loved or carelessly smashed as the whim of larger forces may dictate. When she does act on her own initiative, she is propelled by an instinctive or dream sense beyond conscious control.

Yet, despite her lack of "character," Manty is an effective creation. In her protected childhood, in her bewilderment at being suddenly cast out of a white world into a new status as a succulent object of trade, in her undefined position as slave-mistress in Hamish Bond's household, even in her white marriage, she remains sympathetic, a fully realized and in many ways quite modern figure. If she does not see her analyst once a week, it is only that analysts had not been invented in the 1860's. But she responds to her dilemmas like many an over-protected child of the twentieth century, hurt always by the unfair bruising of circumstance, crying back to her childhood security, acting on her own direction only in impulsive desperation.

Warren's problem in this novel was a difficult one at the outset. Lacking a protagonist and narrator of reflective intelligence—a *sine qua non* of Henry James generally, and of most of his followers in modern times—he is forced to imply his understandings through images and to sustain his interest through events and through subsidiary characters. Several major images suggesting freedom are made explicit on the first page of the novel. A reflective Amantha, who has finally achieved her "freedom," sets them out after propounding her life-long question of self-identification: "Oh, who am I?"

> The world is big and you feel lost in it, as though the bigness recedes forever, in all directions, like a desert of sand, and distance flees glimmering from you in all directions. Or the world is big, and the bigness grows tall and close, like walls coming together with a great weight and you will be crushed to nothingness.

Both of these images, of desert and of closing walls, are immediately associated with Manty's failure to achieve the emotional and intellectual freedom she constantly seeks through the body of the novel. Gradually, as they appear and reappear in her varied experience, these images assume symbolic proportions. When they reoccur, as at her sale into slavery, she becomes, as she has defined herself in retrospect, "nothing." In Hamish's lavish New Orleans home, in the shadowy bayous with Rau-Ru, in all escapes and confinements, these basic images alternate, until finally in a western Kansas setting involving both desert vastness and the constrictive image of small-town life, she is able to transcend the objective symbols of her slavery to things and events and find within herself and her relations the emancipation she has sought.

Supplementing these basic images are those of birds, flickering their wings in sun over water in apparent mockery of Manty's confinement, or, like the ducks over the Mississippi, being shot down for joyless diversion of unfeeling men, or flapping shadowy menacing wings over the night-filled bayous of the Negro retreat. Manty's hopes and fears of irresponsible flight from an oppressive world are figured in these unobtrusive but continuous images.

Manty's dream picture of innocence is, like Jefferson's in *Brother to Dragons*, a vision "of a grassy place, a place with sun, maybe water running and sparkling, or just still and bright." She recognizes the image as a memory of her childhood home at Starrwood, where she was pampered by her father, but ultimately betrayed. As she seeks return to womb-innocence and security from the contamination and compulsions of the world in which she is cast, this dream propels her. In the familiar Warren pattern, she is eventually freed only as she learns to accept the contamination of this image with her acceptance of her father's ultimately decent motives, with his weakness or human frailty.

All of these image patterns are heavily reinforced by a constant play on the black-white, day-night symbolism that projects Manty's ambiguous situation, a play handled with great variety and unforced complexity. In Manty's mind, of course, the black-slavery, white-freedom association predominates through the early sections. It is soon complicated with black-sensual, white-intellectualist ideal connotations. During the war period in New Orleans, the concepts of freed Negroes and bound white soldiers and politicians and businessmen add a new complexity. The snow-white and ice-cold Oberlin idealism which her husband Tobias finally epitomizes must in the end besmirch itself—and warm itself—with the black Negro garbage man realism of an Uncle Slop. The original black-white dichotomy which has dominated Manty's conscious life must undergo a mixing and merging process until it exhibits itself to her as the gray of the actual world, which is the color of her real self.

Symbolism, even when it achieves the control and flexibility which Warren has given it in this novel, cannot in itself produce important fiction, as many younger American novelists have by now unfortunately demonstrated. If character and event do not carry conviction, if the narrative does not provide a sustained propulsion for the reader, the author's cause is lost. Manty does, despite her radical lack of character, convince, as do our own images in a mirror. But, as I have indicated, her weakness demands a cast of supporting characters and a succession of events to sustain interest and to supplement the understanding and vitality which the symbolic development suggests.

Through the early sections, the Starrwood household relations and childhood incidents, school life at Oberlin, and the three-sided relations with the ambitious Miss Idell of pious memory provide ample textural interest. The Oberlin episodes, it must be admitted, suffer from the all but caricatured passionate asceticism of Seth Parton, who dominates them and lends them a somewhat distortedly glacial atmosphere. Later, with Manty's sale into slavery, first events, then the New Orleans scene, and finally the strong character of Hamish Bond take over the story, with Manty, despite an abortive suicide attempt, become largely a set of responses to new situations and sensations. Hamish is an eminently full creation, a forthright realist, possessed of "kindness like a disease," and ultimately, as he painfully discovers, empty; and the Micheles, Jimmees, and Dollies of his household support his central role brilliantly.

Once the War situation strikes New Orleans, Manty is battered about among her three men, realist Hamish, idealist Tobias, and primitive emotionalist Rau-Ru. A vividly portrayed background of military, political, and politico-social skirmishes supports and often determines the foreground action. Only when Manty escapes the turmoil with her ineffectual husband do the exigencies of ideological completeness begin to leave the narrative thin. Since neither Manty nor Tobias sustains a vital character interest, their wanderings, and even their final discovery of a real "joy" which cancels the "old shadows," remains flat and anticlimactic. The enlightenment which the novel seeks to produce, therefore, is considerably less effective than the conflicts which precede it and prepare for it. As a tragedy of mis-orientation on many levels, it succeeds fully, for the tensions among characters and within them and those between characters and the history in which they participate are solidly convincing in the large. The epilogue of rehabilitation, however, like that of Dostoevsky's *Crime and Punishment,* seems forced and gratuitous. Perhaps this is the inevitable fate of "resolved" fiction in an unresolved world. Logically we may accept the resolution, but humanly we cannot.

A final perspective on Warren as a novelist is, of course, impossible since he has reached only a late middle-point in his creative career. His achievement, however, is already very considerable; it is mature, serious, highly varied in its texture if not in its ideological patterns, prodigal of insights and of verbal felicities, brilliant in its descriptive evocations, rich in humor and in dialectical realism. He has weaknesses, and they are typically Fugitive weaknesses, stemming from the highly rational, abstractly philosophical leanings which determined the original orientation of the group. Throughout the novels, and despite the intention to allow the experiences themselves to project the patterns, there is a noticeable tendency toward the imposition of pattern. Warren's direct hold on life prevents him from being often betrayed, but the philosophic mind cannot but regard the pattern of meaning as vital, so that the temptation to impress, Procrustes fashion, is constant.

All the King's Men, in its attempt to deal with the whole range of modern philosophies, of false and pseudo, as well as unrecognized but real, heritages, suffers most from the forcing of event in the interest of prefixed framework. There are the strained father relationships at the end, where the accepted religious father becomes a no-father, then a sort of almost-father, the pragmatic realist father-surrogate a dead one, and the sinful but strongly principled father the real father, all to provide an acceptable heritage for enlightened modern man. But the manipulation of Anne Stanton is more damaging. When Anne gives herself to Willie Stark—we are not allowed to witness the process—our firmly built sense of Anne's fastidiousness is sharply violated. She must, in the interests of the pattern, commit herself to the world of fact, lose her primary innocence and destroy Jack's illusions about her; but humanly, we feel, she simply could not do it, at least not with the crude Willie.

Again, symbolic actions are introduced at times solely, it would seem, for their symbolic value. Several of Jeremiah's and Rachel's actions are of this nature, and the final severance of Jeremiah's head from his body is especially gratuitous in terms of the human narrative alone. (In the original Beauchamp history, the pair were buried "in a double coffin, with his right arm about her neck," a sentimentality which perhaps required alteration in view of Jerry's final insights.)

These tendencies, together with an occasional strain to lift image into symbol or to impose images for their symbolic value, must be cited, together with Warren's growing accent on the commentative element in the novels, as unfortunate movements toward over-abstraction. The compounding of points of view, each with its commentative function, in *World Enough and Time* weakens the human body of the story and sets us too far back from the human center, while it necessarily involves repetitions and undramatic contradictions or rejections by the several commentators. And again, the included stories, despite their oblique commentative value, their value as tonal contrasts, and their inherent excellences, are interruptions of the dramatic sequence, and therefore frequently read with some impatience.

These are all weaknesses, as I have said, stemming from the same overemphasis, and most of them may be seen in more acute form in Tate's *The Fathers*. But Warren's novels are effectively saved by the abundance of his vitality, in addition to his natural narrative and verbal talents. There is a great deal of "felt life" in all the books, and the occasional lapses of the too "philosophic novelist" never destroy the essential life they all contain.

CHAPTER XIV

Brooks and Warren, Critics

FOR A NUMBER of years now, Cleanth Brooks, Jr., has been regarded as the American exemplar of the "New Criticism." In so far as the movement is characterized by its emphasis on linguistic analysis, and in so far as it implies a strain of dogmatism, a "school" of criticism, Brooks's reputation is justly acquired. Certainly no other critic of an aesthetic formalist bias has exerted so much influence on younger men or on college programs (though Warren must be associated with much of the influence) and no other has been engaged in so many public skirmishes over his "approaches" and his readings of literary works.

Like the original Fugitives, Brooks began in college to write poetry under the influence of Ransom, but the magazine excitement had died by the time he became an upperclassman. A native of Kentucky like Tate and Warren, a Rhodes Scholar like Ransom and Warren, Brooks was to become a teacher like all the others, though more directly and immediately. He was already on the faculty at Louisiana State University when Warren joined him there in the highly fruitful collaboration that produced *The Southern Review* and the volumes on *Understanding Poetry* and *Understanding Fiction.*

From the beginning in *The Southern Review,* Brooks was the synthesizer, the applier, and, to a lesser extent, the extender of critical ideas and methods derived from Tate and other "new critics." All of this early work, which was to be collected in his volume *Modern Poetry and the Tradition* (1939), is valuable, and all but indispensable for comprehension of the ways and means of aesthetic formalist criticism. In the previous year, however, he had collaborated with Warren on a volume meant for use as a college textbook in literature courses, *Understanding Poetry*.

Warren, as we have noted, had already published a volume of poetry, and he had printed occasional critical articles on poetry following his return from Europe. Two pieces in particular should be noted, a 1932 contribution to the Southern issue of *Poetry* magazine,[1] and the 1935 critique of Ransom's poetry,[2] which has already been discussed. The earlier essay discusses John Gould Fletcher, Donald Davidson, and Ransom. Theoretically, Warren is preoccupied with the concept of irony, derived from Ransom and I. A. Richards.

"Davidson is not an ironist," he says, for there is "little of the acceptance or resolution ordinarily inherent in irony as a mode." This is clearly a Ransomic emphasis on the "stoic" attributes of the mature ironic mind. But a poet like Davidson who gives the "effect . . . of shock and desperation" clearly cannot be immune from ironic contemplation, the condition which Richards defines as ironic. Warren finds the "source of Ransom's irony" in his sense of the modern "disruption of sensibility," which he projects in fables, never solving the problems, but attempting to "work out a sort of equilibrium."

In the discussion of Fletcher's poetry, Warren implies a Ransomic disagreement with Eliot's emphasis on the emotion and its "objective correlative." Fletcher attempted, he says, to "abstract the emotional from logical composition. The attempt . . . is to give the *structure,* not merely random suggestions, of the emotion." But he is defeated by his "allusive method," by the distractions of his imagery. He writes, therefore, a verse of almost pure texture, as Ransom would later put it. Eliot, in the same predicament, is saved by "a certain historical sense," manifested in "Mr. Eliot's irony of historical basis, the juxtaposition of a degenerate present with the noble

1. "A Note on Three Southern Poets," *Poetry,* XL, 103-113.

2. "John Crowe Ransom: A Study in Irony," *Virginia Quarterly Review,* II, 93-112.

past." This description is hardly adequate for Eliot's method, but it is interesting in its attempt to reconcile the divergent views of Ransom and Tate on Eliot's poetry.

Warren's insistence on the centrality of irony, an insistence which we must feel that Brooks already shared, dominates *Understanding Poetry*. However, the emphases of all the leading aesthetic formalist critics are represented in this volume. If any one influence can be said to be preferred, it would have to be that of Allen Tate. The consistent focus for the authors is the whole poem, seen as a self-sufficient entity—not as a combination of elements, but as an organic thing in which every element is integral. There are no "beauties" which are not aspects of the total effects of the poems analyzed, no ideas apart from their dramatization in terms of all other factors present (unless, indeed, the poem is being overtly or covertly condemned). The individual exegeses of poems, however, though many of them are brilliant and all provocative, do not constitute the permanent value of the book; the vital contribution is one of focus and of techniques for analysis and appreciation. For the first time in textbook history, a valid objective method for introducing poetry to the common reader was offered in this book, and its effect on teaching faculties and on subsequent writers of poetry texts was immense. The poems were not destroyed, as some critics claimed, by the attention given to minute detail, nor were they converted into substitutes for actual living by the stress placed on their revelations or insights. Furthermore, the book was not theory-ridden at the expense of the poems themselves. The authors distinguished clearly between poetry and scientific statement on the one hand, and between poetry and life on the other, without setting up dogmatic definitions about the essence or function of poetry in general. Its examples were varied, illustrative, and often definitive; finally, it did not evade the problem of judgment among bad, mediocre, and good poetry.

If *Understanding Poetry* seems now to have defects, they

are to be discovered chiefly in the Empsonian vice of over-reading. The commentators occasionally succumb to the temptation of reading, not only paradoxes and ironies, but other subtleties into the poems. As Ransom and others have noted, the discussion of the metrics of Yeats's "After Long Silence" is a particularly flagrant example. Though the editors discount the poet's intention and attend only, they say, to what is actually there, they find such an elaboration of special effects as to turn the poem into a fiendishly contrived exercise to baffle students. This fault, however, is rare; and the editors disclaim any dogmatic validity for their readings.

Brooks's volume of the next year, *Modern Poetry and the Tradition,* performed the much-needed service of reducing aesthetic formalism to a semblance of order. Brooks admits indebtedness in his preface to "Eliot, Tate, Empson, Yeats, Ransom, Blackmur, Richards, and other critics," of whom only Yeats cannot easily be fitted into the formalist category. He says furthermore that "such credit as I may legitimately claim, I must claim primarily on the grounds of having possibly made a successful synthesis of other men's ideas rather than on the originality of my own." This is candid and true; it modestly neglects, however, the original contributions, particularly in the studies of Yeats and Eliot. These two studies, both of which appeared in *The Southern Review,* are intelligent and perceptive. Furthermore, they are scholarly beyond anything that Ransom or Tate has written. In both cases, Brooks's interest has been in the explication of the poetry in terms of ideas and symbols, and he has performed a considerable service in each case. These essays, with their necessary concentration on special phases of the poets' work, do not advance particularly the theories insisted upon in the early chapters; but it is a little irritating to find Brooks apologizing for approaching a poem "frankly on the basis of theme," "in view of the state of criticism." "It may well be," he says of *The Waste Land,* that there is a "scaffolding to be got out of the way before we contemplate the poem as poem." This scaffolding is "an explicit intellectual account of the various symbols and a logical account of their relationship." This critic's formulation cannot be got out of the way, of course; it was never there. What Brooks must mean is that the basic intellectual and symbolic structure must be removed—which is ridiculous. The point illustrates the danger to which Brooks, of all the Fugitive critics, is most liable: that of being tyrannized by theory (the scandal of attending to a poem's structure!) and even by words.[3] Fortunately, the essay pays close attention to its business, and the result is enlightenment.

One of the features of *Modern Poetry and the Tradition* is the long section devoted to the Fugitive poets, Ransom, Tate, and Warren. As one would expect, the discussions in these cases are entirely laudatory. The poets are shown to illustrate the theses advanced in the theoretical chapters, and they are tailored exactly to measure. Yet the three are individual enough to exhibit somewhat different modes of irony and various types of paradox. As far as they go, the discussions are valuable, and authoritative, one supposes, of the poets' intentions. The implication, however, that the Fugitives represent the norm of good poetry in our era could be questioned by a number of excellent critics. By the standards of the book, in fact, it is difficult to see why Ransom, Warren, and Tate are not absolutely great lyricists, for in every theoretic particular they meet the requirements in an absolute manner. In a subsequent chapter, Frost, MacLeish, and Auden are measured against the same standards and found deficient in one or more respects; still later, practically every poet between Milton and Yeats is shown similarly deficient. Brooks's "Notes for a Revised History of English Literature," the final essay in the book, illustrates the usefulness and the limitations of the standards.

3. Brooks's subtitle, "A Critique of the Myth," is an instance of word tyranny. The logical subtitle would be something like "An Exposition of Themes and Symbols." "Myth" was already a highly charged word, and "critique" is a rather elegant inaccuracy, as it is applied to the "myth."

The essay ignores every other factor in English literary history except the rise of science, and the resultant "dissociation of sensibility"; but the concept produces analyses of considerable interest and weight. Many of the judgments derive, as does the theory, from Eliot, Ransom, and others; but Brooks makes applications of his own, especially in regard to Thomas Hobbes, the villain of the piece—Ransom had suggested him in this light[4]—and to certain eighteenth-century figures.

The theoretical synthesis which Brooks produces in the early chapters of this book owes much to Ransom, Tate, and Richards, but most perhaps to Eliot. Like Ransom, Brooks is chiefly concerned that poetry express the full complexity of experience, a complexity which necessarily involves the ironic (Richards' self-critical) view. He makes Ransom's distinction between the abstraction of science and the concrete of poetry, adding Tate's condemnation of allegory. From Eliot, he takes his view of the dramatic element in lyric verse, insisting that only in so far as the poem represents a dramatic conflict of attitudes does it escape oversimplification and falsity of representation. The poem partakes, too, of the objectivity and impersonality (Eliot's word) of drama. Like Eliot, also, he stresses "wit": he is tempted to say that "wit is the most serious aspect of the mind." Wit may take the form of the conceit, the pun, ambiguity, or the "yoking by violence together" of the frivolous or bawdy and the intensely serious. These are dramatic devices for Brooks, used to intensify the poetic expression, and their justification is Ransom's: that they "represent [the] sort of mingling" present in "nearly all mature attitudes." Brooks restates the conception of the poet as craftsman, crediting both Eliot and Tate. More importantly, from Eliot originally comes the doctrine that differentiates sharply between the whole poem and its component elements, and insists upon the unique quality of the poetic experience.

Brooks generally avoids the excesses of his originals (Ran-

4. Brooks credits him earlier, p. 52.

som's *mimesis* and "poetry as knowledge," Eliot's emphasis on emotion and its objective correlative) largely by staying clear of the philosophic aspects of his subject. Specifically, he makes no attempt to define the exact nature of the poetic experience or its value. He lets Ransom, Tate, Richards, Eliot, and Kenneth Burke speak for themselves, emphasizing in his own right only what he calls "a complete liberation of the imagination" as characterizing the modern "critical revolution" in poetry. The liberation is from a poetry of ideas, "Platonic" or "exclusive," according to the several formulations. Brooks's summary is essentially negative; it speaks of what poetry is not. What it is, is simply inclusive. There are no absolutes, no ontologies, no religions in Brooks's theoretical statements. There is, however, in Richards' term "myth," which, "not scientifically true, and yet though a fiction, though a symbolic representation, intermeshes with reality. It is imaginatively true, and if most people will take this to mean that it is after all trivial, this merely shows in what respect our age holds the imagination." "Intermesh" is a more cautious word than Ransom, or later Tate, would employ; and it establishes no sort of ontological validity for the myth or for the poetry.

Brooks, unlike Ransom, discounts "logical unity" in poetry, as not a value in itself "unless we value the poem as science or as exhortation to a practical purpose"; and admits only what he calls "imaginative unity," a concept never clearly defined. "Surely a fairer test [than logic]," he says, ". . . is to measure the scope and breadth of experience which . . . poetry assimilates." This extensive test seems an unfortunate substitute for Eliot's (and, for that matter, Dewey's) intensive one, though Brooks would certainly admit the "pressure" of artistic fusion as a valid criterion. The motivation of Brooks's extensive test is clearly his desire to place a premium on the "metaphysical" fusion of incongruous experience, which is Warren's "impure." However, if the accent is placed upon the "breadth," rather than upon the fusion, a Whitman is likely to loom too large for Brooks's taste.

Ultimately, the value of *Modern Poetry and the Tradition* is an academic value, despite an animus which scarcely permits an academic detachment. The Yeats and Eliot essays are the results of careful research and correlation, as well as close textual analysis. Their importance is for the interpretation of the works, and is therefore independent of theory. Similarly, the formulation and illustration of "new critical" doctrine represents a scholarly achievement. By correlating the theories of the leading formalist critics, ignoring their philosophical extremes and scaling down their special emphases, Brooks has performed an intellectual service dependent for its value, not on originality, but on organizational and synthesizing abilities. These are valuable qualities, and they have made *Modern Poetry and the Tradition* the most satisfactory single statement of aesthetic formalist critical doctrine thus far produced.

Cleanth Brooks's second critical volume was not published until 1947. Much of the preliminary work, however, as Brooks says, was done in 1942 and thereafter. The book belongs in the immediate line, not only of *Modern Poetry and the Tradition,* but of Ransom's and Tate's volumes of the same decade. Theoretically, no new concepts are developed in *The Well Wrought Urn,* but the last chapters show the author trying to reach a synthesis of the new positions to which Richards, Tate, and others have arrived. The point of view generally is that of his earlier volume; the obvious departure centers on the attempt to include under the earlier definition of good poetry individual poems from all the major periods of English literature, from Shakespeare and Milton through Herrick, Pope, Gray, Wordsworth, Keats, and Tennyson, to Yeats. All the selected poems are carefully analyzed in terms of "irony," "paradox," "ambiguity," and "dramatic context," and shown to possess "organic structure."

Brooks dedicates this book to a university class which aided with some of the analyses, and one must confess that the illusion of pedagogic exercise carries over into the body of the text. The difficulty seems to center in a general impression that the poems treated were selected on the single principle that they fit, or could fit, certain a priori rules laid down in *Modern Poetry and the Tradition.* It would be unfair to Brooks to suggest that his chief interest in the poems lay in their relation to his theoretical standards, but the effect of the analyses is to give precisely that impression. The total impact of nine close exegeses of very different poems, all ending in similar discoveries, phrased in the same vocabulary, is somewhat overpowering.

The chronological plan of the book, unfortunately, I think, demanded that the *Macbeth* essay appear first. The evidences of strain to fit a preconceived formula are most noticeable in this attempt to reduce a full-bodied tragedy to a paradox. Brooks rightly emphasizes two persistent images in the play, the babe and the robes, both used symbolically at moments; and he makes some excellent interpretations of their use in certain passages, some strained ones, and at least one, I believe, completely mistaken. But to assume, as Brooks does, that the paradoxical use of the two images constitutes the heart of the play is to ignore the heavily underscored theme of fatality. Macbeth's fatal susceptibility to urging against his nature must be distorted, in the interests of anti-positivistic theory, one supposes, into "the over-brittle rationalism on which Macbeth founds his career." Similar evidences of strain appear along with valuable insights throughout the remaining analyses. In general, the earlier poets, Milton, Herrick, and Pope, are better handled than Wordsworth (in whom the paradox is taken largely as unconscious on the poet's part), Keats, and Tennyson (who commonly "fought his doubts," instead of using them "as enriching ambiguities in his poems"). Yeats's "Among

School Children," as we should expect, receives perceptive, if not quite definitive, treatment.

The chief interest of *The Well Wrought Urn* does not appear until the final essays of refutation and theoretical extension. "The Language of Paradox," which opens the book, restates Brooks's familiar thesis that "apparently the truth which the poet utters can be approached only in terms of paradox," and finds illustrations in romantic as well as in metaphysical poems. A later chapter, "The Heresy of Paraphrase," attempts, by accenting the structural unity of the analyzed poems, to demonstrate the total inadequacy of reproducing in a prose paraphrase their "achieved harmony." For the most part, he is here laboring a very dead horse, since those who still believe, after a quarter of a century of "organic" criticism, that the prose paraphrase equals the poem must be a desperately small minority among Brooks's readers. When he accuses Mr. Yvor Winters, however, of the "paraphrastic heresy" because he "assigns primacy to the 'rational meaning' of the poem," he is exaggerating an opponent's position with the recklessness of Winters himself.

The new feature in this essay, to be expanded in the later chapters, is Brooks's attempt to define his "unity of structure." Brooks will not tolerate Ransom's dualism. "The characteristic unity of a poem," he says, "(even of those poems which may accidentally possess a logical unity as well as this unity) lies in the unification of attitudes into a hierarchy subordinated to a total and governing attitude." I believe that Miss Rosemund Tuve has pretty well proved that the pervasive influence of the logical system introduced into England by Ramus about 1570 led Elizabethan and early seventeenth-century poets to employ logic in anything but an accidental manner.[5] Miss Tuve cites Donne in particular as an instance, and Donne is admittedly a norm of the poetry Brooks is describing.

5. Rosemund Tuve, "Imagery and Logic," *Journal of the History of Ideas*, III, 365-400.

The important word for Brooks is "attitude." He evidently wishes to go beyond Eliot's hierarchy of feelings and emotions to include an intellectual element, but the tone of the word Brooks has chosen is essentially affective, "more the product of temperament or of emotion than of thought or conviction." Brooks's bête noire is logic, as Ransom's is emotion, so that each tends to slip over into one of the opposing "heresies" against which the other inveighs. However, Brooks is not content to rest in an attitude. The structure of a poem may be unified by an attitude, but the attitude must represent something more important than a response to an experience. It must represent something in one sense or another "true." So Brooks tackles the philosophic question which has occupied Ransom, Tate, Richards, Morris, and others. Does poetry give us a "complete knowledge," an "ontology"? Is it cognition or "pseudo-statement"?

Brooks has said that his test for poetry enables us "to set up our hierarchy in terms of the organizations of the poems themselves—not by having to appeal to some outside scale of values." The test is strictly internal, involving only "the variety and clash among the elements to be comprehended under a total attitude." However, to establish the validity of poetry itself, one *must* appeal to some outside reference. This repeats Tate's dilemma exactly. The referent for Brooks cannot be that of science, nor that of metaphysics. It can only be Richards'—and Tate's—which is termed "mythic," or, now, Mr. W. B. Urban's, which is "symbolic." Brooks summarizes and quotes Urban:

> The test of "good poetry" is evidently that of "authentication": "We constantly speak of 'good' symbols and, what is even more to the point here, of 'authentic' symbols. By such expressions we always mean that the symbol expresses adequately for our type of consciousness that which could not be fully expressed in 'literal' sentences."

A more subjective test could hardly be proposed, since it depends not only on "our type of consciousness," but also on our sense of "adequacy."

A further quotation from Urban says: " 'Truth, then, is always a function of expression, and the relation between an expression and that which is expressed can only be one of adequacy.' " This is perfectly true as far as it goes, and it enables Brooks to use the "expression" as his sole test for "truth." But adequacy tests only the relational truth, and the expressions of science have at least an equal adequacy in expressing what they wish to express. Since we are not to be concerned with the "what" expressed, Urban, and Brooks here, allow us no means of distinguishing triviality from importance. The expression may be symbolic, as the only adequate means of communicating the poetic experience, but our evaluation must depend on more than the adequacy of the symbols to express it. And necessarily standards external to the expression must be concerned in the evaluation. Unlike the other Fugitive critics, who by 1947 have given up strictly internal standards, Brooks sticks to linguistic concepts; but, as his quotations from Richards and Tate show, he has progressed essentially no farther than the point the others had reached at least five years earlier.

Brooks spends several pages criticizing Ransom's accent on logical coherence. Ransom's much-discussed essay from *The World's Body* on "Shakespeare at Sonnets" compares Shakespeare unfavorably with Donne and Spenser, because his figures do not "work out" in logical fashion. Brooks is able to show that Donne very frequently uses the same technique. He insists, therefore, that the unity in both cases is not logical, but one of "tone." "Or," he asks rhetorically, "does [a poem] find its coherence in a complex of attitudes dramatically related to each other?" The answer probably goes back to Ramus, for Ramus's logic demanded precisely the type of "rapidly shifting" figures which Brooks describes in both Donne and Shakespeare. Says Miss Tuve: "The conceit is sometimes based on one of the more tenuous logical links, but characteristically *is based on multiple parallels,* frequently in three or four predicaments simultaneously."[6] Both Donne and Shakespeare seem rather to be following the logical practice taught in the schools than to be aiming at a unity of tone through a complex of attitudes.

Brooks's objections to Ransom are more valid when he refers to the analyses of dramatic speeches, though even here the governing factor seems to be logical method. However, it is a great deal easier to account for a "ragged and spotty . . . analogical argument" by reference to a dramatic situation in which *non sequiturs* are to be expected than to allow them on the part of a poet speaking in his own right. Brooks is certainly correct in emphasizing, as Ransom does not, the essentially dramatic character of many, if not as he would have it all, good lyric poems. The difficulty lies in Brooks's insistence that the drama is only attitudinal.

The organization of the poem, in this view, must be in terms of what Kenneth Burke, and Winters after him, has called "qualitative progression," and what Eliot has spoken of as the "logic of the imagination," or of the "images." Brooks himself shows that the progression in Donne's "Valediction: forbidding mourning" is "associational ultimately," and Eliot, by making a comparison with Joyce's *Finnegans Wake,* implies the same sort of organization. Any such concept, whether we accept "associational," "qualitative," or "imaginative" as the descriptive focus, takes us again out of the realm of objective criticism. We can only *feel* that the progression on these terms is valid. As Winters says of Eliot's "logic of the imagination": "If it is neither formulated nor formulable (and he admits that it is not formulated), the word *logic* is used figuratively . . . the figure is one which it is hard to pardon a professed classicist."[7] This is Brooks's predicament exactly.

Cleanth Brooks has continued into the 1950's a very active scholar and interpreter of poetry. Though he has published

6. *Ibid.*, p. 377.

7. Yvor Winters, *In Defense of Reason*, p. 62.

nothing to date since 1951, he has been reported hard at work on a new volume in collaboration with Richard Wimsatt at Yale, where Brooks has been teaching for the past nine years.

Brooks's chief recent preoccupation has been with the poetry of John Milton, and his latest collaborative volume intensively re-examines the nonepic and nondramatic poetry of the great Puritan whom "new critics," under the impetus of Eliot's early attack, once rudely pulled down from his high place in literary history. It should be noted, however, that Brooks was not one who joined the hue and cry. As early as his "Notes for a Revised History of English Poetry," published in *Modern Poetry and the Tradition,* he noted Milton's "continual and energetic word play." This emphasis on verbal texture and controlled imagery dominates the discussions in the 1951 volume, *The Poems of Mr. John Milton,* edited with analytic essays and appendices by Brooks and John Edward Hardy, once a student of his present collaborator at Louisiana State University.

This book reveals the complete synthesis of the scholar and formalist critic in Brooks for the first time. Though the major essays on individual poems are couched in the familiar language of "paradox," "irony," and "ambiguity," and though they stress "reading narrowly and precisely," the editors explicitly employ all the resources of historical scholarship. Appendix A, on reading the longer poems, defines the new synthetic approach. The essay allows that the reader "can hardly have too much" of scholarly annotation, but insists also that such information "*may* be stressed at the expense of the reader's participation in the poetry," and that it "*in itself* does not deal with the poetry" (Brooks's italics). However, the editors do constantly employ such resources as *NED* and stress Milton's meanings in their historical context, supporting the interpretations from evidences of contemporary notions and usage. In addition, there are distinctly non-formalist discussions of sources and influences operating on the poetry through Milton's extensive study of earlier poets.

The major insights of this volume—its chief value is to be found in the textural analyses of language and image and their coherence in structure—are concerned with "aesthetic distance," which Ransom once stressed in his essay on "Lycidas,"[8] and the relation of that strategy to the pastoral and epic modes which Milton so favored. The editors credit William Empson for his observation of "the typical ambivalence of attitude characteristic of the pastoral," and they emphasize the pastoral poet's projection of "his problems and themes onto a simpler scene—e.g., that of the shepherd's life—" with the advantage of a "special perspective" thus gained. Brooks and Hardy extend this conception to the epic, which is related to pastoral as major to minor mode of projection, and therefore find that "Milton's progression from pastoral poetry to epic poetry is a perfectly natural one."

Milton scholars must perforce cavil at many of the readings of Milton included in the individual analyses of poems that precede the larger essays, but the total effect of this book must certainly be flattering to their preoccupation. For Milton emerges from these pages a much more complex, subtle, and exciting artist than the Miltonians have generally proved him. Brooks and his colleague have done a service which no scholar can discredit and which modern critics must hail as a further vindication of their methods.

In 1951 Brooks produced two other Milton articles[9] which extend the scholarly and interpretive aspects of the book, one attempting to establish Milton's relation to Donne, and the other examining Milton's reputation as established by a succession of critical reappraisals. Brooks's third 1951 essay[10] is a,

8. In *The World's Body*, pp. 1-28.

9. "Milton and the New Criticism," *Sewanee Review*, LIX, 1-22; and "Milton and Critical Re-estimates," *PMLA*, LXVI, 1045-54.

10. "*Absalom, Absalom*: The Definition of Innocence," *Sewanee Review*, LIX, 543-58.

for him, rare excursion into criticism of fiction. This reappraisal of Faulkner's *Absalom, Absalom*, "in my opinion the greatest of Faulkner's novels," begins as refutation of Harvey Breit's Introduction to the new Modern Library edition and ends with generalizations which tend to explain why Northern-bred critics tend to misinterpret not only Faulkner but Southern novelists as a group. The explanation lies in an awareness of tragedy which Southerners possess by inheritance and a conception of man which "can be subsumed under the old terms of original sin, grace, and expiation." Lack of this awareness brings on Sutpen's tragedy, which he cannot understand, and a similar lack in modern industrially conditioned man leads him to misunderstand the novelist. What the critic fundamentally misses in *Absalom, Absalom* is the nature of the tragic innocence which Sutpen embodies, Brooks finds. And it is perhaps inevitable that he should. For Sutpen's faith in a "design," and courage and shrewdness to fill it out, is the typical belief of modern man, and therefore a largely unquestioned assumption with which he starts. Brooks finds that "Southern novelists of our time have been fascinated by this kind of character and the destruction that he brings," and he cites Warren's Bogan Murdock and Tate's George Posey.

This essay marks one of the few occasions when Brooks has generalized on a set of conceptions which are peculiarly Southern and most particularly Fugitive. Brooks has never advertized his beliefs, since his critical stance has insisted primarily on objective reading and interpretation, on finding what is there in the work. Here, finally, he departs from impersonal analysis long enough to assure us that he is, and has been for long, a committed Fugitive.

Robert Penn Warren becomes an important critic shortly after the demise of *The Southern Review* and his transfer to the University of Minnesota as chairman of the creative writing program. Unlike Ransom, however, he does not immediately shed his aesthetic formalist and modernist prepossessions, nor his concern with tradition and the South. In the main, his critical affinities are closest to those of Eliot; but his chief contributions to criticism have been his independent analyses of modern fiction. More scholarly than Tate, and generally broader in his critical outlook than Brooks, he employs the terminology of aesthetic formalism without allowing it to limit the range of his investigations. By nature, Warren appears to have strong idealistic proclivities, but they are always under the control of a harsh, sometimes bitter, critical spirit. His ideal constructions are plunged into a bath of cold reality, to emerge tempered or completely destroyed—the process followed in his own novels and poetry.

This is substantially what Warren describes in his 1943 essay on "Pure and Impure Poetry."[11] The "pure poem," he tells us, "tries to be pure by excluding, more or less rigidly, certain elements which might qualify or contradict its original impulses." Its merit is simplicity, direct effect, and immediate appeal to the emotions. But the simplicity and effectiveness is achieved only at the cost of excluding whole areas of human experience. In contrast, "impure poetry" submits its original impulse to the full range of the poet's experience. Here, "the poet wishes to indicate that his vision has been earned, that it can survive reference to the complexities and contradictions of experience. And irony is one such device of reference." This account of "impure poetry" coincides with the description and analysis of Warren's own work given by Brooks in *Modern Poetry and the Tradition.* Such a poetry, it should be noted, does not exclude the introduction of abstract statements into poems. The statements, however, are justified only if they have been "earned" by the referential process which Warren describes. As a logical corollary to this doctrine, "impure" poems may include any material, any effects. Warren lists ten characteristics which have been considered undesirable in poetry,

11. *Kenyon Review,* V, 229-54.

including the disagreeable, the "realistic," the complicated, irony, cacophany, ideas. All of these are not only admissible, but often desirable in the interests of a broader inclusiveness of reference.

There is nothing in this article to indicate that Warren has departed in any way from *The Southern Review* positions he held in common with Brooks. His "impure" is equivalent in almost every respect to Brooks's "metaphysical": he implies the same extensive test for poetry that Brooks formulated for *Modern Poetry and the Tradition*, and under the same compulsion.

Warren's examination of modern American prose writers begins in 1944 with an examination of the stories of Eudora Welty.[12] In this, as in the later studies of Faulkner, Hemingway, and Conrad, Warren is concerned to discover by analysis of the works the nature of the fundamental insight or reading of life which the author exhibits. His concentration, therefore, is, like that of Brooks in his Yeats and Eliot essays, on theme, and the devices, symbols, and methods used to present and enforce the theme. He explains that "we do not get any considerable emotional impact unless we sense, at the same time, some principle of organization, some view, some meaning." Increasingly, this is to be Warren's accent, and it is to lead him to reject the strictly internal standards which have been the distinguishing feature of aesthetic formalism.

In 1946 Warren wrote a long, heavily annotated commentary for an illustrated edition of *The Rime of the Ancient Mariner*.[13] "My first purpose in this paper," the critic says, "is to establish that the *Ancient Mariner* does make a statement." Soon he adds:

> I shall try to establish that the statement which the poem does ultimately make is thoroughly consistent with Coleridge's basic theologi-

12. "The Love and Separateness in Miss Welty," *Kenyon Review*, VI, 246-59.
13. S. T. Coleridge, *The Rime of the Ancient Mariner* (New York: Reynal and Hitchcock, 1946), introductory essay.

cal and philosophical views as given to us in sober prose, and that, without regard to the question of the degree of self-consciousness on the part of the poet at any given moment of composition, the theme is therefore "intended."

Warren has set himself in these opening pages against the impressionistic and romantic criticism which would protect the poem against any rational account of its "meaning." He does not desert his own earlier critical methods, but he broadens the territory from which he draws his evidence. His first criterion remains "internal consistency," but the application "cannot be made in a vacuum." The critic must regard "external consistency" as well: "in regard to the intellectual, the spiritual climate of the age in which the poem was composed"; "in regard to the over-all pattern of other artistic work by the author in question"; "in regard to the thought of the author available from non-artistic sources"; and finally, "in regard to the facts of the author's life." These sources are not, of course, to be applied mechanically, but "as factors of control in interpretation."

This essay is, in many ways, an academic piece, and Warren seems to be placating scholarly colleagues of all the traditional types. The display of learning and research data in the copious notes sets this volume apart among Fugitive publications. However, the basic interpretive argument betrays a typical Fugitive point of view. Warren, more obsessively than Ransom or any other of the Fugitives with the possible exception of Andrew Lytle, has been concerned with the evil propensities rooted in human nature. His fiction and his poetry have constantly emphasized a version of original sin which owes more perhaps to secular philosophy than to Augustine or Calvin. In Coleridge, as in Faulkner later, he reads the narrative as an instance of "a contamination implicit in the human condition," from which the individual can manage only a limited redemption.

But the excursion into Coleridge's thought leads Warren into new theoretical depths. Often it becomes impossible to separate the positions of the critic from those of the subject. In elucidating Coleridge's view of symbols, he says that "a symbol implies a body of ideas which may be said to be fused in it. This means that the symbol itself may be developed into a discursive sequence as we intellectually explore its potential." Then he puts the whole matter into what are apparently his own terms: "a symbol may be a condensation of several themes and not a sign for one"; the true symbol is distinguished from the simple allegorical one in that it "is not arbitrary. . . . A symbol may avoid being arbitrary in two ways: by necessity and by congruence." The symbol of necessity "is rooted in our universal natural experience"—and he cites all "phallic symbols" in this class. The symbol of congruence "does not come to us bearing within itself the reason for its appeal to us but is validated by the manipulation of the artist in a special context" —and he cites Yeats's "Byzantium."

Warren is evidently attempting here to keep his discussion of symbols on a rational, objective plane. In the main, as his notes indicate, he is following Mrs. Suzanne Langer's *Philosophy in a New Key*, a book on which Brooks has remarked: "I am not sure that her . . . general position on the function of literary meaning is not somewhat reminiscent of the earlier Richards [i.e., tainted with scientism] and open to the same objections."[14] Warren's note quotes Mrs. Langer:

> "The material of poetry is discursive, but the product—the artistic phenomenon—is not; its significance is purely implicit in the poem as a totality, as a form compounded of sound and suggestion, statement and reticence, and no translation can reincarnate that . . . . An artistic symbol . . . has more than discursive or presentational meaning."

Mrs. Langer escapes the "heresy of paraphrase," while she keeps her concepts in the realm of rational inquiry.

Warren, however, by way of further quotation, both in the

14. *The Well Wrought Urn*, p. 233.

text and in the notes, from C. S. Lewis and from Blake, soon involves himself in transcendental idealism. Before he is through, he is saying in his own right: "If poetry does anything for us, it reconciles, by its symbolic reading of experience (for by its nature it is in itself a myth of the unity of being) the internecine malices which arise at the superficial level on which we conduct most of our living." The parenthesis here seems to echo the quotation from Lewis, which Warren has used in evident assent: "'. . . it is possible that our material world . . . is the copy of an invisible world. . . .'" Having failed to find confirmation of such a view in Warren's other published work, I can only conclude that he has so far absorbed himself in Coleridge's doctrines as to suffer a temporary loss of identity. (I. A. Richards, it seems to me, tends toward a similar confusion in his *Coleridge on Imagination.*)

Warren offers an account of the creative process in this essay in terms again liable to a transcendental construction. He stresses the poem as "discovery." The poet begins with an idea or an image, a "kernel" of some sort "which has, for the poet, a suggestive quality," a "symbolic potential." He proceeds to explore this potential "in the light of his total being and his total experience." This is an act of discovery, for it involves bringing to focus previously buried or unconscious material, though "the degree of self-consciousness may vary from instance to instance." Then Warren continues: "As Coleridge said, and as many other poets and even scientists have said, the unconscious may be the genius in the man of genius." He hastens to add:

> . . . this is not to define the process as an irrational process. What comes unbidden from the depths at the moment of creation may be the result of the most conscious and narrowly rational effort in the past. In any case, the poet retains the right of rejecting whatever seems to violate his nature and his developing concept of the poem.

All the Fugitive critics are alert to disclaim any critical

dictum which smacks of the irrational, though their anti-positivistic bias is constantly forcing them in that direction. To escape the charge here, Warren's basic reliance must be on a Freudian interpretation of the unconscious, not on Coleridge's or Lewis', or even on Jung's "archetypal images." The earlier reference to "universal natural experience" may imply either Jung or Freud, but the illustration by means of "phallic symbols" seems a deliberate Freudian recall. The attempt here as elsewhere, I think, is to skirt the irrational as closely as possible while keeping one foot, at least, in objective rationality. As we have seen, this is the predicament into which all the Fugitives, together with Richards and others, are driven.

Warren's later essays, on Faulkner and Hemingway, are certainly the most penetrating written in their era on either author. They continue certain lines of emphasis from the Coleridge study, without the academic flavor, and finally develop an account of the literary and general intellectual situation from the time of Wordsworth and Coleridge. The stress in the Faulkner piece[15] is again on "a kind of Original Sin"; on violation of nature, floral, animal, and human, with the inevitable punishment, as it was meted out to the Mariner; and on the modern predicament as opposed to traditional order. The Hemingway article[16] develops the predicament itself and reaches back into intellectual history to trace its stages. Though Warren is generally applying the familiar Fugitive doctrines of scientism versus the religious attitude, and though he, like the others, is animated by a bitter opposition to the "Iron ring of mechanism" which squeezes about our daily lives, his acceptance of the situation sounds with a flat finality not paralleled in any of his Fugitive colleagues. His is a Calvinism without an elect, and man can hope to achieve only a little dignity. Speaking of Hemingway's picture of the damned generation, he says that "in a world without supernatural sanctions, in the God-abandoned world of modernity, man can realize an ideal meaning

15. "Cowley's Faulkner," *New Republic*, CXV, 176-80, 234-37.
16. "Hemingway," *Kenyon Review*, IX, 1-28.

only in so far as he can define and maintain the code." Then: "We know where the literary men got this picture. They got it from the scientists of the 19th Century."

Warren discovers a "similarity between Wordsworth and Hemingway on the ground of a romantic anti-intellectualism." Following Wordsworth, the area of possible faiths, of institutions in which one could believe, continued to narrow under the constant hammering of scientific iconoclasts. By the time of Hardy, little remained except a still habitual and ill-founded "meliorism." For Hemingway, there is "only a little secret community of, paradoxically enough, individualists who have resigned from the general community, and who are strong enough to live without any illusions, lies, and big words of the herd." So Hemingway's important symbols are "the sleepless man . . . who hungers for the certainties and meaningfulness of the religious faith," and "the violent man trying to find human values in a naturalistic world."

Faulkner's reading of modern life is much the same, as Warren sees it, though it is set against the background of a decayed Southern tradition. Warren has fewer illusions about traditions in general, and about that of the Old South in particular, than the other Fugitives, though he stresses the values Tate, Ransom, and Davidson have discussed. He finds:

> . . . the old order did not satisfy human needs—the Southern old order or any other—for it, not being founded upon justice, was "accursed" and held the seeds of its own ruin in itself. But . . . the old order . . . allowed the traditional man to define himself as human by setting up codes, concepts of virtue, obligations, and by accepting the risks of his humanity. Within the traditional order was a notion of truth, even if man in the flow of things did not succeed in realizing that truth.

Warren's own historically based novels are proof enough that he takes his qualification quite seriously.

For understanding those novels, both in terms of their dominant themes and in terms of their technical methods, Warren's 1951 essay on Conrad's *Nostromo*[17] is his most valuable

17. "Nostromo," *Sewanee Review*, LIX, 364-91.

piece of critical writing. As a critique of Conrad and the novel it takes as Conrad's central masterpiece, it is both scholarly and highly perceptive, and, as such, it admirably fulfills its function as the introduction to the Modern Library edition of *Nostromo*. Much of its persuasiveness, however, derives from the fact that Warren is writing about his own themes and methods as he discovers them in Conrad. This statement applies to a considerable extent, as we have seen, to the Hemingway and Faulkner essays, but the parallel, particularly in the technical dimension, was never so clear and precise as it is here.

In the previous discussion of Warren's novels, I have had occasion to quote the definition of a "philosophical novelist" from this essay and to apply it directly to Warren's own practice. Further, in the matter of method, Warren cites Conrad's use of the inserted commentary supplied by a character's life history—parallel to Warren's "bumps." And again: "the very personalities of the narrators function as commentary . . . as their voices are interpolated into Conrad's high and impersonal discourse." This, as I have indicated, is a constant practice in Warren's novels, where it serves as a thematic device as well, reinforcing his dualisms.

When Warren discusses Conrad's themes—and he discovers as Conrad's "central fact," "the fable as symbol for exfoliating theme"—he describes his own dualisms, as well as Conrad's, and concludes:

> Man, however, is committed to action. The Heysts, who repudiate action, find their own kind of damnation. Wisdom, then, is the recognition of man's condition, the condition of the creature made without gills or fins but dropped into the sea, the necessity of living with the ever-renewing dilemma of idea as opposed to nature, morality to action, . . . justice to material interests.

If we substitute for "idea as opposed to nature" Warren's own phrasing in *All the King's Men,* "idea versus fact," we have here a major statement of Warren's philosophic premise as it is embodied in his late poems and novels. Furthermore, he describes in terms of Conrad's characters the specific errors of his own "pure idea" and "pure fact" characters:

> Those men [like Willie Stark] who take the purely "natural" view, . . . who deny the dream and man's necessity to submit to the idea, to create values that are, quite literally, "super-natural" and therefore human, are destroyed by the dream.

And for the Jeremiah Beaumonts:

> Man, as a natural creature, is not born to swim in the dream, with gills and fins, but if he submits in his own imperfect "natural" way he can learn to swim and keep himself up.

Or again for Jerry:

> There has been the same contamination of the vision in the very effort to realize the vision.

Redemption is possible, but, as Jack Burden learned, "redemption must be continually re-earned."

Warren's approach to the critical problem in this essay is a broad one, if not so broad as that of his Coleridge piece. He uses Conrad's statements, testimony of his acquaintances, and the social and historical dimensions in a limited way. But the focus remains entirely on *Nostromo* and the author's other fictional works, and the emphasis is on total meaning primarily, technique secondarily. It is, in the main, the kind of eclectic approach which R. P. Blackmur advocated in his "A Burden for Critics," and which Allen Tate has since endorsed.

Warren presents no new aesthetic formulations in this essay, but he is evidently committed to the thesis that literature is a kind of knowledge, "a way of knowing, a way of exploration," as he puts it here. Although his exposition of Conrad's method implies a great deal of intellection, formulation of pattern, and control of symbolism, Warren reiterates his latter-day stress on the unconscious factor in artistic composition, which is "evoked out of the primal fecund darkness that always lies below our imagination." For Warren, too, the rational predilection has led finally to psychology and the edge of the irrational abyss.

CHAPTER XV

Conclusion

IN THE FOREGOING PAGES I have been concerned largely with an assessment of the creative and critical achievements of the Fugitive writers through 1956. That these achievements have been considerable in themselves and influential is beyond question. There remains a perhaps somewhat premature attempt to place the group as a whole in the American, and even in the total Western, cultural complex of our age.

It seems evident now that the Fugitives, despite their Southern accent, have reflected to a considerable degree the intellectual climate of the broader society in which they matured. In the United States, the Vanderbilt nucleus supplied the primary impetus to a modern religio-aesthetic reaction against that progressive liberalism which had dominated the social and political philosophy of our country since Jefferson's day. The aesthetic manifesto carried in the first issue of *The Fugitive* was by no means the first of its kind, and, but for the talents developed by its authors and the cohesiveness of the group, it might have become merely another in a series of protests against faith in scientific and industrial progress.

Ransom's early postwar reactions, contemporaneous with those of such American expatriates as Eliot, Stein, and Hemingway, and those of many European intellectuals, stressed, like theirs, the failure of scientifically oriented disciplines to cope with the needs of modern man. His philosophic dualism, which was the original core of the Nashville movement, echoed at a distance underground rumblings which had been heard on the continent since Kierkegaard, Nietzsche, and Dostoevsky—rumblings which were to culminate in several forms of modern

Existentialism, all of them, like Ransom's, arising from the pessimistic recognition of man's hard situation, born to die, set in an indifferent environment with his once-proud super-animal possession, his reason, proved inadequate to solve his dilemma.

Even on the American scene, many of Ransom's theses had venerable histories. In the writings of Thoreau, of Melville, of Henry James, among others, themes of anti-materialism and emphasis on the "world's body" of direct natural and human experience had been iterated and reiterated. Henry Adams, in the pessimism of his *Education*, had given the whole complex of ideas and feelings a definitive American expression. Adams had yearned back primarily to an eighteenth-century order—much the same as Ransom's ideal ante bellum Southern order—in which purposeful involvement in public affairs had not meant, as it did for him, a constant debasement and soilure in materialistic compromise. Behind the eighteenth century, he had finally discovered his spiritual home in the age of Thomist rational metaphysics and its aesthetic accompaniments. Ransom, who found the basic facts even harsher, by-passed medieval monism, where Eliot, too, was finding rest, and arrived back in a stern Judaistic dualism. At the same time, his pessimism lacked the desperation of Adams', so that he could stand aloofly ironical without failing in humanistic concern. But others of the group, as their quick attachment to Eliot demonstrated, were temperamentally keyed to the Adams tradition and its desperate sense of loss.

The Fugitives, however, are incurably Southern, and have always been quick to repudiate a common heritage with their Northern predecessors, whose underlayer of Puritanism and abstractionism has instinctively repelled them. Their sense of invasion from the North—of a series of invasions culminating in World War I and postwar industrial penetration—and their sense of an agrarian-realist tradition of their own, militated against identification with New England's literary dissenters. The Fugitives continued to see themselves as pioneer American crusaders, first, for pure aestheticism, then for social reform *cum* aestheticism. Their recognitions of kinship, therefore, have generally been with European, rather than with American, counterparts.

The battleground which the group chose in the late twenties and early thirties, however valid the logic of its choice, proved unpropitious. Their earthworks against a mechanistic enemy made little show even during the deep Depression years when the fuels of "progress" had apparently run out. Not only was the Agrarian program impractically retrogressive, given the dynamism of American society as a whole, but it suggested a farm ideal which the newly farm-liberated generation could not stomach, and an ideal ante bellum Southern culture which was historically vulnerable. The practical movement never materialized, but the critical doctrines which accompanied the ideational one, the negative social verdicts and the positive aesthetic creeds, proved viable products. Furthermore, the concrete aesthetic achievements which embodied their doctrines impressed their era and lent substance to the theoretic formulations.

The between-wars generation of the late thirties and the forties reacted strongly against the militant leftist doctrines which had captured the intellectual vanguard of the Depression era. The Fugitives, and such outstanding literary compatriots as Faulkner, Katherine Anne Porter, and Eudora Welty, found themselves in possession of a wide audience. It may be argued, as it was by several contributors to the *Partisan Review,* that the appeal of the new aestheticism, with its religious overtones and traditionalist social component, represented a "failure of nerve," a retreat of the rational intelligence before problems on whose complexities the parent generation had foundered. The younger generation was not, at any rate, socially or even intellectually bold, as Malcolm Cowley continued to point out in derogation. If they were not so complacently conservative as their successors of the fifties, they profoundly distrusted rational progressivism, which was more and more identified with Soviet materialism. Their critical explorations sought out non-rational fundamentals and tended, therefore, to cast backward into the areas of myth and symbol, of emotional and religious motivations and directives.

In this area they found the Fugitives already encamped. In particular, they found that the criticism of the major Fugitive writers had anticipated their attitudes and interests. Aesthetic formalism, as preached and practiced by Tate, Brooks, and Warren, especially, had effectively stripped the work of art from its social and philosophic backgrounds and given it an independent, quasi-religious status. Young intellectuals seeking an orientation or already oriented religiously and aesthetically could embrace easily a doctrine which expressly disavowed the cultural contexts which had appeared to fail them. Despite the opposition of older generations, the influence of Fugitive critics, of Eliot, and of their European allies quickly infiltrated American universities. By 1950, through their vigor and diligence and by virtue of their strong foothold in the literary quarterlies, they were largely in possession of the field.

By 1956, however, enthusiasm for strict "new critical" canons has waned. As the reaction against social philosophies has lost its original impulse, critical interests have broadened, even among the Fugitives themselves. Eliot's emphasis on metaphysical and moral aspects of the work of art has influenced modern attention to extra-formal considerations. But the development of Jungian and anthropologically oriented criticism, with its researches into and applications of myth, ritual, and symbolism, has largely characterized the "newer" new criticism. The account of these developments is for the most part irrelevant here, but it must be noted that several of the Fugitive critics have been forced by their own logic and that of their followers into similar extra-formal directions.

The Fugitives long had what V. S. Pritchett has alluded to in relation to the Catholic novelist, the great advantage of writing against the temper of their times. As a group, they possess a striking record for defying popular conceptions and ideologies. Their list of defiances includes their own literary heritage, all modern creeds of "progress," Marxism, Jeffersonian liberalism, finance capitalism and materialism, philosophic positivism and relativism, and public education. Some of them remain defiant, as Davidson's late title, "Still Rebels, Still Yankees," for example, indicates. But the major Fugitive battle, fought on the literary front, has been largely won. If an avant-garde has continued to move beyond Fugitive positions, it does so in tacit acknowledgement of the achievements of the men who opened the new country to them. These men have established aesthetic formalism as the basic weapon of critical armories, and they have made of symbolic naturalism, by example and by theoretic stress, the most important of modern literary strategies. Finally, they have been the heart of the twentieth-century literary renaissance in the South.

APPENDIX

The Minor Fugitives

OF THE RATHER miscellaneous group of men who are officially entitled to be called Fugitives, since their names appeared on the masthead of the magazine, the majority have no more than passing importance for literary history. Hirsch, Frank, Stevenson, Starr, Jesse and Ridley Wills, and Stanley Johnson produced no significant literary works after the magazine's demise in 1925. The three novels produced earlier by the latter two of this group are all tours de force, with little lasting interest. Ridley Wills's *Hoax* of 1922 remains a quite readable account of the love affairs of an irresponsible, talented, romantic, and generally amused young man, as told by a tolerant and also amused father. Nothing is involved in the story but a marriage, which obviously will not quite take place in the end. Wills's second and last novel, *Harvey Landrum*, of 1924, is predicated on the doctrine of compensation. The protagonist, born physically and morally chinless, succeeds in bluffing his employer and his future wife, among others, with a vigorous display of forcefulness, until he faints at the flow of blood at a prize fight. The story's inherent irony fails for lack of a realistic surface, and it collapses weakly at the end with Harvey's failure to bring off a suicide.

Stanley Johnson's 1925 novel, *The Professor*, though it is badly written, holds considerable interest largely because it novelizes quite uncharitably the role of the chairman of the English Department in the early days of *The Fugitive*. Johnson sets his story of one Professor Parkhurst in a Vermont college which boasts a very strange scholastic atmosphere. Parkhurst is engaged chiefly with making love, in a schoolboy-clever banter, to female graduate students, and in recounting his erotic career to the female librarian. But the publication of *American Quicksilver* by a group of his faculty and students—most of them recognizable as Fugitives in caricature—rouses his professional pride so far that his current affair suffers from the choleric upset. Parkhurst gives inspirational lectures to women's clubs, and finally, after the magazine has been recognized nationally, donates $50 to support what becomes now his own godchild. Johnson introduces a good deal of interesting intra-editorial controversy on the magazine's board, but this, for lack of confirmation, must be regarded as purely fictional. There is little need to speculate about the brevity of Johnson's career at Vanderbilt. He evidently had considerable fun producing this novel, even if he did not, as one reviewer felt, write a satire rivaling those of Sinclair Lewis.

William Frierson, an English professor long at the University of Alabama, and Walter Clyde Curry, Chairman of the English Department and Head of Humanities at Vanderbilt, have produced volumes in critical history which do not come within the scope of this account. Their Fugitiveness, like that of William Yandell Elliott, who turned to political science, is merely technical after the first flurry of excitement, when they dropped creative pretensions to concentrate on their academic specialties, Frierson on the continental and English novel and Curry on Shakespeare and Chaucer.

Merrill Moore was from the beginning a Fugitive-inspired phenomenon, rather than a true Fugitive in attitudes, ideas, or allegiances. Devoted to science and the individual case, rather than to literature or to larger doctrine, he deserted the South and his ancestral home as soon as he had finished his medical studies, and established himself in the center of the old Abolitionist region at Boston. Moore very evidently possesses a minimal critical sense, the sense par excellence of the Fugitives proper. His enormous productivity in "American sonnets," always thrown off, as it were, between cases, perhaps as a kind of continuous therapy, has not abated since the early Fugitive days. He has published, most notably, one large book, *M: One Thousand Autobiographical Sonnets* (1938), a collection selected by others from a fabulous pile of fourteen-liners. The level of this volume is neither higher nor lower than that of his *Fugitive* poems. Almost all contain some felicity of phrase or of image or of conception, but there is no fully realized poem among the thousand. Moore's "naive egotism," as Louis Untermeyer called it in his laudatory introduction to *Six Sides to a Man* (1935), has produced a startlingly large number of privately printed pamphlets of sonnets and comments on Merrill Moore as poet and psychiatrist. There is also a small collection of *Some Poems for New Zealand*, printed there, and a volume of translations of his sonnets into Spanish. None of this activity proves anything about Moore's prowess as a poet. Indeed, such comments as that of William Carlos Williams in his Foreword to *Sonnets from New Directions*—"Merrill Moore's sonnets are magnificent," with their "extremely familiar dialogue unit"—become rather interesting sidelights on the critic's temporary prepossessions than valid criticism of the poems themselves. Moore has remained a man with a fascinating hobby, rather than an artist attempting to discover his world truly in terms of his medium.

Donald Davidson, as I have noted, ceased to be a major Fugitive figure by the end of the 1930's largely because he was unable to accept the collapse of Agrarianism as an active movement and to progress from it into more fruitful attitudes. His two volumes of 1938 mark the limits of Davidson's original contributions. *Lee in the Mountains,* his last collection of poetry, consists in the main of a slightly revised version of *The Tall Men,* with the addition of several dramatic poems which contain the same vigor and the same vehemently Southern bias, as well as the same looseness of structure, as the longer poem exhibits. *The Attack on Leviathan* is a sustained diatribe against finance capitalism and collective economy, together with a complacently uncritical defense of traditional Southern economy and culture.

Since this period, Davidson has published several anthologies, including an excellent and popular *American Composition and Rhetoric*, which has been revised and republished. The disillusion and unreconstructed romantic regionalism that characterized his 1938 volumes has apparently not changed, but Davidson's printed work has skirted direct attack on literary as on socio-economic problems. He has interested himself in folklore and spirituals rather than in literature per se, and in history rather than in immediate issues. His major publication in recent years has been a two-volume history of the Tennessee for the Rinehart Rivers of America series.

Davidson's one late serious effort at pure literary criticism, and it is inevitably impure, appears in his Introduction to the Scribner's Modern Standard Authors edition of Stark Young's *So Red the Rose* (1953). This extended attempt to revitalize for the modern critical reader a long-time Southern best-selling novel of 1934 begins as an account of the form, the point of view, and the treatment of character as defense against charges of romantic formlessness. Before long, however, Davidson has left the book to one side, is quoting Young's contribution to *I'll Take My Stand*, and is interpreting:

> No doubt we are to assume—although Stark Young as author does not say so—that in Hugh McGehee Southern society has produced an example of the unified personality, in tune with its environment while also commanding it; and that Southern society at the outbreak of the war [the Civil War] was tending toward such an ideal. . . . To follow the code of the Bedfords and the McGehees . . . means ownership of the land, respect for God and nature, devotion to agriculture and its allied pursuits, and, with these, a healthy mistrust of what towns and trade, or in the later phrase, "industrialism," may seductively offer.

After this old-line Agrarianist diversion, Davidson returns to the novel. He employs such timely terms as " 'myth,' in the high sense," "Aristotelian principle," "universals"; and he offers comparisons with Sophocles and Shakespeare. But in the end he makes clear the ground of his partiality for *So Red the Rose*. The novel displays for him, in terms of the North-South struggle of almost a century ago, the "two parties of a great conflict recurrent": one which "integrates in terms of a harmonious life that blends substance and spirit"; the other which "disintegrates and, using disintegration itself as a tool of power, presumes to mount beyond good and evil and to make human intelligence a quasi-God." This is, somewhat overstated, good Fugitive doctrine still, except in its identification of the integrated life with the achievement of a historical society. Davidson, like no others of the group except Andrew Lytle, remains romantically committed to the "myth" of the ante bellum South as a nearly perfected society willfully destroyed by power-hungry, abstraction-centered intellectuals.

Andrew Lytle has entered very little into the preceding pages, for, though he contributed to the Agrarian volumes, printed a few stories, and was editor of *The Sewanee Review* for a time, his emergence as writer of fiction and criticism has been slow and unimpressive until recent years. Lytle was an honorrary Fugitive only, since he published nothing in the magazine and was elected to the Board with several others in a final inclusive gesture. Born in Murfreesboro, Tennessee, in 1903, Lytle was completing his undergraduate career at Vanderbilt when *The Fugitive* ceased publication. After graduation, he studied in the Yale University School of Drama, wrote several plays and directed others, and for a year acted professionally on the New York stage.

Lytle came into his heritage as a Fugitive writer only on his return to the South in 1930, when he immediately joined Ransom, Tate, and Davidson in their Agrarian activities. Lytle's first essay was a contribution to *I'll Take My Stand*, but more importantly he set to work, following the example of Tate and Warren, on a biography with a Civil War setting, and published in 1931 *Bedford Forrest and his Critter Company.* Lytle's is a frankly partisan account of one of the Confederacy's most noted, and unrewarded, cavalry commanders: a Tennessean, a "red neck," later a plantation owner, an investor in railroad schemes and the Grand Commander of the Ku Klux Klan. Lytle's early attempts in this book to mix dialect, such as that of the title, with the grand manner of Southern historians is unsuccessful, but when he becomes involved in raids and campaigns, he exhibits a very considerable narrative and descriptive ability. His battles and skirmishes are done with clarity and good narrative pace. He tends, despite occasional disclaimers, to idolize his protagonist as "a strong man of his Culture," though his personal culture, even as detailed here, is less than impressive and his simple success philosophy is hardly typical.

The generalizations in this volume lean heavily on those of Tate's *Jefferson Davis,* but the author has discovered his own particular villain in General Braxton Bragg. First Forrest's superior in the field, and one whom Forrest obeyed only cursorily as he seems to have obeyed all his seniors, he later became Davis's military advisor. Lytle's thesis is that Bragg's personal enmity to Forrest, carried into the heart of the Confederate cause, was largely responsible—rather than Northern arms or abilities—for defeat in the central area of war.

Already from this book it seems clear that Lytle's talents are narrative rather than broadly analytic. His blanket endorsement of Klan activities without regard to the injustices perpetrated by the group in the name of restoration of justice is typical of his simplifications. Throughout the book, Lytle fails in any way to distinguish between means, often exhibited as over-violent and angrily unjust on Forrest's part, and the ends they are meant to serve. The author is, in effect, a success-worshipper, the war situation justifying any action that could be demonstrated to have accomplished its end, the winning of battles.

Lytle's first novel, *The Long Night,* was published five

years later. From a structural point of view, it is unfortunate that the author chose for his evident model *The Count of Monte Cristo*. Young Cameron McIvor, son of an unjustly persecuted and murdered Alabamian, pursues his revenge during the early 1860's, fighting in underground organizations, living perilously as still an adolescent, killing off one by one his father's persecutors. Despite its often excellent local color in terms of place and character, the novel does not truly survive the contrived quality of its central action. Inevitably episodic, since each retributive act requires a distinct plan and campaign, the novel becomes a series of romantic adventures, which culminate in a full-scale treatment of the Battle of Shiloh, where the revenge theme is overwhelmed.

At the Moon's Inn, Lytle's second novel, is a very different matter. A venture in historical fiction at a difficult remove, this re-creation of DeSoto and his conquests and failures among the Indians of Florida and the deep-Southern areas remains an impressive work. Particularly in its descriptions of the Indian spirit and their customs, the novel succeeds, where few historical and anthropological studies have succeeded, in conveying a way of life, a coherent set of values beyond the comprehension of the single-minded Spanish adventurers. The Spanish, it would appear, have been somewhat oversimplified in Lytle's account, DeSoto in particular being interpreted as a man of pure will-power, defying man and God alike in his thirst for gold. The early Spanish section of the novel is somewhat confused, and Tovar's narrative is sometimes out of key and character. But when the story proper begins in American surroundings, a new authenticity begins to assert itself. In the final sections, again, when the Indian way of life is equated obviously with an agrarian devotion to the land—though their blood-thirstiness and wiliness are fully portrayed—and the Spanish with an early version of capitalistic exploitation, the novelist resorts to visions and symbols which are a disappointment following the central sections. Like several of the other Fugitives, Lytle is constantly subject to the danger of forcing patterns of meaning which his narratives cannot always bear.

Shortly after the publication of *At the Moon's Inn*, Lytle printed in *The Kenyon Review*[1] a novelette called "Alchemy," narrating the conquest of Peru by Pizarro and DeSoto. Here the story is all of a piece, unified by the consistent first-person point of view from which it is told—sub-commander DeSoto's chief aide—and unmarred by intrusive symbolic constructions. The Inca and his people are rather shadowly portrayed here, but their treatment is consistent with the point of view, while the suspenseful progress of the hopelessly placed Spanish invaders into the puzzling unknown land is done in Lytle's best narrative manner. Only at the climax of their incredible victory, which Pizarro and DeSoto see as a miracle, does the narrator transcend his commanders' insights. He senses an invisible companion with his leaders and, "As they reached out their hands to clasp their desires, that other—the dark thing—stepped forward to receive them." Lytle does not develop or define the symbolic presence, but allows our own knowledge of the commanders' history, the history of the whole Spanish adventure, to complete the extension.

Three other short stories preceded the publication of the Spanish pieces, and one more followed before the next novel, *A Name for Evil*, appeared in 1947. All three of the earlier stories are set in the Long Gourd, evidently a rich, somewhat secluded Tennessee valley, and each of them features a strong-willed woman who represents the traditional strength of an agrarian people. The first two of these stories are slight: "Old Scratch in the Valley,"[2] a kind of Southern Stephen Benét piece; and "Mister McGregor,"[3] which features a long "stomp and gouge" fight between Negro and white employer. Lytle felt called upon to defend editorial objections to the inconsistent speech of his narrator in the latter piece—the narrator

1. Vol. VI, 273-327.
2. *Virginia Quarterly Review*, VIII, 237-46.
3. *Ibid.*, XI, 218-37.

being a degenerate descendent of the title character—but the "action story" is hardly redeemed by what the author calls the "ironic" mixture, of unconvincing dialect and intelligent analytical comment.

"Jericho, Jericho, Jericho," of 1936,[4] a several times anthologized short story, is effectively done. It seems to owe something to Warren's early story, "When the Light Goes Green," and perhaps more to Katherine Anne Porter, but it succeeds admirably in its own right as a portrait of matriarchal assertiveness on the threshold of death. Old Mrs. McCowan, in her recollections of the past, in her immediate antipathy toward her prospective granddaughter-in-law, and in her consciousness of sin in defense of property, is a convincing rebel against death, which will cost her the gratification of seeing to it that the area is properly and efficiently tended. Only in the final sentence, where the dying woman is allowed escape from her knowledge of guilt by the sound of the hymn tune in her ears, "Joshua fit the battle of Jericho," does a sense of author contrivance intervene. The justification of the old woman's rapacity in the interest of taking care of property is managed by a kind of *deus ex machina*. The hymn arrives, not certainly out of the story proper, but out of the need of the author to bestow a gratuitous accolade.

"Guide," printed in 1945,[5] like most of Lytle's stories has a derivative ring, this time of such Faulkner stories as "The Bear," and of the Hemingway stories of Nick Adam's earlier experiences. The setting is clearly Reelfoot Lake, which lies on the southwestern borders of Tennessee and Kentucky. Like its models, it is the story of the maturation of a young boy in intimate association with nature. The fine description of duck-hunting inevitably brings to mind the opening of Hemingway's *Across the River and Into the Trees*, published several years later, and in its evocation of atmosphere and suspense it is

4. *Southern Review*, I, 411-22.
5. *Sewanee Review*, LIII, 362-87.

almost as effective. Lytle's story, however, more directly resembles Faulkner's in its thematic concern with tradition. The young protagonist enters on his initiatory experience with the ideal image of his great-grandfather before him. His uncle and the guides on the lake seem to conspire to destroy the image, especially when the uncle depicts the great-grandfather as a heartless playboy, exploiting his wife while he amused himself with his hunting and his women. The revelation occurs when the boy suddenly sees the uncle looking at him with his great-grandfather's eyes. The recognition of continuity of a tradition, however fallible, as traditions must be, becomes therefore the burden of the story—and the reader of Warren's novels will have discovered an additional source for Lytle's fiction.

The 1947 novel, *A Name for Evil,* suggests again a model, this time Henry James, and in particular, "The Turn of the Screw." Lytle's story begins realistically, with the problems of a young couple engaged in renovating an old house. This section, told in the first person, so lacks aesthetic distance that it is automatically read as an autobiographical account, especially since it is weighted with Davidsonian comments on tradition, industrialism, and modern education. When the "Turn of the Screw" element enters, with ghostly appearances, the effect is not only startling, but unconvincing, since it violates completely the immediate factual atmosphere that has been created. Once the ghostly phenomenon enters the story, it grows out of hand. Like James's ghost, it represents an essentially evil principle, but at the same time it here belongs to historical tradition, which, as the commentary makes clear, is the desideratum for the narrator. In actual effect, it is the intrusion of the past as evil which causes Major Brent's disturbance. His actions become less a symbolic reaction to industrial invasion, which the author seems to have intended, than a kind of madness induced by an obsession with tradition. Ideologically, love is supposed, one feels, to be destroyed by the lack of a solid traditional grounding, but the fable recalcitrantly refuses to support any such interpretation. As a whole, in fact, this novel seems the best single refutation of Agrarian-traditionalist positions that has been produced either by its enemies or its supporters, which is to say that it is Lytle's least effective fictional work. Clearly Henry James is a dangerous model.

In his latest story,[6] which is introduced in *The Sewanee Review* as a section of a novel still uncompleted, Lytle has reverted to a more congenial model, William Faulkner. Meanwhile, his essays in criticism have focused on fiction, and particularly on fiction historically based. His four most important critical pieces, all dating from after his commitment to the teaching of literature—he had earlier taught history—establish a limited aesthetic for the novel and provide a series of essentially aesthetic formalist analyses of fiction. The end of the novel, as Lytle defines it in a critique of Caroline Gordon's fiction,[7] is to "force the meaning of experience to show beneath appearance," or to recover the quality of innocence "out of the contamination of experience." Its prime method is the practice of the "averted eye," which gives author and reader alike a "focusing and controlling image." This image is further defined in an essay on the historical novel[8] as "a central image, which might also be a dominating symbol, placed at the post of observation and at the center of the author's seeing eye." Lytle further insists, in Jamesian fashion, on the sense of humanity, the "very illusion of life," and on craftsmanship. In an excellent review of *Intruder in the Dust,*[9] he stresses the necessity of a controlled view and of a style. Lytle has studied Percy Lubbock's *Craft of Fiction* with care and has drawn upon it heavily, though he explicitly disagrees with certain specific judgments.

Lytle's Fugitiveness appears most directly in his analyses,

6. "What Quarter of the Night," *Sewanee Review,* LXIV, 349-97.

7. "Caroline Gordon and the Historic Image," *Sewanee Review,* LVII, 560-86.

8. "Image as Guide to Meaning in the Historical Novel," *Sewanee Review,* LXI, 408-26.

9. "Regeneration for the Man," *Sewanee Review,* LVII, 120-27.

though he commonly expresses some trepidation about violating the "mysteries" of creation, or protests that analysis is "a kind of bloody operation" on a work that is perfectly fused. The analyses themselves, of Caroline Gordon's short story, "Brilliant Leaves," and of her *Green Centuries*, of *War and Peace*, and of Faulkner's novels, *Intruder in the Dust* and *The Fable*, are excellent examples of a close reading which never loses sight of the larger implications, of aesthetic formalist criticism at its best. The effect of Lytle's analyses is anything but "bloody"; they are uniformly illuminating and should lead the reader immediately to, or back to, the works themselves. The essay on *The Fable*[10] is certainly the most thorough and attentive yet written. If it seems overly complex and even at times turgid in its elucidations, one can only feel, as many readers have, that the primary fault lies here with the author, not the critic. Faulkner has indeed given the reader, and, I think, himself, more problems, of more complexity, than can be handled in presentational narrative terms.

The section of a novel "now approaching completion" was printed in 1956 under the title "What Quarter of the Night" in *The Sewanee Review*,[11] of which Lytle is now an advisory editor. The story, as printed in four parts, seems complete in itself, and it immediately adds to Lytle's stature as a creative artist. Though the setting and the characters are distinctly Tennessean, the form and the images, even to an extent the style, recall Faulkner in his most authentic and forceful phase. The section begins with a dialect passage describing the semi-willed and clearly symbolic death of Capt. Joe Cree by the felling of a huge old tree he wanted down. Part II shifts to Cree's supposed son, intensely blond where Joe was dark, and a narrator uncle driving to the funeral, both of them aware now for the first time that Lucius is not actually Cree's son, but the offspring of a premarital affair. In this part, the old Indian

10. "The Son of Man: He Will Prevail," *Sewanee Review*, LXIII, 114-37.
11. Vol. LXIV, 349-97.

path through the wilderness, the "War Trace," still open as an image of the past, is suggested by the uncle as an alternate route for their journey, less sun-blinded than the more direct pike, less harsh in the boy's present disturbance. It is this path into the past which the dozing uncle takes to re-create for himself the human situation, of refusal of inheritance by his own elder primitive-minded brother, of the semi-incestuous relationship between his younger brother and sister, and of the adolescent sister's ill-fated affair with "that new man Peter Legrand" on the spot of the elder brother's all but sacred retreat, the "deer's sanctuary." The uncle's extended spiraling back through the corridors of time and finally back out to the sun's "blind light" of history is the heart of the story. Though the final meaning eludes the uncle, with the complication of sex repression and the "flaming sword" of retribution with which the younger brother splits the seducer's abdomen, in Lucius' final admission of an affair of his own paralleling his mother's it is clear that the initial tree-felling, the renunciation of inheritance which deprives the girl of her natural status, and the land-clearing new type man, who is the seducer, form an intricate pattern amounting finally to betrayal of tradition. Lytle's long excursion into a dim past has lighted the present dilemma with a distinctly Faulknerian glow. Yet the texture, the particularity of the vision, is distinctly Lytle's. Out of his deep understanding of Faulkner, Lytle has apparently found himself as a creative writer of real power and authenticity.

Selected Bibliography

I. General

Magazines

The Fugitive, Vols. I-IV, 1922-1925.
The Double-Dealer, Vols. I-VI, 1921-1926.

Books

Blackmur, Richard P. *The Double Agent; Essays in Craft and Elucidation.* New York: Arrow Press, 1935.

———. *The Expense of Greatness.* New York: Arrow Editions, 1940.

———. *Language as Gesture; Essay in Poetry.* New York: Harcourt, Brace and Co., 1952.

Daniels, Jonathon. *A Southerner Discovers the South.* New York: Macmillan Co., 1938.

Eliot, T. S. *Selected Essays, 1917-1932.* New York: Harcourt, Brace and Co., 1932.

Elton, William. *A Glossary of the New Criticism.* Chicago: University of Chicago Press, 1948.

Hicks, Granville. *The Great Tradition; An Interpretation of American Literature since the Civil War.* New York: Macmillan Co., 1935.

Hoffman, Frederick J., Allen, Charles, and Ulrich, Carolyn. *The Little Magazine, A History and a Bibliography.* Princeton: Princeton University Press, 1946.

Hyman, Stanley Edgar. *The Armed Vision.* New York: Alfred A. Knopf, 1948.

Kazin, Alfred. *On Native Ground, An Interpretation of Modern American Prose Literature.* New York: Reynal and Hitchcock, 1942.

Kunitz, Stanley J. and Haycraft, Howard. *Twentieth Century Authors.* New York: H. W. Wilson Co., 1942.

Langer, Suzanne. *Philosophy in a New Key: A Study in the Symbol-*

ism of Reason, Rite, and Myth. Cambridge, Mass.: Harvard University Press, 1942.

Mencken, H. L. *Prejudices, 2nd Series.* New York: Alfred A. Knopf, 1920.

Mims, Edwin. *The Advancing South, Stories of Progress and Reaction.* Garden City, N. Y.: Doubleday, Page and Co., 1926.

———. *Adventurous America; A Study of Contemporary Life and Thought.* New York and London: Charles Scribner's Sons, 1929.

Odum, Howard. *An American Epoch; Southern Portraiture in the National Picture.* New York: Henry Holt and Co., 1930.

Parks, Edd Winfield. *Segments of Southern Thought.* Athens, Ga.: University of Georgia Press, 1938.

Richards, I. A. *Coleridge on Imagination.* New York: Harcourt, Brace and Co., 1935.

———. *Principles of Literary Criticism.* New York: Harcourt, Brace and Co., 1925.

Smith, Bernard. *Forces in American Criticism, A Study in the History of American Literary Thought.* New York: Harcourt, Brace and Co., 1939.

Stauffer, Donald A. (ed.). *The Intent of the Critic.* Princeton: Princeton University Press, 1941.

Winters, Yvor. *In Defense of Reason.* New York: Swallow Press and W. Morrow Co., 1947.

Anthologies

Fugitives: An Anthology of Verse. New York: Harcourt, Brace and Co., 1928.

Southern Renascence: The Literature of the Modern South. Eds. Louis D. Rubin, Jr., and Robert D. Jacobs. Baltimore: Johns Hopkins Press, 1953.

A Southern Vanguard. Ed. Allen Tate. New York: Prentice-Hall, 1947.

Vanderbilt Miscellany, 1919-1944. Ed. Richard Croom Beatty. Nashville, Tenn.: Vanderbilt University Press, 1944.

Unpublished Dissertations

Stewart, John Lincoln. "The Fugitives." Ohio State University, 1947.

Stocking, Frederick. "Poetry as Knowledge: The Critical Theories of John Crowe Ransom and Allen Tate." University of Michigan, 1946.

Unger, Leonard Howard. "Donne's Poetry and Modern Definitions of 'Metaphysical': A Critical Study." State University of Iowa, 1941.

Woodward, Barbara C. C. "Theories of Meaning in Poetry, 1915-1940: A Critical History." University of Michigan, 1946.

Essays

Abel, Darrell. "Intellectual Criticism," *American Scholar*, XII (Autumn, 1944), 414-28.

"American Scholar Forum: The New Criticism," *American Scholar*, XX (Winter, Spring, 1951), 86-104, 218-31.

Baum, Bernard. "Corpus Delicti; Some Letters Mainly Concerned with the New Criticism," *South Atlantic Quarterly*, LI (1952), 261-75.

Bush, Douglas. "The New Criticism: Some Old-fashioned Queries," *PMLA*, LXIV (1949), 13-21.

Daiches, David. "The New Criticism: Some Qualifications," *English Journal*, XXXIX (1950), 64-72.

Davis, Robert G. "The New Criticism and the Democratic Tradition," *American Scholar*, XIX (Winter, 1950), 9-19.

Fitzell, Lincoln. "The Sword and the Dragon," *South Atlantic Quarterly*, L (1951), 214-32.

Fogle, R. H. "Romantic Bards and Metaphysical Reviewers," *Journal of English Literary History*, XII (Summer, 1945), 221-50.

Jarrell, Randall. "Contemporary Poetry Criticism," *New Republic*, CV (July 21, 1941), 88-90.

Mizener, Arthur. "Recent Criticism," *Southern Review*, V (Autumn, 1939), 376-400.

Muller, H. J. "The New Criticism in Poetry," *Southern Review*, VI (Spring, 1941), 811-39.

———. "Pathways in Recent Criticism," *Southern Review*, IV (Summer, 1939), 187-208.

O'Connor, William Van. "A Short View of the New Criticism," *English Journal*, XXXVIII (November, 1949), 489-97.

Olson, Elder. "Recent Literary Criticism," *Modern Philology*, XL (1943), 275-83.

Ong, W. J. "The Meaning of the New Criticism," *Modern Schoolman*, XX (1943), 192-209.

Pritchard, J. P. "Aristotle's *Poetics* and Certain American Literary Critics," *Classical Weekly*, XXVII (1934), 81-85, 89-93, 97-99.

Roellinger, Francis X., Jr. "Two Theories of Poetry as Knowledge," *Southern Review*, VII (Summer, 1942), 690-701.

Thorpe, C. D. and Nelson, N. E. "Criticism in the Twentieth Century; A Bird's-Eye View," *English Journal*, XXXVI (April, 1947), 165-73.

Trowbridge, Hoyt. "Aristotle and the 'New Criticism,'" *Sewanee Review*, LII (Autumn, 1944), 537-55.

Tuve, Rosamund. "Imagery and Logic," *Journal of the History of Ideas*, III (October, 1942), 365-400.

Wilson, Edmund. "Tennessee Poets," *New Republic*, LIV (March 7, 1928), 103-4.

Winters, Yvor. "Fugitives," *Poetry*, XXXII (May, 1928), 102-6.

II. John Crowe Ransom

Books

Poems about God. New York: Henry Holt and Co., 1919.

Chills and Fever. New York: Alfred A. Knopf, 1924.

Grace after Meat. London: L. and V. Woolf, 1924.

Two Gentlemen in Bonds. New York: Alfred A. Knopf, 1927.

God without Thunder: An Unorthodox Defense of Orthodoxy. New York: Harcourt, Brace and Co., 1930.

The World's Body. New York: Charles Scribner's Sons, 1938.

The New Criticism. Norfolk, Conn.: New Directions, 1941.

Selected Poems. New York: Alfred A. Knopf, 1945.

Editor

The Kenyon Critics: Studies in Modern Literature from the Kenyon Review. New York: World Publishing, 1951.

Essays and Reviews

"Waste Lands," *Literary Review*, III (July 14, 1923), 825-26.

"The Poet Laureate," *Literary Review*, IV (March 29, 1924), 625-26.

"Freud and Literature," *Saturday Review of Literature*, X (October 4, 1924), 161-62.

"Man without a Country," *Sewanee Review*, XXXIII (July, 1925), 301-7.

"South—Old or New," *Sewanee Review*, XXXVI (April, 1928), 138-47.

"Flux and Blur in Contemporary Art," *Sewanee Review*, XXXVII (July, 1929), 353-66.

"Classical and Romantic," *Saturday Review of Literature*, VI (September 14, 1929), 125-27.

"The Aesthetics of Regionalism," *American Review*, II (January, 1934), 290-310.

"Modern with the Southern Accent," *Virginia Quarterly Review*, XI (April, 1935), 184-200.

"The Tense of Poetry," *Southern Review*, I (Autumn, 1935), 221-38.

"Fiction Harvest," *Southern Review*, II (Autumn, 1936), 399-418.

"Characters and Character," *American Review*, VI (January, 1937), 271-88.

"The Content of the Novel," *American Review*, VII (June, 1938), 301-18.

"Yeats and his Symbols," *Kenyon Review*, I (Summer, 1939), 309-22.

"The Aesthetic of *Finnegans Wake*," *Kenyon Review*, I (Autumn, 1939), 424-28.

"The Pragmatics of Art," *Kenyon Review*, II (Winter, 1940), 76-87.

"An Address to Kenneth Burke," *Kenyon Review*, IV (Spring, 1942), 219-37.

"Inorganic Muses," *Kenyon Review*, V (Spring, 1943), 278-300.

"Positive and Near-Positive Aesthetics," *Kenyon Review*, V (Summer, 1943), 443-47.

"The Bases of Criticism," *Sewanee Review*, LII (October, 1944), 556-71.

"Art and the Human Economy," *Kenyon Review*, VII (Autumn, 1945), 683-88.

"Poetry," *Kenyon Review*, IX (Spring, Summer, 1947), 436-56, 640-58.

"On Shakespeare's Language," *Sewanee Review*, LV (April, 1947), 181-98.

"The Understanding of Fiction," *Kenyon Review*, XII (Spring, 1950), 189-218.

"William Wordsworth," *Kenyon Review*, XII (Summer, 1950), 498-519.

"Poetry, 1900–1950," *Kenyon Review*, XIII (Summer, 1951), 445-54.

"Why Critics Don't Go Mad," *Kenyon Review*, XIV (Spring, 1952), 331-39.

"Age of Criticism," *New Republic*, CXXVI (March 31, 1952), 18.

"Hardy, Old Poet," *New Republic*, CXXVI (May 12, 1952), 16-17.

"Art of Prose," *New Republic*, CXXVII (October 6, 1952), 17-18.

"Humanism at Chicago," *Kenyon Review,* XIV (Autumn, 1952), 647-59.

"Poems of T. S. Eliot; A Perspective," *New Republic,* CXXVII (December 8, 1952), 16-17.

"The Shores of Criticism," *Partisan Review,* XX (January–February, 1953), 108-11.

"Responsible Criticism," *Sewanee Review,* LXI (Spring, 1953), 300-3.

"Symbolism, American Style," *New Republic,* CXXIX (November 2, 1953), 18-20.

"The Concrete Universal: Observations on the Understanding of Poetry," *Kenyon Review,* XVI (Autumn, 1954), 554-64; XVII (Summer, 1955), 383-407.

About Ransom

Special "Homage to John Crowe Ransom" Issue, *Sewanee Review,* LVI (July, 1948), 365-476.

Baker, Joseph E. "Philosopher and New Critic," *Sewanee Review,* L (April, 1942), 167-71.

Beatty, Richard C. "John Crowe Ransom as Poet," *Sewanee Review,* LII (July, 1944), 344-66.

Blum, Morgan. "The Fugitive Particular," *Western Review,* XIV (Winter, 1950), 85-102.

Burgum, Edwin B. "An Examination of Modern Critics: John Crowe Ransom," *Rocky Mountain Review,* VIII (Spring, 1944), 87-93.

Eberhard, Richard. "Search for Perfection," *Poetry,* LXVII (January, 1946), 213-15.

Gamble, Isabel. "Ceremonies of Bravery: John Crowe Ransom," *Southern Renascence: The Literature of the Modern South.* Eds. Louis D. Rubin, Jr., and Robert D. Jacobs. Baltimore: Johns Hopkins Press, 1953. Pp. 341-51.

Lynshey, Winifred. "A Critic in Action; Mr. Ransom," *College English,* V (February, 1944), 239-49.

Schwartz, Delmore. "Instructed of Much Mortality," *Sewanee Review,* LIV (July, 1946), 439-48.

Stauffer, Donald. "Critical Principles and a Sonnet," *American Scholar,* XII (Winter, 1942), 52-62.

Winters, Yvor. *In Defense of Reason.* New York: Swallow Press and W. Morrow Co., 1947. Pp. 502-55.

III. Allen Tate

Books

The Golden Mean and Other Poems. Tate and Ridley Wills. Nashville, Tenn.: Privately printed, 1923.

Mr. Pope and Other Poems. New York: Minton, Balch and Co., 1928.

Stonewall Jackson: The Good Soldier. New York: Minton, Balch and Co., 1928.

Jefferson Davis: His Rise and Fall. New York: Minton, Balch and Co., 1929.

Poems: 1928-1931. New York and London: Charles Scribner's Sons, 1932.

The Mediterranean and Other Poems. New York: Alcestis Press, 1936.

Reactionary Essays on Poetry and Ideas. New York: Charles Scribner's Sons, 1936.

Selected Poems. New York and London: Charles Scribner's Sons, 1937.

The Fathers. New York: G. P. Putnam's Sons, 1938.

Reason in Madness, Critical Essays. New York: G. P. Putnam's Sons, 1941.

The Vigil of Venus. Cummington, Mass.: Cummington Press, 1943.

The Winter Sea. Cummington, Mass.: Cummington Press, 1944.

Poems: 1922-1947. New York: Charles Scribner's Sons, 1948.

On the Limits of Poetry. New York: Swallow Press, 1948.

The Hovering Fly. Cummington, Mass.: Cummington Press, 1949.

The Forlorn Demon. Chicago: Henry Regnery Co., 1953.

Editor

I'll Take My Stand; The South and the Agrarian Tradition, by Twelve Southerners. New York and London: Harper and Bros., 1930.

Who Owns America? A Declaration of Independence. Eds. Herbert Agar and Tate. Boston and New York: Houghton Mifflin Co., 1936.

The Language of Poetry. Princeton: Princeton University Press and London: Oxford University Press, 1942.

Princeton Verse between Two Wars. Princeton: Princeton University Press, 1942.

American Harvest. Eds. Tate and John Peale Bishop. New York: L. B. Fischer, 1942.

A Southern Vanguard. New York: Prentice-Hall, 1947.

The Collected Poems of John Peale Bishop, 1892-1944. New York: Charles Scribner's Sons, 1948.

The House of Fiction. Eds. Caroline Gordon and Tate. New York: Charles Scribner's Sons, 1951.

Essays and Reviews

"Last Days of a Charming Lady," *Nation,* CXXI (October 28, 1925), 485-86.

"Fundamentalism," *Nation,* CXXII (May 12, 1926), 532-34.

"Tiresias," *Nation,* CXXIII (November 17, 1926), 509.

"The Holy War," *Nation,* CXXIII (December 29, 1926), 694.

"Poetry and the Absolute," *Sewanee Review,* XXXV (January, 1927), 41-52.

"The Revolt against Literature," *New Republic,* XLIX (February 9, 1927), 329-30.

"A Tendency Yearbook," *Bookman,* LXVIII (November, 1928), 353-58.

"American Poetry since 1920," *Bookman,* LXIX (January, 1929), 503-8.

"Mr. Cabell's Farewell," *New Republic,* LXI (January 8, 1930), 201-2.

"The Fallacy of Humanism," *Hound and Horn,* III (January, 1930), 234-57.

"Confusion and Poetry," *Sewanee Review,* XXXVIII (April, 1930), 133-49.

"A Fully Matured Art," *Nation,* CXXXI (October 1, 1930), 352-53.

"Post-Symbolism," *Hound and Horn,* IV (June, 1931), 619-24.

"A Note on Milton," *New Republic,* LXVIII (October 21, 1931), 266-68.

"Editorial Note," *Poetry,* XL (May, 1932), 90-94.

"Laundry Bills," *Poetry,* XLI (November, 1932), 107-12.

"The Whole Image of Man," *Hound and Horn,* VI (January, 1933), 345-49.

"Poetry and Politics," *New Republic,* LXXV (August 2, 1933), 308-11.

"The Fugitive—1922–1925," *Princeton University Library Chronicle,* III (April, 1942), 75-84.

"The Post of Observation in Fiction," *Maryland Quarterly,* II (1944), 61-64.

"Three Commentaries: Poe, James and Joyce," *Sewanee Review,* LVIII (Winter, 1950), 1-15.

"Homage to St-John Perse," *Poetry*, LXXV (January, 1950), 213-16.

"Orthodoxy and the Standard of Literature," *New Republic*, CXXVIII (January 5, 1953), 24-25.

"Clarity, Elegance and Power," *New Republic*, CXXVIII (March 2, 1953), 17-18.

"Self-Made Angel," *New Republic*, CXXIX (August 31, 1953), 17-18.

"Christ and the Unicorn," *Sewanee Review*, LXIII (April, 1955), 175-81.

"Reflections on American Poetry, 1900-1950," *Sewanee Review*, LXIV (January, 1956), 59-70.

Short Stories

"The Immortal Woman," *Hound and Horn*, VI (July, 1933), 592-609.

"The Migration," *Yale Review*, XXIV (September, 1934), 83-111.

Recent Poetry

"The Maimed Man," *Partisan Review*, XIX (May, 1952), 265-67.

"Buried Lake," *Sewanee Review*, LXI (April, 1953), 175-80.

"The Swimmers," *Hudson Review*, V (Winter, 1953), 471-73.

About Tate

Abraham, E. "The Reading of Poetry," *English Literary History*, IX (September, 1942), 235-44.

Amyx, Clifford. "The Aesthetics of Allen Tate," *Western Review*, XIII (Spring, 1949), 135-44.

Beatty, Richard C. "Allen Tate as a Man of Letters," *South Atlantic Quarterly*, XLVII (April, 1948), 226-41.

Bentley, Eric R. "Romanticism—A Re-Evaluation," *Antioch Review*, IV (March, 1944), 6-20.

Berland, Alwyn. "Violence in the Poetry of Allen Tate," *Accent*, XI (Summer, 1951), 161-71.

Burke, Kenneth. "Tentative Proposal," *Poetry*, L (May, 1937), 96-100.

Daiches, David. "Notes for a Reply to Mr. Tate," *Southern Review*, VI (Autumn, 1941), 843-46.

Dupee, F. W. "Frost and Tate," *Nation*, CLX (April 21, 1945), 465-66.

Flint, F. Cudworth. "Poems, 1928–31," *Symposium*, III (July, 1932), 407-14.

Glicksberg, Charles I. "Allen Tate and Mother Earth," *Sewanee Review*, XLV (July, 1937), 384-95.

Hook, Sidney. "The Late Mr. Tate," *Southern Review*, VI (Spring, 1941), 840-43.

Knickerbocker, W. S. "Friction of Powder Puffs; Tatian Esoterics," *Sewanee Review*, XLVIII (July, 1940), 315-21.

Koch, Vivienne. "The Poetry of Allen Tate," *Kenyon Review*, XI (Summer, 1949), 355-78.

Mizener, Arthur. "*The Fathers* and Realistic Fiction," *Accent*, VII (Winter, 1947), 101-9.

Morse, Samuel F. "Second Reading," *Poetry*, LI (February, 1938), 262-66.

Nemerov, Howard. "The Current of the Frozen Stream: An Essay on the Poetry of Allen Tate," *Furioso*, III (February, 1948), 50-61.

Rubin, Louis D. "The Serpent in the Mulberry Bush," *Southern Renascence: The Literature of the Modern South*. Eds. Louis D. Rubin, Jr., and Robert D. Jacobs. Baltimore: Johns Hopkins Press, 1953. Pp. 352-67.

Schwartz, Delmore. "The Poetry of Allen Tate," *Southern Review*, V (Winter, 1940), 419-38.

Shafer, Robert. "Humanism and Impudence," *American Bookman*, LXX (January, 1930), 489-98.

Spears, Monroe K. "The Criticism of Allen Tate," *Sewanee Review*, LVII (Spring, 1949), 317-34.

Thorp, Willard. "Allen Tate: A Checklist," *Princeton University Library Chronicle*, III (April, 1942), 85-98.

Vivas, Elisio. "Allen Tate as a Man of Letters," *Creation and Discovery*. New York: The Noonday Press, 1955. Pp. 267-81.

Winters, Yvor. "In Vindication of Poetry," *New Republic*, LVI (October 17, 1928), 255-56.

Zabel, Morton. "A Critic's Poetry," *Poetry*, XXXIII (February, 1929), 281-84.

———. "The Creed of Memory," *Poetry*, XL (April, 1932), 34-39.

IV. Robert Penn Warren

Books

John Brown: The Making of a Martyr. New York: Payson and Clarke, Ltd., 1929.

Thirty-six Poems. New York: Alcestis Press, 1935.

Night Rider. Boston: Houghton Mifflin Co., 1939.

Eleven Poems on the Same Theme. Norfolk, Conn.: New Directions, 1942.

At Heaven's Gate. New York: Harcourt, Brace and Co., 1943.

Selected Poems, 1923-1943. New York: Harcourt, Brace and Co., 1944.

All the King's Men. New York: Harcourt, Brace and Co., 1946.

Blackberry Winter. Cummington, Mass.: Cummington Press, 1946.

Circus in the Attic and Other Stories. New York: Harcourt, Brace and Co., 1948.

World Enough and Time; A Romantic Novel. New York: Random House, 1950.

Brother to Dragons; A Tale in Verse and Voices. New York: Random House, 1953.

Band of Angels. New York: Random House, 1955.

(*Proud Flesh,* a play. Unprinted, 1945?)

Editor

See Brooks, Editor.

A Southern Harvest: Short Stories by Southern Writers. Boston: Houghton Mifflin Co., 1937.

Introductory Essays

Coleridge, Samuel Taylor. *The Rime of the Ancient Mariner; Illustrated by Alexander Calder, with an Essay by Robert Penn Warren.* New York: Reynal and Hitchcock, 1946.

Conrad, Joseph. *Nostromo.* New York: Modern Library, 1951.

Hemingway, Ernest. *A Farewell to Arms.* New York: Charles Scribner's Sons, 1949.

Essays and Reviews

"Hawthorne, Anderson and Frost," *New Republic,* LIV (May 16, 1928), 399-401.

"Merrill Moore's Sonnets," *New Republic,* LXI (January 29, 1930), 280.

"Not Local Color," *Virginia Quarterly Review,* XIII (January, 1932), 153-60.

"A Note on Three Southern Poets," *Poetry,* XL (May, 1932), 103-13.

"Blind Poet: Sidney Lanier," *American Review,* II (November, 1933), 27-45.

"Georgian Middle Life," *Poetry,* XLIII (February, 1934), 287-90.

"T. S. Stribling: A Paragraph in the History of Critical Realism," *American Review,* II (February, 1934), 463-86.

"Working toward Freedom," *Poetry,* XLIII (March, 1934), 342-46.

"John Crowe Ransom: A Study in Irony," *Virginia Quarterly Review,* II (January, 1935), 93-112.

"Notes on the Hamlet of Thomas Wolfe," *American Review,* V (May, 1935), 191-208.

"Some Don'ts for Literary Regionalists," *American Review,* VIII (December, 1936), 142-50.

"Jeffers on the Age," *Poetry,* XLIX (February, 1937), 279-82.

"The Present State of Poetry III: In the United States," *Kenyon Review,* I (Autumn, 1939), 384-98.

"The Snopes World," *Kenyon Review,* III (Spring, 1941), 253-57.

"Principle and Poet," *Nation,* CLIV (April 11, 1942), 438-39.

"Katherine Anne Porter," *Kenyon Review,* IV (Winter, 1942), 29-42.

"Pure and Impure Poetry," *Kenyon Review,* V (Spring, 1943), 229-54.

"The Love and Separateness in Miss Welty," *Kenyon Review,* VI (Spring, 1944), 246-59.

"Melville the Poet," *Kenyon Review,* VIII (Spring, 1946), 208-23.

"Cowley's Faulkner," *New Republic,* CXV (August 12, 1946), 176-80, and (August 26, 1946), 234-37.

"Hemingway," *Kenyon Review,* IX (Winter, 1947), 1-28.

"Nostromo," *Sewanee Review,* LIX (Summer, 1951), 364-91.

"The Themes of Robert Frost," *The Writer and his Craft,* Robert Morse Lovett *et al.* Ann Arbor, Mich.: University of Michigan Press, 1954. Pp. 218-33.

"Knowledge and the Image of Man," *Sewanee Review,* LXIII (Spring, 1955), 182-92.

"Divided South Searches its Soul," *Life,* XLI (July 9, 1956), 98-99, 101-2, 105-6, 108, 111-12, 114.

Recent Poetry

"To a Little Girl, one year old, in a ruined fortress," *Partisan Review,* XXII (Spring, 1955), 171-78.

About Warren

Anderson, Charles R. "Violence and Order in the Novels of Robert Penn Warren," *Southern Renascence: The Literature of the Modern South.* Eds. Louis D. Rubin, Jr., and Robert D. Jacobs. Baltimore: Johns Hopkins Press, 1953. Pp. 207-24.

Bentley, Eric. "All the King's Men," *Theatre Arts,* XXXI, (November, 1947), 72-73.

———. "The Meaning of Robert Penn Warren's Novels," *Kenyon Review,* X (Summer, 1948), 407-24.

Campbell, Harry Modean. "Warren as Philosopher in *World Enough and Time,*" *Southern Renascence: The Literature of the Modern South.* Eds. Louis D. Rubin, Jr., and Robert D. Jacobs. Baltimore: Johns Hopkins Press, 1953. Pp. 225-35.

Cargill, Oscar. "Anatomist of Monsters," *College English,* IX (October, 1949), 391-98.

Fiedler, Leslie A. "On Two Frontiers," *Partisan Review,* XVII (September-October, 1950), 739-43.

———. "Romance in the Operatic Manner," *New Republic,* CXXXIII (September 26, 1955), 28-30.

Ford, N. F. "Kenneth Burke and Robert Penn Warren: Criticism by Obsessive Metaphor," *Journal of English and Germanic Philology,* LIII (April, 1954), 172-77.

Frank, Joseph. "Romanticism and Reality in Robert Penn Warren," *Hudson Review,* IV (Summer, 1951), 248-58.

Girault, Norton. "The Narrator's Mind as Symbol: An Analysis of *All the King's Men,*" *Accent,* VII (Summer, 1947), 220-34.

Heilman, Robert B. "Melpomene as Wallflower," *Sewanee Review,* LV (January, 1947), 154-66.

———. "Tangled Web," *Sewanee Review,* LIX (January, 1951), 107-19.

Hendry, Irene. "Regional Novel," *Sewanee Review,* LIII (January, 1945), 84-102.

Humbolt, Charles. "The Lost Cause of Robert Penn Warren," *Masses and Mainstream,* I (July, 1948), 8-23.

Hynes, Samuel. "Robert Penn Warren: The Symbolic Journey," *University of Kansas City Review,* XVII (Summer, 1951), 279-85.

Lowell, Robert. "Prose Genius in Verse," *Kenyon Review,* XV (Autumn, 1953), 619-25.

McDowell, Frederick P. W. "Psychology and Theme in *Brother to Dragons,*" *PMLA,* LXX (September, 1955), 565-86.

———. "Robert Penn Warren's Criticism," *Accent,* XV (Summer, 1955), 173-96.

Mizener, Arthur. "Amphibian in Old Kentucky," *Kenyon Review,* XII (Autumn, 1950), 697-701.

O'Connor, William Van. "The Burden of Innocence," *Sewanee Review,* LXII (Winter, 1954), 143-50.

———. "Robert Penn Warren, Provincial Poet," *A Southern Vanguard*. Ed. Allen Tate. New York: Prentice-Hall, 1947. Pp. 92-99.

———. "Robert Penn Warren's Short Fiction," *Western Review*, XII (Summer, 1948), 251-53.

Schwartz, Delmore. "Dragon of Guilt," *New Republic*, CXXIX (September 14, 1953), 17.

Southard, W. P. "The Religious Poetry of Robert Penn Warren," *Kenyon Review*, VII (Autumn, 1945), 653-76.

Stallman, Robert. "Robert Penn Warren: A Checklist of his Critical Writings," *University of Kansas City Review*, XIV (Autumn, 1947), 78-83.

Stewart, John L. "The Achievement of Robert Penn Warren," *South Atlantic Quarterly*, XLVII (October, 1948), 562-79.

Zabel, Morton. "Problems of Knowledge," *Poetry*, XLVIII (April, 1936), 37-41.

Unpublished Dissertation

Coleman, Emmett, Jr. "Form as Function in the Novels of Robert Penn Warren." University of Louisville, 1950.

V. Cleanth Brooks, Jr.

Books

Modern Poetry and the Tradition. Chapel Hill, N.C.: University of North Carolina Press, 1939.

The Well Wrought Urn; Studies in the Structure of Poetry. New York: Reynal and Hitchcock, 1947.

Editor

Approach to Literature. Eds. Brooks, R. P. Warren, and John T. Purser. Baton Rouge, La.: Louisiana State University Press, 1936.

Understanding Poetry. Brooks and R. P. Warren. New York: Henry Holt and Co., 1938.

Undersanding Fiction. Brooks and R. P. Warren. New York: F. S. Crofts and Co., 1943.

The Percy Letters. David Nichol Smith and Brooks. Baton Rouge, La.: Louisiana State University Press, 1944.

Understanding Drama. Brooks and Robert B. Heilman. New York: Henry Holt and Co., 1945.

Modern Rhetoric. Brooks and R. P. Warren. New York: Harcourt, Brace and Co., 1949.

The Poems of Mr. John Milton, with Essays in Analysis. Brooks and John Edward Hardy. New York: Harcourt, Brace and Co., 1951.

Poetry

"When Chemistry Failed," *Christian Century,* XLVI (September 18, 1929), 1151.

"Geometry of Sunset," *New Republic,* LX (November 6, 1929), 318.

"Maelstrom," *Sewanee Review,* LIV (January, 1946), 116-18.

Essays and Reviews

"Note on Symbol and Conceit," *American Review,* III (May, 1934), 201-11.

"History of Percy's Edition of Surrey's Poems," *English Studies,* LXVIII (1934), 424-30.

"Chaucer: Saturn's Daughter," *Modern Language Notes,* XLIX (November, 1934), 459-61.

"The Modern Southern Poet and Tradition," *Virginia Quarterly Review,* XI (April, 1935), 305-20.

"Modern Poetry: a Symposium," with R. P. Warren and Mark Van Doren, *American Review,* VIII (February, 1937), 427-56.

"Poetry and Political Faith," *Poetry,* L (August, 1937), 280-84.

"The Poem as Organism: Modern Critical Procedure," *English Institute Annual, 1940.* Ed. Rudolf Kirk. New York: Columbia University Press, 1941. Pp. 21-41.

"The Language of Paradox," *The Language of Poetry.* Ed. Allen Tate. Princeton: Princeton University Press, 1942. Pp. 37-61.

"What Deep South Literature Needs," *Saturday Review of Literature,* XXV (September 18, 1942), 8-9.

"Mr. Kazin's America," *Sewanee Review,* LI (January, 1943), 52-61.

"The Case of Miss Arabella Fermor," *Sewanee Review,* LI (October, 1943), 505-24.

"The New Criticism: a Brief for the Defense," *American Scholar,* XIII (Summer, 1944), 285-95.

"Empson's Criticism," *Accent,* IV (Summer, 1944), 208-16.

"Shakespeare as a Symbolist Poet," *Yale Review,* XXXIV (June, 1945), 642-65.

"Allen Tate," *Poetry,* LXVI (September, 1945), 324-29.

"Mrs. Colum and Mr. Jones," *Sewanee Review,* LIV (Spring, 1946), 334-43.

"The Intimations of the Ode," *Kenyon Review,* VIII (Winter, 1946), 80-102.

"The New Criticism and Scholarship," *Twentieth Century English.* Ed. W. S. Knickerbocker. New York: Philosophic Society, 1946. Pp. 371-83.

"Criticism and Literary History: Marvell's Horatian Ode," *Sewanee Review,* LV (Spring, 1947), 199-222.

"Irony and Ironic Poetry," *College English,* IX (February, 1948), 231-37.

"The Place of Creative Writing in the Study of Literature," *Association of American Colleges Bulletin,* XXXIV (May, 1948), 225-33.

"The Limits of Poetry," *Hudson Review,* II (Spring, 1949), 27-33.

"The Relative and the Absolute: An Exchange of Views," with Herbert J. Muller, *Sewanee Review,* LVII (Summer, 1949), 357-77.

"My Credo: Formalist Critic," *Kenyon Review,* XIII (Winter, 1951), 72-81.

"Milton and the New Criticism," *Sewanee Review,* LIX (January, 1951), 1-22.

"*Absalom, Absalom:* The Definition of Innocence," *Sewanee Review,* LIX (October, 1951), 543-58.

"Milton and Critical Re-estimates," *PMLA,* LXVI (December, 1951), 1045-54.

About Brooks

Bush, Donald. "Marvell's Horatian Ode (as Interpreted by Cleanth Brooks)," *Sewanee Review,* LX (July, 1952), 363-76.

Crane, Ronald S. "Cleanth Brooks: or, The Bankruptcy of Critical Monism," *Modern Philology,* XLV (May, 1948), 226-45.

Empson, William. "Thy Darling in an Urn," *Sewanee Review,* LV (Winter, 1947), 691-99.

Hardy, John Edward. "The Achievement of Cleanth Brooks," *Southern Renascence: The Literature of the Modern South.* Eds. Louis D. Rubin, Jr., and Robert D. Jacobs. Baltimore: Johns Hopkins Press, 1953. Pp. 412-26.

Hecht, Roger. "Paradox and Cleanth Brooks," *Bard Review,* II (Spring, 1947), 47-51.

Pearce, Roy Harvey. " 'Pure' Criticism and the History of Ideas," *Journal of Aesthetics and Art Criticism,* VII (December, 1948), 122-32.

Stallman, Robert W. "Cleanth Brooks: A Checklist of his Critical Writings," *University of Kansas City Review,* XIV (Summer, 1948), 317-24.

Strauss, A. B. "The Poetic Theory of Cleanth Brooks," *Centenary Review,* I (Fall, 1949), 10-22.

VI. Donald Davidson

Books

An Outland Piper. Boston and New York: Houghton Mifflin Co., 1924.

The Tall Men. Boston and New York: Houghton Mifflin Co., 1927.

Lee in the Mountains and Other Poems, Including The Tall Men. Boston: Houghton Mifflin Co., 1938.

The Attack on Leviathan: Regionalism and Nationalism in the United States. Chapel Hill, N.C.: University of North Carolina Press, 1938.

The Tennessee. ("Rivers of America Series.") 2 vols. New York and Toronto: Rinehart and Co., 1946, 1948.

Editor

British Poetry of the 1890's. Garden City, N. Y.: Doubleday, Doran, 1937.

American Composition and Rhetoric. New York: Charles Scribner's Sons, 1939.

Reading for Composition, from Prose Models. Davidson and Sidney Erwin Glenn. New York: Charles Scribner's Sons, 1942.

Twenty Lessons in Reading and Writing Prose. New York: Charles Scribner's Sons, 1955.

Essays and Reviews

"Criticism Outside New York," *Bookman,* LXXIII (May, 1931), 247-56.

"The Southern Poet and his Tradition," *Poetry,* XL (May, 1932), 94-103.

"Erskine Caldwell's Picture Book," *Southern Review,* IV (Winter, 1938), 15-25.

"The Traditional Basis in Thomas Hardy's Fiction," *Southern Review,* VI (Winter, 1940), 162-70.

"Yeats and the Centaur," *Southern Review,* VII (Summer, 1942), 510-16.

"White Spirituals and their Historian," *Sewanee Review,* LI (October, 1943), 589-98.

"Preface to Decision," *Sewanee Review,* LIII (Summer, 1945), 394-412.

"In Memory of John Gould Fletcher," *Poetry,* LXXVII (December, 1950), 164-51.

"Theme and Method in *So Red the Rose,*" *Southern Renascence: The Literature of the Modern South.* Eds. Louis D. Rubin, Jr., and Robert D. Jacobs. Baltimore: Johns Hopkins Press, 1953. Pp. 262-77.

"In Justice to So Fine a Country," *Sewanee Review,* LXIII (Winter, 1955), 142-52.

About Davidson

Beatty, Richmond C. "Donald Davidson as Fugitive-Agrarian," *Southern Renascence: The Literature of the Modern South.* Eds. Louis D. Rubin, Jr., and Robert D. Jacobs. Baltimore: Johns Hopkins Press, 1953. Pp. 392-412.

Millspaugh, C. A. "A Long Perspective," *Poetry,* LIV (May, 1939), 108-11.

Monroe, Harriet. "Tennesseans," *Poetry,* XXXI (January, 1928), 222-24.

VII. Merrill Moore

Books

The Noise that Time Makes. New York: Harcourt, Brace and Co., 1929.

Six Sides to a Man, New Sonnets. New York: Harcourt, Brace and Co., 1935.

M: One Thousand Autobiographical Sonnets. New York: Harcourt, Brace and Co., 1938.

Some Poems for New Zealand. Wellington, N. Z.: Wellington Progressive Publishing Society, 1945.

Clinical Sonnets. New York: Twayne Publishers, 1949.

Illegitimate Sonnets. New York: Twayne Publishers, 1950.

Case Record from a Sonnetarium. New York: Twayne Publishers, 1951.

Clinical Sonnets. New York: Twayne Publishers, 1953.

More Clinical Sonnets. New York: Twayne Publishers, 1953.

Verse Diary of a Psychiatrist, New Sonnets. Baltimore: Contemporary Poetry, 1954.

War Diary of an Army Psychiatrist. Baltimore: Contemporary Poetry, 1955.

A Doctor's Book of Hours, Including Some Dimensions of the Emotions. Springfield, Ill.: Thomas, 1955.

Pamphlets

The Fugitive: Clippings and Comment. Boston: Privately printed, 1937.

Numerous reprints of poems and reviews.

About Moore

Burden, J. "Prolific Dr. Moore," *Poetry*, LXXXIV (April, 1954), 32-37.

Eberhart, Richard. "Warmth and Ease and Charm and Aptitude," *Poetry*, LIV (June, 1939), 160-63.

Fitts, Dudley. "Quick Fingers," *Hound and Horn*, III (January, 1930), 285-87.

———. "The Sonnets of Merrill Moore," *Sewanee Review*, XLVII (Spring, 1939), 268-93.

Holden, Raymond. "Activities of an Amateur," *Poetry*, XLVII (October, 1935), 49-52.

Honig, Edwin. "Psychiatrist as Poet," *Poetry*, LXXX (April, 1952), 58-59.

McCord, David. "M-m-m-m-m," *Saturday Review of Literature*, XIX (January 7, 1939), 10.

Ransom, John C. Foreword to Moore, *The Noise that Time Makes*. New York: Harcourt, Brace and Co., 1929.

Untermeyer, Louis. "A New Hybrid," *Saturday Review of Literature*, VI (November 9, 1929), 364.

———. "More Moore," *Saturday Review of Literature*, XXXVII (January 16, 1954), 20.

Warren, Robert Penn. "Merrill Moore's Sonnets," *New Republic*, LXI (January 29, 1930), 280.

Wells, F. L. "The Mental Measure of Merrill Moore," *Life and Letters Today*, XXI (March, 1939), 27-35.

Wells, Henry W. "Poet and Psychiatrist: Merrill Moore," *Southern Renascence: The Literature of the Modern South*. Eds. Louis D. Rubin, Jr., and Robert D. Jacobs. Baltimore: Johns Hopkins Press, 1953. Pp. 427-35.

Williams, William Carlos. Foreword to *Sonnets from New Directions* (pamphlet). Reprinted at end of Moore, *M: One Thousand Autobiographical Sonnets*. New York: Harcourt, Brace and Co., 1938.

Winters, Yvor. "Merrill Moore's Poetry," *Poetry*, XXXVI (May, 1930), 104-6.

VIII. Andrew Nelson Lytle

Books

Bedford Forrest and his Critter Company. New York: Minton, Balch and Co., 1931.
The Long Night: A Novel. Indianapolis and New York: Bobbs-Merrill Co., 1936.
At the Moon's Inn. Indianapolis and New York: Bobbs-Merrill Co., 1941.
A Name for Evil. Indianapolis and New York: Bobbs-Merrill Co., 1947.
Several unpublished early plays.

Short Stories

"Old Scratch in the Valley," *Virginia Quarterly Review*, VIII (April, 1932), 237-46.
"Mr. McGregor," *Virginia Quarterly Review*, XI (April, 1935), 218-37.
"Jericho, Jericho, Jericho," *Southern Review*, I (Fall, 1936), 411-22.
"Alchemy," *Kenyon Review*, IV (Summer, 1942), 273-327.
"Guide: A Story," *Sewanee Review*, LIII (Summer, 1945), 362-87.
"What Quarter of the Night," *Sewanee Review*, LXIV (Summer, 1956), 349-97.

Essays and Reviews

"Caroline Gordon and the Historic Image," *Sewanee Review*, LVII (Fall, 1949), 560-86.
"Regeneration for the Man," *Sewanee Review*, LVII (Winter, 1949), 120-27.
"How Many Miles to Babylon?" *Southern Renascence: The Literature of the Modern South*. Eds. Louis D. Rubin, Jr., and Robert D. Jacobs. Baltimore: Johns Hopkins Press, 1953. Pp. 31-34.
"Image as Guide to Meaning in the Historical Novel," *Sewanee Review*, LXI (July, 1953), 408-26.
"The Son of Man: He Will Prevail," *Sewanee Review*, LXIII (Winter, 1955), 114-37.

IX. Ridley Wills

Novels

Hoax. New York: Doran, 1922.
Harvey Landrum. New York: Simon and Schuster, 1924.

X. Stanley Johnson

Novel

The Professor. New York: Harcourt, Brace and Co., 1925.

XI. Walter Clyde Curry

Books

Chaucer and the Medieval Sciences. New York and London: Oxford University Press, 1926.

Shakespeare's Philosophical Patterns. Baton Rouge, La.: Louisiana State University Press, 1937.

XII. William C. Frierson

Book

The English Novel in Transition, 1885-1940. Norman, Okla.: University of Oklahoma Press, 1942.

Index